America's Best Pies
2014-2015

Nearly 200 Recipes You'll Love

American Pie Council with Linda Hoskins

Skyhorse Publishing

Editor's Note:

Crisco® is a trademark of The J. M. Smucker Company.

The Great American Pie Festival and the National Pie Championships are trademarks of American Pie Council.

Skyhorse Publishing books may be purchased in bulk at special discounts for sales promotion, corporate gifts, fund-raising, or educational purposes. Special editions can also be created to specifications. For details, contact the Special Sales Department, Skyhorse Publishing, 307 West 36th Street, 11th Floor, New York, NY 10018 or info@skyhorsepublishing.com.

Skyhorse® and Skyhorse Publishing® are registered trademarks of Skyhorse Publishing, Inc.®, a Delaware corporation.

Visit our website at www.skyhorsepublishing.com.

10 9 8 7 6 5 4 3 2 1

Library of Congress Cataloging-in-Publication Data is available on file.

Print ISBN: 978-1-62914-672-0
Ebook ISBN: 978-1-62914-857-1

Printed in China

Table of Contents

INTRODUCTION

As the Executive Director of the American Pie Council, I wanted to be able to share our award-winning collection of recipes with you. We've added some new categories, like Innovation, to the APC National Pie Championships—these recipes will bring you traditional pie baking recipes with new, innovative twists on flavors and concepts. This collection of 200 recipes guarantees to get your mouth watering in the first few pages.

The American Pie Council, founded in 1983, is the only organization dedicated solely to PIE, America's favorite dessert. We believe in the total enjoyment, consumption, and pursuit of PIE. We believe that the art of PIE making shouldn't be forgotten. We believe that the enjoyment of PIE should be continued. We believe that the pursuit of finding the perfect PIE should be eternal. And it is in these beliefs that we hold the APC National Pie Championships® every year.

Usually in the month of April, the APC Crisco National Pie Championships is held to determine who makes the best pies in America. Pie Bakers from all over the country descend upon Celebration, Florida to compete. Pies are entered into five divisions: commercial, independent/retail bakers, amateur bakers, professional chefs, and junior chefs. The entries are then divided into price point and flavor categories. Then, the judging begins. Close to one thousand pies are judged each year over the course of three days. Two hundred judges (food professionals, chefs, cookbook authors, food editors, suppliers to the PIE Industry, and everyday PIE lovers) are chosen in the months before the event. And then the best pies are chosen. . . .

We would love for you to come to the National Pie Championships and experience this pie baking extravaganza first hand. You can come as a contestant, volunteer, pie judge, or simply to take it all in. Being a part of our pie baking family is an experience you won't want to miss.

I hope you enjoy this new collection of recipes as much as our pie bakers enjoyed being a part of the National Pie Championships. We hope to see you at the National Pie Championships soon!

To learn more about the American Pie Council and membership, visit www.piecouncil.org.

AMERICAN PIE COUNCIL'S TIPS FOR A GREAT PIE

1. Read the recipe in its entirety before beginning. Make sure you have all of the ingredients and utensils and that you understand all of the directions. Many mistakes have been made by skipping steps.

2. All ingredients for the piecrust should be cold. It even helps to have cold bowls and utensils.

3. Don't overwork or over-handle the dough. Your shortening/butter should be coated with flour mixture, not blended with it.

4. To ensure that your bottom crust is finished, bake pie in the lower third of the oven. You may have to cover the edges with foil or a crust protector to avoid overbrowning the edges.

5. Make sure that all of your ingredients are really fresh. Try making fruit pies when the fruits are in season to ensure a wonderful pie.

How to crimp the perfect pie

6. Carefully transfer the dough into your Emile Henry pie dish.

7. Fit the dough into the dish (avoid stretching).

8. Trim the dough to 1" inch overhang and tuck it under itself to create a thick rim.

9. With the index finger on one hand, press the dough against the thumb and forefinger of the opposite hand; continue around the perimeter of the crust and dish following the natural flute of the Emile Henry pie dish.

APPLE

<‹ *Apple Pie (recipe page 6)*

APPLE-PRALINE PIE

Raquel Hammond, St. Cloud, FL
2005 American Pie Council Crisco National Pie Championships
Amateur Division 1ˢᵗ Place Apple

CRUST
2 cups unbleached flour
1 cup cake flour
1½ tablespoons sugar
1 teaspoon salt
8 tablespoons (1 stick) frozen
  unsalted butter, cut up
½ cup plus 2 tablespoons frozen
  shortening, cut up
2 tablespoons vinegar
1 large egg yolk
4 to 5 tablespoons ice water, or as
  needed
1 large egg white with 1 tablespoon
  water added
¼ cup crushed cornflakes

FILLING
5 cups Granny Smith apples, peeled,
  cored, and sliced

4 cups Braeburn apples, peeled,
  cored, and sliced
½ cup apple cider
½ cup sugar
3 tablespoons cornstarch
¾ teaspoon cinnamon
¼ teaspoon nutmeg
⅛ teaspoon salt
2 tablespoons unsalted butter, cut up

PRALINE TOPPING
½ cup chopped pecans
½ cup brown sugar
¼ cup unsalted butter
Pinch of salt
2 tablespoons heavy cream
¼ teaspoon cinnamon

For the Crust: Preheat oven to 425°F. Whisk together dry ingredients in large bowl. Add the butter and shortening. Using a pastry blender, cut in fat until mixture resembles dry rice. Add egg yolk, vinegar, and a minimum amount of water. Lightly toss until mixture just begins to clump together. If dough looks too dry, sprinkle on a little more water. Dough should cling together and feel pliable, but not sticky. Form dough into a cohesive ball on a piece of waxed paper by lifting opposite corners and pressing them together. Flatten into a 6-inch disk for single shell, or divide dough in half and make two disks for two-crust pie. Wrap dough in plastic wrap and refrigerate for at least 1 hour or even overnight (the longer the better). Soften dough at room temperature for a few minutes before rolling out. Roll out bottom crust and line 9-inch pie plate. Roll out top crust and refrigerate both for 15 minutes. Whisk egg white and 1 tablespoon water together. Brush on the bottom crust. Carefully spread ¼ cup of crushed cornflakes on the bottom shell over the egg wash.

For the Filling: Combine apples and cider in large pot. Bring to boil, cover, and cook over medium-high heat for about 5 minutes, stirring once or twice. Drain apples, reserving juice. Transfer juice to small saucepan and reduce to ¼ cup over medium-high heat. Stir into apples and set aside to cool. In a small bowl, combine sugar, cornstarch, cinnamon, nutmeg, and salt. Stir into apple cider mixture. Pour filling into pie shell

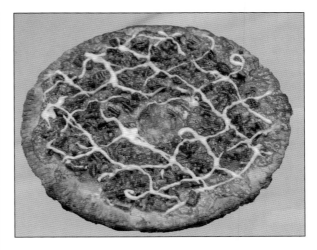

Apple-Praline Pie

and dot with butter. Attach top crust and flute edge. Poke several steam vents in top with fork or paring knife. Bake for 15 minutes in lower third of oven. Raise rack to center and bake an additional 45 to 50 minutes. Check halfway through baking and cover pastry with foil if browning too quickly. Transfer pie to wire rack and cool.

For the Topping: Melt butter in small saucepan. Stir in brown sugar, salt, cinnamon and heavy cream. Bring slowly to a boil. Remove from heat and stir in chopped pecans. Spread evenly over cooled pie and broil until topping bubbles and turns golden brown.

Transfer pie, once again, to wire rack and cool for at least 2 hours. Slice and serve. Cover leftovers with loosely tented foil and refrigerate.

COUNTY FAIR APPLE RHUBARB PIE

Evette Rahman, Orlando, FL
2011 American Pie Council Crisco National Pie Championships
2nd Place Apple

CRUST
3 cups flour
3 tablespoons sugar
1½ teaspoons salt
¾ teaspoon baking powder
½ cup shortening
½ cup unsalted butter, cold, cubed
½ cup heavy cream
1½ tablespoons vinegar
1½ tablespoons oil
1 egg mixed with 1 tablespoon heavy cream
Sugar for sprinkling

FILLING
5½ cups cooking apples, peeled, cored, and cut into ⅛-inch thick slices
1½ cups cut-up rhubarb (weighing 7.5 ounces while frozen), thawed completely
2 teaspoons fresh lime juice
2 tablespoons salted butter, melted
1 cup plus 3 tablespoons sugar
⅓ cup cornstarch
½ teaspoon ground cinnamon
¼ teaspoon freshly ground nutmeg

For the Crust: Mix flour, sugar, salt, and baking powder. Cut in shortening and butter. Stir together oil, vinegar, and cream. Add by tossing with flour. Knead briefly. Form dough into 2 disks. Cover with plastic wrap and refrigerate for at least 1 hour before rolling out.

For the Filling: Preheat oven to 400°F. Mix together apples, rhubarb, and lime juice. Add melted butter. Mix together sugar, cornstarch, and spices. Add to fruit and coat thoroughly.

Roll out one disk of dough on a lightly floured surface and place in a deep dish pie plate. Add filling. Roll out remaining disk of dough to make a full top crust or cut into strips for a lattice design. Cover filling with dough and crimp edges. Brush with egg wash and sprinkle with sugar. Bake for 25 minutes. Reduce heat to 375°F. Bake for another 25 to 30 minutes or until golden and bubbly. Cover pie edges with pie shield or aluminum foil during baking to prevent excess browning. Cool completely on wire rack before serving.

County Fair Apple Rhubarb Pie

CARAMEL APPLE PIE

Marles Riessland, Riverdale, NE
2003 American Pie Council Crisco National Pie Championships
Amateur Division 1st Place Apple

CRUST
3 cups all-purpose flour
1 teaspoon salt
1 teaspoon sugar
1 cup plus 1 tablespoon butter-
  flavored shortening, chilled
1/3 cup ice water
1 tablespoon vinegar
1 egg, beaten

FILLING
6 cups Jonathan or Granny Smith
  apples, peeled, cored, and sliced
1/2 cup packed light brown sugar
1/2 cup sugar
1/4 cup flour

1 teaspoon cinnamon
1/4 teaspoon nutmeg
1/4 teaspoon salt
1 tablespoon lemon juice
1 teaspoon vanilla
4 tablespoons heavy cream
4 tablespoons butter

STREUSEL TOPPING
1/2 cup flour
3 tablespoons sugar
1 tablespoon butter
2 toffee bars or 3 ounces chocolate
  covered peanut or pecan brittle
Egg white and sugar for brushing
  and sprinkling on pie

For the Crust: Chill all ingredients, including the flour and vinegar. Combine the flour, salt, and sugar. Cut in shortening with a pastry blender until the mixture resembles cornmeal. In another bowl, mix water and vinegar with the beaten egg. Add the liquid mixture, one tablespoon at a time, to the flour mixture, tossing with a fork to form a soft dough. Form dough into a ball and divide in two. Roll out half the dough and place in a 9-inch pie dish. Roll out the remaining half for top crust and set aside.

For the Filling: Preheat oven to 450°F. Sprinkle apples with lemon juice. Combine dry ingredients in large bowl and add apples. Toss to mix. Add vanilla and cream. Melt butter in heavy skillet. Add apple mixture and cook approximately 8 minutes to soften apples. Turn into pie shell.

For the Topping: Combine the flour and sugar. Mix in butter with fork until coarse crumbs form. Crumble toffee bars and add to crumbs. Sprinkle over pie. Add top crust. Seal, flute edge, and vent top. Brush with beaten egg white and sprinkle with sugar. Bake at 450°F for 15 minutes. Reduce heat to 350°F and bake 45 minutes longer. Let cool before serving.

FRENCH APPLE PIE

Linda Pater, Coloma, MI

2005 American Pie Council Crisco National Pie Championships
Amateur Division 2nd Place Apple

CRUST
2 cups flour
1 teaspoon salt
¾ cup Crisco
¼ cup cold water

FILLING
4 cups Granny Smith apples, peeled, cored, and sliced

3 cups Braeburn or Jonagold apples, peeled, cored, and sliced
¾ cup sugar
1 teaspoon cinnamon

TOPPING
½ cup butter
½ cup brown sugar
1 cup flour

For the Crust: In a medium bowl, combine flour and salt. With a pastry blender, cut Crisco into flour and salt mixture until mixture looks like small pebbles. Mix in cold water. Form dough into 2 balls. Roll out one ball on floured surface until evenly thin. Place the crust into a 9-inch pie pan. Save the remaining ball of dough for another pie.

For the Filling: Preheat oven to 400°F. In a large bowl, mix sugar and cinnamon. Add apples and mix lightly. Place apples in a heap in the prepared pie crust.

For the Topping: Using a pastry cutter, mix all ingredients until crumbly. Sprinkle on top of apples in pie crust before baking. Bake for 45 to 55 minutes.

French Apple Pie

NANA'S CRUMB DUTCH APPLE PIE

Mary Foley, Stanfordville, NY
2007 American Pie Council Crisco National Pie Championships
Amateur Division 3rd Place Apple

CRUST
½ cup butter
8 teaspoons granulated sugar
⅔ cup Crisco shortening
3⅓ cups sifted flour
½ teaspoon salt
⅓ cup cold water

FILLING
6 or 7 Granny Smith apples
3 tablespoons butter

¾ cup sugar
1 teaspoon cinnamon

STREUSEL TOPPING
1⅛ cups flour
¾ teaspoon cinnamon
½ cup light brown sugar
½ cup butter

For the Crust: Blend butter with sugar using a fork. Blend in shortening. Combine flour to the fats with a fork. Blend mixture into lumps, leaving sides of the bowl clean. Add water and use hands to bring together. Roll out dough when ready and place in 9-inch pie plate. Makes three crusts per batch. Use one crust for this recipe.

For the Filling: Peel, core, and quarter apples. Cut each quarter into 4 slices lengthwise. Melt butter in saucepan, add apples, and toss until coated. Mix cinnamon with sugar and add to apples. Toss to distribute. Arrange apples compactly in unbaked pie crust, heaping slightly in center.

For the Topping: Preheat oven to 425°F. Mix flour, cinnamon, and brown sugar. Cut in butter using two knives or pastry blender. Mix using fingers until particles are the size of rice grains. Sprinkle mixture over apples before baking. Bake for 20 minutes. Reduce heat to 325°F and continue baking for 30 minutes or until apples are tender when tested with a fork.

Nana's Crumb Dutch Apple Pie

TERRIFIC TOPSY-TURVY APPLE PECAN PIE

Shirley J. Myrsiades, Pinellas Park, FL
2005 American Pie Council Crisco National Pie Championships
Amateur Division 3rd Place Apple

CRUST
3 cups all-purpose flour
9 tablespoons unsalted butter
9 tablespoons Crisco butter-flavored shortening
9 tablespoons ice water
1 teaspoon salt

CARAMEL BASE
2 pounds light brown sugar
½ cup honey
½ cup butter
1 ounce water
3 tablespoons Crisco butter-flavored shortening

1 package pecan halves
1 egg white

FILLING
5 to 6 Granny Smith apples, cored, peeled, and sliced
2 tablespoons lemon juice
1 cup light brown sugar
½ teaspoon salt
1 tablespoon ground cinnamon
1 teaspoon ground nutmeg
Pinch of ground allspice
5 tablespoons flour
5 tablespoons cubed butter

For the Crust: Pre-chill a mixing bowl, cubed butter, cubed shortening, salt, and pastry cutter. Cut in fats with cutter until they resemble small peas. Drizzle water 1 tablespoon at a time and blend with a fork; continue adding water 1 tablespoon at a time until dough forms a ball. Do not overhandle dough. Split dough in half and press into two 6-inch disks. Chill and let rest for 1 hour.

For the Caramel Base: Beat together all ingredients except the pecan halves and the egg white. Use a thin layer of shortening to coat a 9½-inch deep-style glass pie pan. Use about 1½ cups of base on bottom and sides of pie pan, making a nice thick layer. Carefully arrange pecan halves with the flat side facing you in three circles on the bottom and sides of pie pan. Chop remaining pecans and place them in the center of pie pan. Press in slightly. Roll out first crust and carefully place over nuts. Leave 1-inch overhang. Brush inside of shell with egg white.

For the Filling: Preheat oven to 350°F. Mix all ingredients except the butter. Arrange the apples neatly inside the shell. Level the top of the filling and dot with butter. Roll out second dough disk and place on top of pie. Trim to fit over pie, leaving no overhang. Dampen edge with water, bring up overhang and fold over edge and seal. Prick several times with a fork to vent steam. Put the pie on a foil-lined cookie sheet and place in center of oven. Bake for 45 to 50 minutes. Let rest 15 minutes and then place serving platter over pie and carefully invert. Be very careful, as hot sugar burns very badly. Remove pie pan and rearrange any pecans that have stuck to the pan. Do not cover until completely cooled. Best if served the same day baked.

Terrific Topsy-Turvy Apple Pecan Pie

THE APPLE OF MY EYE PIE

John Sunvold, Orlando, FL
2012 American Pie Council Crisco National Pie Championships
Amateur Division 1st Place Apple

CRUST
1½ cups graham cracker crumbs
3 tablespoons sugar
5 tablespoons butter, melted

FILLING
8 ounces cream cheese
½ cup powdered sugar
8 ounces Cool Whip
½ teaspoon vanilla extract

APPLE TOPPING
4 cups apple slices
3 tablespoons butter
5 tablespoons brown sugar
1 to 1½ tablespoons cornstarch
1 teaspoon cinnamon
½ cup apple juice
2 tablespoons apple butter

GARNISH
Whipped cream, simple nut granola
(without fruit), caramel sauce

For the Crust: Mix all ingredients together and press mixture into pie plate. Chill for 10 minutes. Bake in a 375°F oven for 10 minutes, or until brown. Allow to cool down to room temperature before filling.

For the Filling: Beat vanilla, cream cheese, and powdered sugar until smooth. Fold in the Cool whip. Gently spread into crust and chill.

For the Topping: Mix apple juice and cornstarch and set aside. Combine the rest of the ingredients in a saucepan and cook on the stove over medium heat until apples are appropriately tender. Once apples are tender, add the apple juice mixture. Bring to a boil and cook until thickened. Remove from heat and cool. When cool, generously top the pie with the apple topping, leaving some room for your favorite whipped topping.

Garnish with whipped cream, nut granola, or caramel sauce.

Drizzle with caramel sauce, if desired. Chill.

The Apple of My Eye Pie

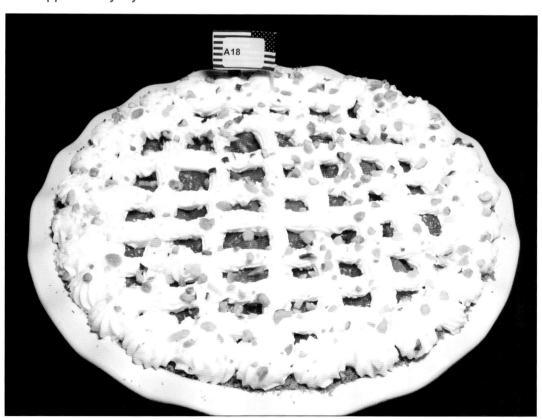

FULL MOON APPLE PIE

Michael Mochizuki, Chicago, IL
2013 Pie Town Chicago 1st Place

CRUST
2 cups flour
½ tablespoon sugar
1 egg
½ tablespoon vinegar
1 teaspoon salt
11 tablespoons butter
4 tablespoons lard
3 tablespoons cold vodka
   (if desired)
5 ginger snap cookies (ground)

FILLING
¼ cup brown sugar
¼ cup white sugar
½ teaspoon cinnamon
¼ teaspoon nutmeg
Pinch salt
5 Braeburn apples, cored, peeled and
   sliced
1 cup of toasted pecans
1 tablespoon lemon juice
2 tablespoons cornstarch

For the Crust: Preheat oven to 450°F. Mix flour, sugar, and salt, and cut in butter and lard. Add the egg, vinegar, and vodka and mix until it comes together (may be slightly sticky). Roll into 2 balls and wrap with plastic wrap, flatten, and refrigerate for 30 minutes. Pound out on floured surface then roll out bottom crust. Place in pie dish. Distribute crushed ginger snap cookies on bottom of pie crust.

For the Filling: Toss together the sugars, spices, and salt. Add sliced apples and cornstarch. Pour filling over gingersnaps. Place top crust over filling on pie.

Bake at 450°F for 10 minutes, lower to 350°F for 50 minutes, and raise to 400°F for last 10 minutes.

MAMA FLIPPED IT AND I HELPED APPLE PECAN PIE

Francine Bryson, Pickens, SC
2012 American Pie Council Crisco National Pie Championships
Amateur Division 2nd Place Apple

CRUST
4 cups flour
1¾ cups butter-flavored shortening
  (chilled)
1 tablespoon sugar
1 tablespoon apple cider vinegar
1 egg
½ cup water

PECAN CRUST
½ stick butter (softened)
2⅓ cups pecan halves

1 cup chopped pecans
1 cup brown sugar (packed)

APPLE FILLING
4½ cups Granny Smith apples,
  peeled, cored, and sliced
2 tablespoons cinnamon
3 tablespoons fresh lemon juice
3 tablespoons all-purpose flour
¾ cup white sugar
½ cup brown sugar
2 tablespoons vanilla extract

For the Crust: Preheat oven to 450°F. Mix flour, shortening, sugar, and apple cider vinegar. In separate dish, beat egg and water. Combine the mixtures, stirring with a fork. Roll to combine, split into 2 balls, and wrap in wax paper. Chill 30 minutes while you make the pecan crust.

For the Pecan Crust: Grease a deep dish pie dish with butter until completely covered. Cover the bottom and sides of the dish with pecans and then sprinkle the brown sugar over the pecans. Sprinkle chopped pecans over the brown sugar and then press one rolled out pie crust firmly to cover the nuts.

For the Filling: Mix all ingredients except apples in bowl, combining thoroughly. Add apples and stir until all apples are covered. Pour apples into pie shell, making sure to mound apples up in the middle. Cover with second rolled out pie crust, and press sides to crimp and seal edges. Poke holes with fork to vent steam.

Bake in 450°F oven for 10 minutes, then drop temperature to 350°F. Bake for an additional 35 to 45 minutes until the top is golden brown. Let sit 10 minutes to cool. Place serving plate over pie and flip over. Remove dish while pie is still hot, and serve.

Mama Flipped It And I Helped Apple Pecan Pie

CRUNCHY CARAMEL APPLE PIE

Sarah Spaugh, Winston Salem, NC
2002 American Pie Council National Pie Championships
Amateur Division 1st Place Apple

CRUST

2 cups all-purpose flour
1 teaspoon salt
¾ cup Crisco shortening
5 tablespoons cold water

FILLING

6 medium (6 cups) cooking apples,
　　peeled, cored, and thinly sliced
½ cup white sugar
3 tablespoons all-purpose flour
1 teaspoon ground cinnamon
⅛ teaspoon salt

CRUMB TOPPING

1 cup packed light brown sugar
½ cup all-purpose flour
½ cup quick cooking rolled oats
½ cup chilled butter

GARNISH

½ cup chopped toasted pecans
Caramel ice cream topping

For the Crust: Spoon flour into measuring cup and level. Combine flour and salt in medium bowl. Cut in Crisco using pastry blender until flour is blended to form pea-size chunks. Sprinkle with cold water, 1 tablespoon at a time. Toss lightly with fork until dough forms a ball. Roll out pastry. Line a 9-inch pie plate with pastry; set aside.

For the Filling: Preheat oven to 375°F. In a large mixing bowl, stir together sugar, flour, cinnamon, and salt. Add apple slices and gently toss until coated. Transfer the apple mixture into the pastry-lined plate.

For the Crumb Topping: Stir sugar, flour, and rolled oats together in medium mixing bowl. Using a pastry blender, cut in chilled butter until the topping mixture resembles coarse crumbs. Sprinkle on top of the apple mixture in the pastry lined plate. To prevent over browning, cover edge of pie with foil. Bake for 25 minutes. Remove foil. Bake for another 25 to 30 minutes or until top is golden. Remove from oven.

For the Garnish: Sprinkle with ½ cup chopped toasted pecans and drizzle caramel ice cream topping over the pecans

STREUSEL APPLE PIE

Dave Hulett, Richfield, MN
2012 American Pie Council Crisco National Pie Championships
Professional Division 1st Place Apple

CRUST
2 cups sifted all-purpose flour
1 cup butter-flavored Crisco
    shortening, cold
½ teaspoon salt
1 teaspoon white sugar
¼ to ½ cup whipping cream
1 teaspoon vinegar

FILLING
6 to 8 cups (6 to 8 apples) tart apples
    peeled, cored, and thinly sliced
¾ cup brown sugar

½ teaspoon ground cinnamon
¼ teaspoon nutmeg
2 tablespoons cornstarch
2 teaspoons fresh lemon juice
1 egg white, lightly beaten
¼ cup butter

STREUSEL TOPPING
1 cup flour
¾ cup brown sugar
¼ teaspoon salt
¼ pound butter (1 stick)
½ cup walnuts

For the Crust: Preheat oven to 350°F. Combine flour, salt, and 1 teaspoon sugar in mixing bowl. Add Crisco butter (must be cold) and cut into crumb size bits using a pastry fork or by using 2 butter knives working in a crisscross motion. Add vinegar to whipping cream, then add to flour mixture. Mix until you have a nice sticky clay substance. Roll out pastry for bottom crust and line a 9-inch pie plate.

For the Filling: Peel apples and thinly slice. In a large bowl, combine apple slices, ¾ cup brown sugar, cinnamon, nutmeg, and cornstarch; stir. Allow to stand for 15 minutes. Mix in lemon juice. Brush inside of bottom crust with egg white to moisture-proof crust. Arrange apple slices in pie shell in flat, snug layers. Create a higher mound of apple slices in center because apples cook down as they bake. Pour juices from bowl over apples; dot with butter.

For the Streusel Topping: In a mixing bowl, add flour, salt, brown sugar, and walnuts, mixing well. Finally, add butter (make sure it is 100 percent real butter) and incorporate until you have a coarse meal mixture. It should resemble small peas. Pour this crumb mixture over the apple filling. Cover with foil and bake for 1 hour. After 1 hour, remove foil and bake for another 45 to 50 minutes.

Streusel Apple Pie

GJELINA'S APPLE PIE

Nicole Mournian, Los Angeles, CA
2013 American Pie Council Crisco National Pie Championships
Professional Division 1st Place Perfect Apple Pie

PINK LADY COOKED APPLES
5 cups raw Pink Lady apples, peeled
½ cup white sugar
¼ to ½ cup water
Juice of one lemon

GJELINA'S PIE DOUGH
1 pound cold unsalted butter (I prefer Strauss European Style or Plugrá) cut into 1-inch cubes
1 pound plus 7½ ounces all-purpose flour (King Arthur is my preferred brand)
1 teaspoon fine sea salt
2½ ounces hot water
2½ ounces ice
3½ ounces granulated sugar
½ ounce white vinegar

FILLING
6 medium-large Black Arkansas or Honey Crisp apples
3 cups cooked Pink Lady apples (see recipe above)
¾ cup plus 1 tablespoon granulated sugar
4 tablespoons flour
Pinch of salt
½ tsp cinnamon
½ tsp nutmeg
1 tablespoon ginger syrup
1 tablespoon butter, chilled
¼ cup heavy cream, reserved for the crust

For the Pink Lady Apples: To make three cups of cooked Pink Lady apples, place the Pink Lady apples, sugar, lemon juice, and ¼ cup water in a large pot and bring to a simmer over low-medium heat. Cook for about 45 minutes, adding more water if necessary, until the apples are transparent and shiny and appear to be candied. Cool before using in pie.

For the Crust: First make sure everything is cold, then preheat oven to 375°F. Mix the hot water, vinegar, and sugar into a syrup then add the ice and stir until ice has melted. Pulse the flour, salt, and butter in a food processor until it is the size of medium peas. Dump this fatty flour out onto a work surface and gather it into a pile.

Add half of the sugar syrup to the flour and butter dough and mix it all together gently; this is messy work. Squeeze the dough together and lightly rub the butter peas into the syrup. Use the palm of your hand and press against the table gently and smear/rub the dough together.

Sprinkle on more of the syrup, keep squeezing and rubbing. Try to work quickly so that the butter does not melt. When the dough comes together in a shaggy ball, wrap the whole thing in plastic and let it chill in the fridge for an hour. Portion the dough into two 14 ounce balls and roll them out, usually very thick, depending on the pie, roughly ⅛ of an inch. Lay the dough into your desired pie plate and chill (do not freeze) it for half an hour while you mix your filling.

Gjelina's Apple Pie

For the Filling: Mix all ingredients except for the cream and 1 tablespoon of sugar together and place into your bottom crust. Paint the edges of the crust with the heavy cream.

Lay the top crust on a floured board and slice into 1-inch thick strips. Lattice them on top of the apples. Brush the lattice generously with heavy cream. Sprinkle with 1 tablespoon sugar. Crimp with your fingers or seal with a fork, your choice. Place the whole pie in the freezer for 10 minutes. Bake at 375°F for 15 minutes and then turn the oven down to 325°F for another 30 to 45 minutes. You know it's done when it's golden brown and a little thickened juice bubbles through the lattice. Cool for at least two hours before cutting.

CHEDDAR CRUSTED CRAN-APPLE PIE

Catherine Colombo, Chicago, IL
2013 Pie Town Chicago 3rd Place

CRUST
3 cups flour, sifted
5 tablespoons salted butter, very cold
8 tablespoons Crisco, very cold
4 ounces Cabot Seriously Sharp Cheddar cheese, grated and very cold
1 teaspoon salt
½ to ¾ cup ice water

FILLING
6 cups Granny Smith apples cut into 1-inch pieces (cut each apple into 8 wedges and each wedge into 4 pieces) plus ½ apple chopped into small pieces.

¾ to 1 cup granulated sugar, depending on the sweetness of the apples
1 tablespoon lemon juice
1 cup Craisins
1 teaspoon cinnamon
2 tablespoons Instant Clearjel. (source: King Arthur Flour)
2 tablespoons unsalted butter

For the Crust: Preheat oven to 375°F. Sift flour into food processor fitted with a regular blade. Sift salt in with the flour. Add butter cut into small pieces and pulse 12 to 15 times. Repeat with Crisco and cheddar cheese. While pulsing, add water and pulse until dough comes together in a ball. Turn out on floured counter and divide in half. Wrap in plastic wrap and chill for a minimum of 30 minutes.

Roll chilled dough into an 11-inch circle between ¼ and ⅛ inch thick for a 9-inch deep dish pie plate. Place dough in pie plate and trim, leaving about ½ inch all around. Refrigerate until ready to fill. Roll out top crust in the same manner. Refrigerate on parchment covered baking sheet if not ready to fill pie immediately.

For the Filling: Toss apples, sugar, and lemon juice. Let apples sit for at least an hour to begin to release their juice. Add Craisins, cinnamon, and Clearjel. Mix well.

Add apple mixture to prepared pie crust. Dot apples with butter. Top with top crust, fold edges over, and crimp. Cut steam vents. Place pie on a parchment lined baking sheet and bake for 60 to 75 minutes until golden brown. Cover edges with pie crust shields or foil about half way through baking to prevent them from over browning.

Allow to cool before serving.

CARAMEL APPLE APPLE PIE

Grace Thatcher, Delta, OH
2012 American Pie Council Crisco National Pie Championships
Amateur Division 3rd Place Apple

CRUST
2 cups flour
½ teaspoon salt
10 tablespoons shortening
3 to 4 tablespoons cold water

CARAMEL
¼ cup plus 2 tablespoons heavy cream
¼ cup water
2 tablespoons light corn syrup
1¼ cups sugar
2 tablespoons salted butter
1 teaspoon vanilla extract

FILLING
3 pounds apples, peeled, cored, and thinly sliced

⅔ cup sugar
2 tablespoons butter
1 tablespoon lemon juice
1 teaspoon cinnamon
2 teaspoons cornstarch
2 tablespoons water
¼ teaspoon vanilla

TOPPING
¼ cup sugar
¼ cup brown sugar
½ cup quick rolled oats
2 tablespoons toasted wheat germ
4 tablespoons all-purpose flour
¼ teaspoon cinnamon
¼ teaspoon nutmeg
⅓ cup butter
¼ cup chopped pecans

For the Crust: Preheat oven to 425°F. Into a large mixing bowl, sift together the flour and salt, then add all of the shortening. Cut the shortening into the flour with a pastry blender until the mixture develops a coarse texture. Sprinkle the water over the mixture one spoonful at a time and toss until the dough begins to cohere. Gather the dough into a ball and press together with your hands, cover with plastic wrap, and refrigerate for at least one hour before using.

Prepare pie crust in a 9-inch pie pan and prebake for 10 to 15 minutes at 425°F.

For the Caramel: Measure cream and set aside. Combine the water and corn syrup in a medium saucepan, pour the sugar into the saucepan, making sure not to splash any sugar crystals onto the sides of the saucepan. Gently stir to thoroughly moisten the sugar. Bring to a boil over medium high heat and cook without stirring until sugar is completely dissolved and the liquid is clear. Continue to cook without stirring, but gently swirl the saucepan occasionally until the caramel is a pale golden color. Reduce the heat to medium low and continue to cook until the caramel is light amber colored and registers 360°F with a candy thermometer. Remove the pan from the heat and with great care, pour the cream into the center of the pan; the mixture will steam and bubble vigorously. Mix gently with a whisk until bubbling subsides and then stir in butter and vanilla. Cool until able to handle and then pour ½ cup of the caramel onto the prebaked crust.

Caramel Apple Apple Pie

For the Filling: In a saucepan on medium heat, cook apples with sugar, butter, and lemon juice until apples are softened and have lost volume. In a small bowl, mix cornstarch with water to a smooth consistency and then add mixture to the apples and cook while stirring for 2 minutes until thickened. Then add the cinnamon and vanilla. Let the filling cool while preparing streusel topping.

For the Topping: Mix all ingredients except butter and pecans together in a medium-sized mixing bowl. Crumble in the butter with a pastry blender. Once blended, add chopped pecans and toss well.

Turn pie filling into pie shell on top of caramel layer. Bake at 400°F for 10 minutes, turn heat down to 350°F, and continue baking 20 minutes. Add streusel to top and bake a final 15 to 20 minutes. Cover edges with foil if crust browns too quickly. Drizzle finished pie with remainder of caramel once pie has cooled.

COMSTOCK APPLE RAISIN STREUSEL CUSTARD PIE

Carol Socier, Bay City, MI
2013 American Pie Council Crisco National Pie Championships
Amateur Division 1st Place Comstock Apple and Best of Comstock

CRUST
1¼ cups all-purpose flour
1 teaspoon sugar
½ teaspoon salt
¼ cup butter-flavored Crisco shortening, cold
¼ cup unsalted butter, cold
1 egg yolk
3 to 4 tablespoons cold milk

FILLING
1 can Comstock Apple Pie Filling
1 cup golden raisins
1 (14 ounce) can sweetened
condensed milk

2 eggs, beaten
½ cup hot water
1 teaspoon vanilla
1 teaspoon cinnamon

TOPPING
½ cup light brown sugar, packed
½ cup all-purpose flour
⅛ teaspoon salt
¼ cup butter
½ cup chopped pecans

GARNISH
½ cup powdered sugar
1 to 2 teaspoons apple juice

For the Crust: Preheat oven to 375°F. In medium-sized bowl, combine flour, sugar, and salt. Add cold shortening and butter, cutting with pastry blender until coarse pieces form. Beat egg yolk, then add to cold milk. Add egg mixture to flour mixture small amounts at a time until dough holds. Shape into a disk. Roll to fit a 9-inch pie pan.

For the Filling: Mix all filling ingredients in a large bowl until combined. Gently spoon mixture into prepared pie crust.

For the Streusel Topping: Mix all streusel ingredients except pecans in bowl until crumbly. Stir in pecans. Sprinkle mixture over filling. Bake for 30 to 40 minutes or until golden brown in 375°F oven. Cool on wire rack.

For the Garnish: Whisk powdered sugar with apple juice and drizzle over cooled pie. Cover and keep refrigerated.

Comstock Apple Raisin Streusel Pie

SMOKEY MOUNTAIN APPLE PIE

Andrea Spring, Braeden, FL
2012 American Pie Council Crisco National Pie Championships
Professional Division Honorable Mention Apple

CRUST
½ cup ground pecans
1½ cups flour
1 tablespoon sugar
½ teaspoon salt
½ cup Crisco
4 tablespoons water

FILLING
7 large Braeburn apples
¼ cup apple juice

½ cup sugar
3 tablespoons cornstarch
½ teaspoon cinnamon

TOPPING
½ cup flour
½ cup brown sugar
¼ cup ground pecans
2 tablespoons butter
2 tablespoons butter flavored Crisco

For the Crust: Preheat oven to 400°F. Cut Crisco into flour, salt, sugar, and nuts. Mix in water and form dough into a ball. Chill dough for at least 4 hours. Roll out dough and place in 10-inch deep dish pie plate. Chill crust while you prepare apples.

For the Filling: Peel, core, and slice apples, and then mix with juice, sugar, cornstarch, and cinnamon. Place in pie crust.

For the Topping: Mix topping ingredients until crumbly and top pie. Bake at 400°F for 10 minutes. Lower heat to 325°F and bake for 1 hour or until apples are tender. Cover with foil if pie browns too quickly.

Smokey Mountain Apple Pie

LATTICE-TOPPED APPLE PIE

Linda Schiessl, Fond du Lac, WI
2013 American Pie Council Crisco National Pie Championships
Professional Division Honorable Mention Perfect Apple Pie

CRUST
2½ cups flour
1 teaspoon salt
½ tablespoon sugar
1 cup Crisco, chilled
1 egg, beaten
1 tablespoon vinegar
Water

FILLING
1 cup sugar
⅓ cup flour

1 teaspoon cinnamon
1 teaspoon nutmeg
Dash salt
8 cups apples, peeled, pared, sliced
2 tablespoon maple syrup
3 tablespoon butter

FOR THE TOP CRUST
Egg wash
1 tablespoon sugar
Freshly grated nutmeg

For the Crust: Sift together flour, sugar and salt. With pastry cutter, cut in chilled Crisco until particles are pea-sized. Beat egg and vinegar in a small bowl with a fork. Add enough water to egg mixture to measure ⅓ cup liquid. Pour egg mixture into dry mixture; stir to combine. Divide dough into two balls. Flatten into disks. Wrap in plastic and chill at least 30 minutes. On lightly floured board, roll out bottom pastry. Spray 10-inch deep-dish pie pan with cooking spray. Place bottom pastry into pie plate. Trim bottom crust to ¼-inch edge of pie plate.

For the Filling: Whisk together sugar, flour, cinnamon, nutmeg, and salt. Toss apple slices with sugar mixture. Drizzle with maple syrup. Pour mixture into prepared bottom pie crust. Top with butter. Fill bottom crust with apple filling. Top with lattice work. Brush with egg wash; sprinkle with sugar and freshly grated nutmeg. Bake at 350°F for 1 hour until golden brown and bubbly.

Lattice-Topped Apple Pie

CHERRY

BLACK FOREST CHERRY PIE

Andrea Spring, Bradenton, FL
2011 American Pie Council Crisco National Pie Championships
Professional Division Honorable Mention Crisco Classic Cherry

CRUST
1½ cups flour
½ teaspoon salt
2 tablespoons cocoa
2 tablespoons sugar
½ cup Crisco shortening
4 to 5 tablespoons cold water

FILLING
½ pound semisweet chocolate
½ pound white chocolate

1¼ sticks butter
4 eggs, separated
1 tablespoon flour
Pinch salt
1 tablespoon sugar

TOPPING
2 (15 ounce) cans cherry pie filling
4 Oreo cookies

For the Crust: Preheat oven to 400°F. Mix dry ingredients in food processor and add shortening. Process until crumbly. Add water and process into ball. Wrap and chill 2 hours. Roll out dough and place in 10-inch deep dish pie pan. Line with sprayed foil and bake at 400°F for 5 minutes. Reduce to 325°F and bake for 5 minutes or until lightly browned. Set aside.

For the Filling: Melt semisweet chocolate. Add half the butter and mix well. In a different bowl, melt white chocolate. Add the rest of the butter and mix well. Beat egg yolks in stand mixer until light and fluffy, about 5 minutes. Fold in flour and salt. Divide eggs and add half to the chocolate mix and half to the white chocolate mix. Whip egg whites until they hold shape and then add sugar. Split in half and add half to chocolate mix and half to white chocolate mix. Spread white chocolate mix in the bottom of the pie crust, bake for 8 minutes. Spread chocolate mix on top and bake until just done, 10 to 15 minutes. Set aside.

For the Topping: Cook cherries over medium heat until most of the liquid reduces. Set aside to cool. When pie is cool, put cherries on top. Crush Oreos and sprinkle over cherries. Chill overnight.

Black Forest Cherry Pie

CHERRY BERRY DOUBLE CRUST CRUMB PIE

Evette Rahman, Orlando, FL
2011 American Pie Council Crisco National Pie Championships
Amateur Division 3rd Place Crisco Classic Cherry

CRUST
3 cups flour
3 tablespoons sugar
1½ teaspoons salt
¾ teaspoon baking powder
½ cup Crisco shortening
½ cup unsalted butter, cold, cubed
½ cup heavy cream
1½ tablespoons vinegar
1½ tablespoons oil
1 egg beaten with 1 tablespoon cream
Sugar for sprinkling

FILLING
1 cup tart cherry juice
1 teaspoon lemon juice
⅛ cup minute tapioca
2 tablespoons salted butter
¼ teaspoon pure almond extract
3 cups fresh pitted dark sweet cherries, divided
2 cups fresh blueberries, divided
1⅛ cups sugar
⅛ cup cornstarch

TOPPING
½ cup flour
¼ cup light brown sugar, packed
⅛ teaspoon ground cinnamon
Pinch salt
¼ cup unsalted butter, cold, cubed
1 to 2 tablespoons sliced blanched almonds

For the Crust: Mix flour, sugar, salt, and baking powder. Cut in shortening and butter. Stir together oil, vinegar, and cream. Add to flour and butter mixture by tossing lightly. Knead briefly. Form into 2 disks. Cover with plastic wrap and refrigerate for at least 1 hour.

For the Filling: In saucepan over medium heat, reduce tart cherry juice and lemon juice to ½ cup. Stir in tapioca. Add in 1 cup cherries and ½ cup blueberries. Cook until thickened. Remove from heat and stir in butter and almond extract. Place remaining fruit in large bowl. Add in cooked fruit and stir to coat well. Mix together sugar and cornstarch. Add to fruit to coat thoroughly. Roll out 1 disk of dough on a lightly floured surface and place in a deep dish pie plate. Add filling. Roll out remaining disk of dough and cut into strips to cover pie, leaving spaces between strips, such as in a lattice design. Crimp edges. Brush with egg wash and sprinkle with sugar.

For the Topping: Preheat oven to 400°F. Stir together flour, sugar, cinnamon, and salt. Cut in butter and combine well until small crumbs form. Refrigerate until use. Bake pie for 25 minutes at 400°F. Reduce heat to 375°F. Bake for 15 minutes. Sprinkle with crumb topping and almonds. Bake for an additional 15 to 20 minutes or until bubbly and golden. Cover edges with pie shield or aluminum foil during baking, if needed, to prevent excess browning. Place on rack to cool completely before serving.

Cherry Berry Double Crust Crumb Pie

CHERRY PIE

Andy Hilton, Davenport, FL
2010 American Pie Council Crisco National Pie Championships
Professional Division Honorable Mention Crisco Classic Cherry

CRUST
½ cup butter, cold
½ cup Crisco
2½ cups flour, sifted
½ teaspoon salt
1 tablespoon sugar
½ teaspoon baking powder
6 to 9 tablespoons cold water
Egg wash: 1 egg white with 1 teaspoon water

FILLING
4½ cups sour cherries (frozen)
1 cup dark sweet cherries (frozen)

¾ cup dried cherries, keeping these separate from other cherries
1 tablespoon lemon juice
¾ cup sugar
4 teaspoon modified cornstarch
½ teaspoon almond flavoring
1 tablespoon cherry extract
3 drops red food coloring
Butter to dot the top

For the Crust: Preheat oven to 400°F. Sift together dry ingredients in a bowl. Add the butter and shortening. With a pastry cutter, cut the butter and shortening into the flour mixture until the butter and shortening are about the size of peas. Sprinkle the cold water into the mixture 2 or 3 tablespoons at a time. Fluff with a fork and add the rest of the water until the mixture holds together. Cover the dough and place it into the refrigerator to chill for 30 minutes. Form the dough into a ball and cut it in half, one for the bottom crust and one for the top crust. Roll out on a lightly floured surface.

For the Filling: Thaw sour cherries and dark sweet cherries for 2 minutes in the microwave, saving about ¼ cup of the juice. Sprinkle 1 tablespoon of lemon juice over the cherries. Blend in the sugar, dried cherries, cornstarch, food coloring, juice, and almond and cherry flavorings. Place cherry mixture into the pie crust and dot with butter. Cover with the second crust, cut vent holes, brush the top crust with egg wash, and sprinkle the top with sugar. Place pie on foil on the bottom rack of the oven and bake at 400°F for 15 minutes. Reduce oven temperature to 350°F and bake for 45 minutes.

FIVE STAR CHERRY PIE

Karen Hall, Elm Creek, NE
2008 American Pie Council Crisco National Pie Championships
Amateur Division 3rd Place Crisco Classic Cherry

CRUST
3 cups unbleached flour
1 cup plus 1 tablespoon butter-
    flavored Crisco, cold
½ teaspoon baking powder
1 egg
1 teaspoon sea salt
¼ cup plus 1 tablespoon ice cold
    water
1 tablespoon sugar
1 tablespoon rice vinegar

FILLING
2 (14.5-ounce) cans sour pitted
    cherries, drained and reserving
    ¾ cup cherry juice

1¼ cups sugar
1 tablespoon tapioca
2 tablespoons cornstarch
¼ cup pear nectar
½ teaspoon almond flavoring
¼ teaspoon red food coloring
2 tablespoons butter

GLAZE
1 egg white, slightly beaten
1 tablespoon sugar

For the Crust: In a large bowl, combine flour, baking powder, salt, and sugar. With a pastry blender, cut in Crisco until mixture resembles coarse crumbs. In a small bowl, beat egg, water, and vinegar together. Add egg mixture slowly to flour mixture, tossing with a fork until mixture is moistened. Do not over mix. Divide dough and shape into 3 balls, flatten each to form a disk. Wrap each disk with plastic wrap and refrigerate for at least 30 minutes before using. Makes 3 single crusts. Use two disks for this recipe.

For the Filling: In a medium saucepan, combine sugar, tapioca, and cornstarch. Add reserved cherry juice, pear nectar, almond flavoring, red food coloring, and butter; cook and stir over medium-high heat for 5 to 6 minutes or until mixture thickens. Stir in cherries and simmer for 3 minutes. Refrigerate until completely cooled or overnight.

Preheat oven to 425°F.

Roll out bottom crust and line a 9-inch pie dish. Roll out top crust and cut for a lattice top. Pour filling into pie shell. Create a pretty lattice top, trim, and flute edge. Brush lattice top gently with slightly beaten egg white and sprinkle with sugar. Protect edge of pie with foil. Bake at 425°F for 10 minutes. Reduce oven to 375°F and bake 30 to 35 minutes or until golden.

Five Star Cherry Pie

CHERRY PEACH BLACKBERRY PIE

Linda Hundt, DeWitt, MI
2010 American Pie Council Crisco National Pie Championships
Professional Division 1st Place Crisco Classic Cherry

CRUST
1½ cups flour
¼ teaspoon baking powder
½ teaspoon salt
1 teaspoon sugar
½ cup Crisco butter-flavored shortening, refrigerated

FILLING
4 cups frozen tart cherries, thawed
¾ cup sugar

¼ cup cornstarch
½ teaspoon lime zest
1 cup frozen blackberries, thawed
1 cup frozen peaches, thawed

CRUMB TOPPING
½ cup butter, softened
¼ teaspoon salt
1 cup flour
½ cup brown sugar
½ cup sugar

For the Crust: Mix flour, baking powder, salt, and sugar in KitchenAid style mixer on medium speed swiftly until dough texture appears "pea-like." Carefully sprinkle water in crust mix until it starts to become moistened and gathers together. Pat into a disk, wrap, and refrigerate for at least half an hour. Roll out on to floured surface and place in pie pan. Crimp crust. Freeze until ready to use.

For the Filling: Preheat oven to 400°F. Mix cherries, sugar, and cornstarch in medium saucepan. Stir constantly on medium heat until boiling. Boil for 1 minute. Add lime zest. Place 1 cup blackberries and 1 cup peaches on bottom of uncooked pie shell. Pour cherry mixture over blackberries and peaches.

For the Topping: Mix butter, salt, flour, and brown and white sugar until mixture is fine in texture. Top pie with crumb topping so no pie filling is showing. Bake for 45 to 60 minutes until pie is bubbling over sides.

Cherry Peach Blackberry Pie

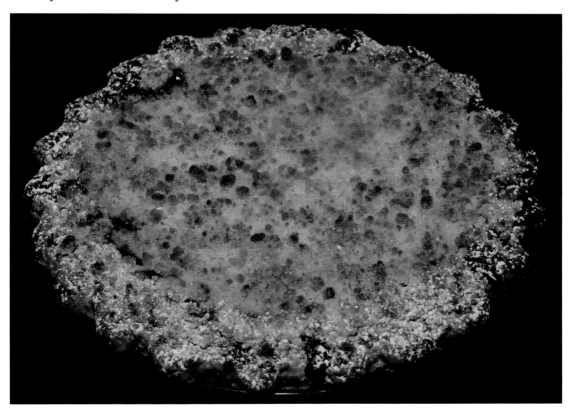

BETTER THAN GRANDMA'S CHERRY PIE

Valarie Enters, Sanford, FL
2008 American Pie Council Crisco National Pie Championships
Professional Division 1st Place Crisco Classic Cherry

CRUST

2 cups all-purpose White Lily flour
½ cup Softasilk cake flour
3 teaspoon powdered sugar (10X)
Additional flour as needed, up to ¼ cup
½ cup butter-flavored Crisco shortening
½ cup real butter, salted
½ teaspoon salt
1 egg
2 teaspoons vinegar
¼ cup ice water (add more water as needed for high altitude)

FILLING

2 jars Morello cherries
4 tablespoons tapioca
Pinch of salt
1 cup sugar
1 teaspoon lemon juice
1 teaspoon vanilla
¼ teaspoon almond extract
¼ cup cherry juice, reserved from jars
3 tablespoons of butter, dotted
Egg wash
Coarse sugar (for garnish)
Apricot glaze (for finish)

For the Crust: Using two pastry blenders, blend the butter, shortening, flours, powdered sugar, and salt. Whisk the liquids in a 2-cup measure and pour over dry ingredients. Incorporate all the ingredients without overworking the dough. Toss additional flour on top and scrape sides of bowl. Roll out dough and make bottom crust. Set in fridge while working on filling.

For the Filling: Mix fruit, tapioca, salt, sugar, lemon juice, vanilla, almond extract, and cherry juice in a large bowl. Let macerate for at least 15 minutes.

Preheat oven to 450°F. Put filling into pie shell and dot with butter. Brush edges with egg wash before covering with a lattice top crust. (Use a pie bird to vent pie filling if making a regular top crust.) Top with coarse sugar. Bake with pie crust shields on and an extra cookie sheet lined with foil on the rack below. Bake at 450°F for 10 minutes. Bring temperature down to 350°F for 40 to 50 more minutes and until juices are visibly thick and crust is golden. Brush hot pie with apricot glaze.

Better Than Grandma's Cherry Pie

SENSATIONAL CHERRY PIE

Kathleen Costello, Tallmadge, OH
2004 American Pie Council Crisco National Pie Championships
Amateur Division 2nd Place Crisco Classic Cherry

CRUST
1½ cups Crisco butter-flavored shortening, plus some extra shortening to grease pie pan
½ cup sugar
2 tablespoons almond extract
1 egg, beaten
2¼ cups flour, plus some extra for flouring work surface
1 egg white, beaten, for egg wash

FILLING
1½ cups sugar
5 tablespoons cornstarch

4 cups cherries (canned cherries in water, reserve ½ cup water, drain the rest)
2 tablespoons caramel syrup
Pinch of salt
½ cup water from cherries
1 egg white, beaten for egg wash
Sugar for sprinkling on pie top

For the Crust: Stir the shortening, sugar, almond extract, and egg together until creamy. Add 2¼ cups flour, a third at a time, until incorporated. Do not over mix dough. Cover dough in bowl with plastic wrap. Chill for 30 minutes in refrigerator.

Lightly grease pie pan with some Crisco butter flavored shortening. Remove dough from refrigerator and take half from bowl, form a ball, and lightly flour the dough, work surface, and hands. Flatten dough and sprinkle a little flour on top. Roll dough out to form a circle. Line bottom of pie pan with dough, poking holes in dough with a fork. Brush lightly with beaten egg white. Roll out other half of dough for top crust.

For Decorative Cherries for Top of Pie (Optional): Take a small amount of left over pie dough and add several drops of red food coloring in center and mix well. Make 3 or more small marble size balls and place on top of pie. Mix small amount of cocoa into dough to make stems and place under each cherry. Use 2 tablespoons of dough and place several drops of green food coloring in center and mix well. Press dough flat and cut out leaves using knife. Place on top of pie as desired.

For the Filling: Preheat oven to 375°F. In a saucepan, combine sugar, salt, cornstarch, and water. Cook over medium heat and stir until cornstarch is dissolved. Add cherries and caramel syrup, stirring occasionally, and continue to cook mixture until it becomes thick and clear. Remove from heat and set aside to cool.

Place cherry filling in prepared pie shell. Put top crust on pie and crimp edges. Place small slits in top of pie for steam to escape. Beat 1 egg white until foamy and brush top of pie. Lightly sprinkle sugar on top of pie.

Before placing pie in oven, put aluminum foil around crimped pie edge to prevent overbrowning. Spray the inner side of foil with cooking spray to prevent sticking when removing foil. Remove foil 10 minutes before pie is done. Bake for 45 to 50 minutes.

MAMA MIA'S CHERRY PIE

Phyllis Szymanek, Toledo, OH
2013 American Pie Council Crisco National Pie Championships
Amateur Division 1st Place Cherry

CRUST
1½ cups Pillsbury all-purpose flour
½ teaspoon salt
1 tablespoon sugar
½ cups chilled Crisco shortening
3 tablespoons chilled butter
3 to 4 tablespoons ice water
1 teaspoon vinegar
1 egg plus 1 teaspoon water
    (egg wash)

FILLING
1 cup sugar
⅛ teaspoon salt

¼ cup cornstarch
2 (24-ounce) jars pitted cherries
    (about 5 cups), drained, reserving
    1 cup cherry juice
1 tablespoon butter
¼ teaspoon almond extract
½ teaspoon orange extract
¼ teaspoon red food coloring

TOPPING
1 cup sugar
1 cup Pillsbury all-purpose flour
¼ teaspoon salt
1 stick butter (softened)

For the Crust: In a mixing bowl, combine flour, salt, and sugar. Cut in Crisco and butter until crumbly. Add vinegar to ice water. Add vinegar/ice water mixture one tablespoon at a time until dough forms into a ball. Shape dough into a disk shape, wrap in plastic wrap, and chill for one hour. Roll out on floured surface to fit a 9-inch pie dish. Trim crust and flute edges. Brush with egg wash. Set aside.

For the Filling: Drain cherries, reserving 1 cup of cherry juice. In a saucepan, add juice, sugar, salt, and cornstarch. Bring to a boil over medium heat, add cherries. Cook and stir until thickened and bubbly. Remove from heat, stir in butter, food coloring, and almond, and orange extracts. Pour into pie shell.

For the Topping: Mix together sugar, flour, and salt, cut in butter until crumbly. Cover pie filling with topping. Bake at 400 °F for 15 minutes. Reduce heat to 375 °F and bake for 40 to 45 minutes or until juice starts to bubble. Cool on wire rack.

Mama Mia's Cherry Pie

CHERRY PRALINE PIE

Raquel Hammond, St. Cloud, FL
2006 American Pie Council Crisco National Pie Championships
Amateur Division 2nd Place Crisco Classic Cherry

CRUST
2 cups unbleached flour
1 cup cake flour
2 tablespoons sugar
1 teaspoon salt
8 tablespoons (1 stick) unsalted butter, cut up
½ cup plus 2 tablespoons Crisco shortening, cut up
1 large egg yolk
2 teaspoon vinegar
½ cup ice water
1 large egg white with 1 tablespoon water for egg glaze

FILLING
5½ cups canned sour cherries, drained
1¼ cups sugar
¼ cup cornstarch
½ teaspoon almond extract
¼ teaspoon nutmeg
¼ teaspoon salt
Few drops red food coloring (optional)

TOPPING
½ cup Demerara sugar
4 tablespoons unsalted butter
2 tablespoons heavy cream
Pinch of salt
¼ teaspoon cinnamon
½ cup slivered almonds, coarsely chopped

For the Crust: Place butter and shortening either on a plate or in plastic wrap in freezer for at least 30 minutes. In a large bowl, whisk flour, cake flour, sugar, and salt until thoroughly combined. Add cut up butter and shortening. With pastry blender or fingertips, cut in until mixture resembles dry rice. Add yolk and vinegar. Drizzle ¼ cup ice water over mixture. Lightly toss until dough just begins to cling together in clumps. Sprinkle on a little bit more water if dough looks too dry. The consistency should feel pliable like clay and cling together, but should not be sticky.

Turn dough out onto waxed paper. Lift opposite corners and press them together, squeezing dough into a cohesive ball. Flatten into disk. Divide in half. Wrap each disk in plastic wrap and refrigerate at least 30 minutes, preferably overnight. When ready to use, allow chilled dough to sit out at room temperature a few minutes to soften it slightly before rolling out.

Lightly butter 10-inch pie pan. Roll out both bottom and top crusts. Line pan with bottom pastry. Brush with egg glaze. Refrigerate both pastries until needed.

For the Filling: Preheat oven to 425°F. In a large bowl, combine cherries, sugar, cornstarch, almond extract, nutmeg, salt, and red food coloring. Set aside to juice for 10 minutes. Gently stir filling together, then spoon into pie shell. Attach top crust, seal, then flute as desired. Cut small hole in the middle and few slashes to vent steam. Glaze or leave plain. Bake 15 minutes in lower third of oven. Reduce temperature to 375°F. Bake an additional 30 to 45 minutes or until juices bubble thickly through vents. If necessary, cover edge and top with foil to prevent over-browning. Remove from oven and cool on wire rack.

For the Topping: Melt butter in small saucepan. Add sugar, heavy cream, and salt. Bring to gentle boil and boil until sugar is dissolved. Remove from heat. Stir in cinnamon and almonds. Cool about 2 to 3 minutes. Spoon praline over top of pie. Return to oven and broil until topping is bubbly and golden brown. Cool on wire rack at least 2 hours.

FOURTH OF JULY CHERRY PIE

John Sunvold, Winter Park, FL
2013 American Pie Council Crisco National Pie Championships
Amateur Division 3rd Place Cherry

CRUST
1½ cups graham cracker crumbs
⅓ cup sugar
½ cup melted butter-flavored Crisco

FILLING
8 ounces cream cheese
½ cup powdered sugar
8 ounces Cool Whip

TOPPING ONE (CHERRY)
3½ cups frozen tart cherries thawed
    with juices
1 cup sugar
¼ to ⅓ cup cornstarch (the more you
    use, the thicker it will be)
1 cup water
1 tablespoon lemon juice
⅛ teaspoon cinnamon
2 cups extra cherries if you like a lot
    of cherries.

¼ teaspoon almond extract.
6 drops red food coloring (optional)

TOPPING TWO (BLUEBERRY)
1¾ cups thawed frozen blueberries
    with juices
⅜ cup sugar
⅛ to ¼ cup cornstarch (the more you
    use, the thicker it will be)
¼ cup water
2 tablespoons lemon juice
3 to 6 drops blue food coloring
    (optional)

GARNISH
Whipped cream
Red, white, and blue candies or
    garnish

For the Crust: Mix all ingredients together and press mixture into pie plate. Chill for 10 minutes. Bake in a 375°F oven for 10 minutes, or until brown. Allow to cool down to room temperature.

For the Filling: Beat cream cheese and powdered sugar until smooth. Fold in the Cool Whip. Gently spread into crust and chill.

For Topping One (Cherry): Place cornstarch and sugar in a pot and whisk. Add the rest of the ingredients except the cherries and cook over medium heat until boiling. Boil for 1½ to 2 minutes. Fold in cherries. Cool.

For Topping Two (Blueberry): Place cornstarch and sugar in a pot and whisk. Add the rest of the ingredients except the berries and cook over medium heat until boiling. Boil for 1½ to 2 minutes. Fold in berries. Cool.

Top cream cheese filling with ¼ of cherry filling and drops of blueberry filling, then swirl into cream cheese to create a marble effect. Top pie with most of remaining cherry filling and periodic teaspoons of the blueberry filling on top, but don't mix the two fillings together.

For the Garnish: Garnish with favorite whipped cream topping and decorate the top as desired using cherries, blueberries, or anything red, white, blue.

Fourth of July Cherry Pie

CHECKERBOARD CHERRY PIE

Ron Bronitsky, Bernalillo, NM
2013 American Pie Council Crisco National Pie Championships
Amateur Division 2nd Place Cherry

**PLAIN CRUST
(MAKES 2 CRUSTS)**
2½ cups flour
2 tablespoons sugar
1 teaspoon salt
12 tablespoons unsalted butter, cut in cubes (chilled)
½ cup Crisco vegetable shortening (chilled)
½ cup ice water

**CHOCOLATE CRUST
(MAKES 2 CRUSTS)**
2½ cups minus 3 tablespoons flour
3 tablespoons sugar
1 teaspoon salt
3 tablespoons Dutch processed cocoa
12 tablespoons unsalted butter, cut in cubes

½ cup Crisco vegetable shortening
1 tablespoon vanilla
2 tablespoons chocolate extract
Add ice water to vanilla and chocolate extract to equal ½ cup

FILLING
5 to 6 cups sour pie cherries (frozen or fresh cherries, if using frozen do not defrost)
1 cup sugar
3 tablespoons tapioca flour
⅛ teaspoon cinnamon
¼ teaspoon fresh ground nutmeg
¼ teaspoon almond extract
1 tablespoon sour cherry concentrate
Fresh grated lemon rind, about 1 teaspoon
1 tablespoon unsalted butter

For the Plain Crust: Blend all solid ingredients together, cutting in with food processor using one second pulses until forming pea-size particles. Pour into bowl and lightly add water until moist. Form into ball. Cut into 2 halves and form into two 6-inch patties. Refrigerate for at least 1 hour then roll out one patty for bottom of 9-inch pie. Roll out the other patty and use for lattice crust.

For the Chocolate Crust: Blend all solid ingredients together, cutting in with food processor using 1 second pulses until forming pea-size particles. Pour into bowl. Add water, vanilla, and chocolate extract to flour mixture. Form into ball. Cut into 2 halves. Form into two 6-inch patties. Refrigerate for at least 1 hour and then roll one patty to use for lattice crust. The other patty can be saved for another pie.

For the Filling: Mix all ingredients except butter together. Place in unbaked plain pie crust. Dot filling with butter.

For the Lattice Crust: Roll both the chocolate and plain crusts out for a 9-inch pie. Cut into lattice strips. Weave into a checkerboard pattern, using chocolate strips going one way, the plain strips the other.

Brush top of crust with slightly beaten egg white. Sprinkle decorative sugar on top.

Bake at 420°F for 20 minutes. Reduce oven heat to 375°F and bake for 50 to 60 more minutes until filling is bubbling. Protect edge of crust with aluminum foil to prevent over browning. Remove from oven and let it cool for at least 8 hours, better if overnight.

Checkerboard Cherry Pie

SIMPLE PLEASURES CHERRY PIE

Susan Boyle, Debary, FL
2013 American Pie Council Crisco National Pie Championships
Professional Division 1st Place Crisco Classic Cherry

CRUST
1 cup Crisco original or butter flavored (cold)
¼ teaspoon salt
¼ cup toasted almonds
2½ cups all-purpose flour
1 egg
1 tablespoon white distilled vinegar
¼ cup ice water

FILLING
½ teaspoon almond extract
2 cups of frozen dark red sweet cherries
2 cups of drained dark Morella cherries
2 cups of drained King Orchards red tart cherries
A few drops red food coloring
1¼ cups sugar
⅛ teaspoon cinnamon
3 tablespoons of Clearjel (mix with sugar before adding to cherries)

For the Crust: Mix together Crisco, salt, and flour until it resembles coarse crumbs. Mix together in another bowl egg, water, and vinegar whisk and add all at once to flour mixture. Toss with fork until mixture forms a ball. Knead in almonds and pat into a disk. Refrigerate until ready to use. Roll out pastry and crimp edges. Chill before filling.

For the Filling: In a large bowl, gently mix all cherries. In a separate bowl, mix sugar and Clearjel together, add cinnamon, and sprinkle on top of cherries, then add almond extract and red food coloring. Toss well and fill chilled pie crust. Top with lattice strips. Bake at 375°F for 30 to 40 minutes. Cool before slicing.

Simple Pleasures Cherry Pie

CRUMBLING CHERRY PIE

Lisa Sparks, Atlanta, IN
2013 American Pie Council Crisco National Pie Championships
Professional Division Honorable Mention Crisco Classic Cherry

CRUST
¾ cup butter-flavored Crisco
2 cups all-purpose flour
1 teaspoon sugar
5 tablespoons cold water

FILLING
4 cups tart cherries
1 cup red raspberries

3 tablespoons tapioca
3 tablespoons butter
1 teaspoon lemon juice

TOPPING
¾ cup sugar
½ cup flour
¼ cup butter, cubed

For the Crust: Cut Crisco, flour, and sugar together, add cold water, and toss until dough forms a ball. Refrigerate overnight.

For the Filling: Combine all ingredients and pour into pie shell.

For the Topping: Mix dry ingredients. Cut in butter until it forms pea size crumbles. Spread over cherry mix and bake at 350°F for 1 to 1½ hours.

Crumbling Cherry Pie

FROSTING CREATIONS CHERRY SUNDAE PIE

Phyllis Szymanek, Toledo, OH
2013 American Pie Council Crisco National Pie Championships
Amateur Division 1st Place Comstock Cherry

CRUST
1½ cups Pillsbury all-purpose flour
½ teaspoon salt
1 tablespoon sugar
½ cups chilled Crisco shortening
3 tablespoons chilled butter
3 to 4 tablespoons ice water
1 teaspoon vinegar
1 egg plus 1 teaspoon water
   (egg wash)

FILLING
1 (21-ounce) can Comstock More
   Fruit Cherry Pie Filling
⅛ teaspoon orange extract
⅛ teaspoon almond extract
1 teaspoon melted butter
1 teaspoon maraschino cherry juice
1 teaspoon lemon juice

TOPPING ONE
1 (10-ounce) jar of maraschino
   cherries with stems (drained)
8 ounces cream cheese, softened
1 cup water
⅔ cup sweetened condensed milk
1 (3.4-ounce) package instant vanilla
   pudding
¼ teaspoon almond extract
12 ounces whipped topping
1 cup chopped pecans

TOPPING TWO
4 ounces cream cheese
1 cup powdered sugar
1 teaspoon vanilla
1 package Duncan Hines Frosting
   Creations Cherry Vanilla flavor
   packet
1½ cups whipped topping
1 cup chopped pecans

For the Crust: In a mixing bowl, combine flour, salt, and sugar. Cut in Crisco and butter until crumbly. Add vinegar to ice water. Add vinegar/ice water mixture one tablespoon at a time until dough forms into a ball. Shape dough into a disk shape, wrap in plastic wrap, and chill for one hour. Roll out on floured surface to fit a 9-inch pie dish. Trim crust and flute edges. Brush with egg wash. Set aside.

For the Filling: In a small bowl combine all filling ingredients. Pour into pie shell, prick sides with fork, and cover crust edges with foil. Bake at 375°F for 20 minutes. Remove foil. Bake an additional 15 to 20 minutes until crust is golden brown. Cool on wire rack.

For Topping One: Set aside 5 maraschino cherries with stems for garnish. Remove the stems and cut up the remaining cherries. In a mixing bowl, beat cream cheese until light and fluffy; gradually beat in water and condensed milk. Add pudding mix and extract. Fold in 2 cups of whipped topping; add ½ cup nuts and maraschino cherries (chopped). Pour onto filling. Chill 4 to 6 hours.

For Topping Two: Beat cream cheese and sugar until combined. Add vanilla. Add Duncan Hines Frosting Creations package. Fold in whipped topping. Cover entire pie with topping. Sprinkle with pecans and place 5 maraschino cherries in center of pie.

Frosting Creations Cherry Sundae Pie

CHOCOLATE

CARAMEL PECAN GERMAN CHOCOLATE FRENCH SILK PIE

Beth Campbell, Belleville, WI
2005 American Pie Council Crisco National Pie Championships
Amateur Division 1st Place Crisco Classic Chocolate

CRUST
1 cup flour
½ cup shortening
¼ cup cold water
Pinch of salt

CARAMEL PECAN LAYER
20 caramels
2 tablespoons milk
½ cup chopped pecans

GERMAN CHOCOLATE FRENCH SILK LAYER
1½ cups whipping cream
6 ounces German sweet chocolate
1 ounce semisweet chocolate square
⅓ cup butter
⅓ cup sugar
2 egg yolks, lightly beaten

For the Crust: Combine flour and salt in a bowl. Cut shortening into the flour and salt until the particles are about the size of small peas. Sprinkle the water into the particles until all the flour is moistened (don't mix too much or crust will be tough). Gather the pastry into a ball and refrigerate until dough is chilled (overnight or at least for a few hours). Preheat oven to 475°F. Roll out on a lightly floured board until it is about two inches larger than the pie pan you are using. Fold the pastry into quarters, unfold, and ease into the pie plate, pressing firmly against the bottom and sides, and pinching the crust edges into whatever designs you prefer. For baked pie shell, prick the bottom and side thoroughly with a fork and bake at 475°F until lightly browned, about 8 to 10 minutes. Let it cool.

For the Caramel Pecan Layer: Combine 20 caramels with 2 tablespoons of milk in a saucepan on low heat, stirring frequently until smooth. Stir in ½ cup chopped pecans. Pour into the baked piecrust and cool. When totally cooled, pour in the chocolate French silk mixture and refrigerate.

For the German Chocolate French Silk Layer: In a heavy saucepan, combine cream, both chocolates, butter, and sugar. Cook over low heat for 10 minutes or until the chocolate

Caramel Pecan German Chocolate French Silk Pie

melts, stirring constantly. Remove from the heat. Gradually stir half of the hot mixture into the beaten egg yolks. Return all to the saucepan. Cook over medium to low heat for 5 minutes or until it begins to bubble. Remove from the heat. Place the saucepan in a bowl of ice water or in the freezer, stirring often, for about 25 minutes or until the mixture stiffens and it is difficult to stir. Put the chocolate mixture into a medium mixing bowl. Beat the cooled chocolate mixture for 2 to 3 minutes or until the mixture is light and fluffy. Spread the filling over the caramel mixture in the crust. Cover and refrigerate for 5 to 24 hours. Garnish as desired.

CHOCOLATE CARAMEL PECAN PIE

Dionna Hurt, Longwood, FL
2005 Crisco National Pie Championships
Amateur Division 1st Place Crisco Classic Chocolate

CRUST
1 bag Oreos, crushed
¾ stick butter, melted

FILLING ONE
½ cup cream
1 bag caramels
1 cup pecans

FILLING TWO
2 (8-ounce) packages cream cheese
1 cup powdered sugar
½ cup cocoa
1 tablespoon half and half
2 cups heavy cream

For the Crust: Mix Oreos and butter together, and press into 9-inch pie pan.

For Filling One: In medium saucepan, heat ½ cup cream until steamy. Add caramels and stir until smooth. Add pecans to caramel and stir. Pour into prepared crust.

For Filling Two: In a medium bowl, mix together cream cheese and sugar until smooth. Add cocoa and 1 tablespoon half and half and beat until very smooth. Set aside. In a separate bowl, whip heavy cream until stiff. Fold whipped cream into cocoa mixture until incorporated. Layer cocoa mixture onto caramel mixture and chill.

Chocolate Caramel Pecan Pie

CHOCOLATE CREAM PIE

Phyllis Bartholomew, Columbus, NE
2004 Crisco National Pie Championships
Amateur Division 1st Place Crisco Classic Chocolate

CRUST
2 cups flour
1 cup cake flour
1 cup butter-flavored Crisco
   shortening
1 whole egg
1 tablespoon cider vinegar
½ teaspoon salt
⅓ cup ice water

FILLING
3 egg yolks
1½ cups sugar
3 tablespoons cornstarch

⅓ to ½ cup unsweetened cocoa
   powder
½ teaspoon salt
3 cups milk or half-and-half
1 tablespoon butter
1½ teaspoons vanilla

MERINGUE
¾ cup egg whites
¾ teaspoon cream of tartar
2 tablespoons cornstarch
⅛ teaspoon salt
½ cup sugar
½ teaspoon vanilla

For the Crust: Preheat oven to 425°F. Cut the shortening into the flour until it resembles coarse crumbs. Beat together the other ingredients and stir into the flour. Mix just until incorporated. Form dough into a disk and wrap in plastic wrap. Refrigerate to chill. Roll out about ⅓ of the dough between 2 sheets of plastic wrap. Place in a 9-inch pie dish. Bake for about 10 minutes or until golden. Cool.

For the Filling: In a bowl, mix together the yolks and sugar. Mix in the cornstarch, cocoa powder, and salt. Add the milk and stir gently. Put into a large saucepan and cook over medium heat, stirring constantly until it boils. Remove from heat and add the butter and vanilla. Pour into baked pie shell and top with meringue (recipe follows) or whipped topping.

For the Meringue: Preheat oven to 350°F. Beat the egg whites until frothy. Add the cream of tartar. Continue to beat until soft peaks form. Combine the sugar, cornstarch, and salt. Slowly start adding the sugar to the whites while whipping on high speed. Whip until the sugar is dissolved. Add the vanilla, mix, and add to the top of pie. Bake 12 to 15 minutes or until golden brown.

TURTLE PIE

Jeanne Ely, Mulberry, FL
2011 American Pie Council National Pie Championships
Amateur Division 3rd Place Crisco Classic Chocolate

CRUST
3 cups flour
1 teaspoon salt
¼ cup shortening
1 cup butter-flavored shortening
1 egg
5 tablespoons cold water
1 tablespoon vinegar

LAYER ONE
1 cup pecan halves
Butter-flavored Crisco spray
Salt

LAYER TWO
14-ounce can sweetened condensed
    milk, label removed

LAYER THREE
½ cup margarine
¾ cup sugar
4 squares melted unsweetened
    chocolate, cooled
2 eggs
2 cups heavy cream, whipped

For the Crust: Preheat oven to 350°F. Cut together flour, salt, and shortening until oatmeal-like in consistency. Beat egg in a cup; add water, vinegar, and almond flavoring. Beat together and pour into flour mixture. Blend well. Roll out dough and place in 9-inch pie plate. Bake until golden brown. Cool.

For Layer One: Place pecan halves in baking dish, spray with butter flavor Crisco spray, and sprinkle with salt. Bake on a cookie sheet at 350°F for 10 minutes. Cool and place in bottom of pie shell.

For Layer Two: Boil with the label removed, 1 can sweetened condensed milk for 3 hours, turning every half hour. Cool completely, and then spread sweetened condensed milk on top of the roasted pecans.

For Layer Three: Cream together margarine and sugar. Stir in cooled chocolate. Add 1 egg at a time, beating 5 minutes between each egg. Fold in whipped cream. Spread on top of pie. Chill until firm. Decorate as desired.

Turtle Pie

CHOCOLATE SIN PIE

Christine Montalvo, Windsor Heights, IA
2007 American Pie Council Crisco National Pie Championships
Amateur Division 2nd Place Crisco Classic Chocolate

CRUST
½ cup chopped pecans
½ cup butter, melted
¼ cup sugar
1 cup all-purpose flour

FILLING ONE
1 cup frozen whipped topping,
  thawed
8-ounce package cream cheese
1 teaspoon vanilla
1 cup confectioners' sugar
1 cup toffee chips, divided

FILLING TWO
5.9-ounce package instant chocolate
  pudding mix
1⅓ cups milk

TOPPING
2 cups frozen whipped topping,
  thawed

GARNISH
Mini chocolate chips for garnish

For the Crust: Preheat oven to 350°F. Mix together pecans, sugar, melted butter, and flour. Pat into bottom and up the sides of a 9-inch pie pan. Bake until lightly browned, about 20 to 25 minutes.

For Filling One: In a mixing bowl, blend 1 cup whipped topping, cream cheese, vanilla, and confectioners' sugar until creamy. Spread into cooled crust. Sprinkle ¼ cup of toffee chips evenly over cream cheese mixture.

For Filling Two: Whisk together pudding mix and milk. Spread evenly over cheese layer.

For the Topping: Spread the whipped topping on top of the pudding layer.

For the Garnish: Sprinkle top with remaining toffee chips. Garnish with mini chocolate chips. Chill 1½ to 2 hours.

MINT CHOCOLATE CHIP CREAM PIE

Johnna Poulson, Celebration, FL
2004 American Pie Council Crisco National Pie Championships
Amateur Division 3rd Place Crisco Classic Chocolate

CRUST
1⅓ cups flour
¼ teaspoon salt
2 teaspoons sugar
½ cup Crisco shortening
3 to 4 tablespoons ice cold water

FILLING
2 cups half-and-half
1 cinnamon stick
2 cups heavy whipping cream
1 cup sugar
¼ cup flour
3 tablespoons cornstarch
4 large egg yolks

¼ cup unsweetened cocoa powder
2 ounces bittersweet chocolate, chopped (Ghirardelli or Lindt chocolate)
1 teaspoon vanilla extract
1 tablespoon butter
2 tablespoons crème de menthe

TOPPING
1¼ cups whipping cream
1 tablespoon powdered sugar
½ teaspoon pure peppermint extract
3 tablespoons finely chopped plain chocolate bar
Fresh mint for garnish

For the Crust: Combine flour, salt, and sugar in a bowl; blend in shortening with fingers until mixture resembles coarse meal. Sprinkle cold water over mixture until ingredients are moist. Form into a ball and chill overnight. On the following day, preheat oven to 425°F and then roll dough between two sheets of waxed paper to ⅛-inch thickness. Place into pie tin. Dock bottom and sides of pastry shell. Spray the bottom of an additional pie tin and place on top of pastry. Flip pans over so they are upside down and bake for 10 to 12 minutes. Remove from oven and turn the pans right side up. Lift the additional pie tin off carefully. Let cool to room temperature.

For the Filling: Pour half-and-half in saucepan, add the cinnamon stick, and heat to almost boiling. Remove from heat and place in the refrigerator for half an hour to combine flavors.

Remove cinnamon stick and add the whipping cream to the mixture. In a separate mixing bowl, mix sugar, flour, and cornstarch. Add egg yolks one at a time. Blend with a fork until incorporated. Fold in cocoa powder. Add mixture to the cream mixture and heat slowly while constantly stirring. When the mixture begins to thicken, add bittersweet chocolate. Continue cooking the mixture until thick. Once it has reached a smooth consistency, remove from heat; add vanilla, butter, and crème de menthe. Pour directly into prebaked pie shell. Press plastic wrap directly on the surface of the pie and refrigerate overnight.

For the Topping: Whip cream until almost stiff. Add powdered sugar and peppermint extract. Gently fold in chopped chocolate. Remove pie from refrigerator and gently lift plastic. Spoon or tube whipped cream on top of pie. Garnish with fresh mint.

CHOCOLATE MOUSSE MINT PIE

Andy Hilton, Davenport, FL
2013 American Pie Council Crisco National Pie Championships
Professional Division 1st Place Crisco Classic Chocolate

CRUST
½ cup butter-flavored Crisco
18 ounces Oreo cookies

FILLING ONE—SWEETENED MINT CREAM CHEESE
16 ounces cream cheese, at room temperature
¾ cup sugar
1½ teaspoons mint extract

FILLING TWO—CHOCOLATE MOUSSE
16 ounces semisweet chocolate
3 egg yolks
8 ounces milk chocolate
3 egg whites
8 tablespoons butter, unsalted
¼ cup powdered sugar
3 teaspoons mint extract
3 cups heavy cream

For the Crust: Preheat oven to 350°F. In a food processor, process the Oreo cookies to a crumb. Melt the butter Crisco in a microwave and pour into the cookie crumbs mixing with a fork until everything is moist. Place buttery crumb into a 9-inch pie pan. Spread the crumb out evenly along the bottom and sides of the pan. (Use a second pie pan to press down on the crumb.) Bake for 7 minutes and remove from the oven to cool.

For Filling One—Sweetened Mint Cream Cheese: Beat cream cheese with a mixer until smooth, add sugar, and beat again until smooth. Blend in mint. Fill half of the pie crust with sweetened mint cream cheese layer.

For Filling Two—Chocolate Mousse: Gently melt butter, milk chocolate, and chocolate chips in a double boiler; this will be thicker than not. Set aside to cool. Beat egg whites and salt to form soft peaks. Add powdered sugar and beat to stiff peaks. Beat the 3 cups of heavy cream to stiff peaks. Add egg yolks to the cooled chocolate and blend. Fold egg whites into the chocolate. Fold whipped cream into the egg whites and chocolate, and add mint and gently blend. Pour over the sweetened mint cream cheese layer. Cover with plastic wrap and place in refrigerator overnight. Garnish with whipped cream before serving.

Chocolate Mousse Mint Pie

HAPPY PIGS IN CHOCOLATE PIE

Valarie Enters, Sanford, FL
2013 American Pie Council Crisco National Pie Championships
Professional Division Honorable Mention Crisco Classic Chocolate

CRUST
18 ounces Crushed Oreos
½ cup butter-flavored Crisco
3 tablespoons cocoa

FILLING ONE
2 (8-ounce) packages softened
    cream cheese
⅓ cup sugar
1 egg
¼ cup sour cream
1½ teaspoons vanilla
2 tablespoons cocoa
4 ounces melted sweet chocolate

BROWNIES
⅔ cup unsalted butter
½ cup sugar
¼ cup water
12 ounces chocolate chips
4 eggs
2 teaspoons of vanilla

1½ cups flour
½ teaspoon baking soda
½ teaspoon salt

FILLING TWO—MOUSSE
1 gelatin envelope
¾ cups milk
1 teaspoon vanilla
1 teaspoon chocolate extract
1 cup marshmallow cream
1 cup chocolate chips
½ cup sugar
1 cup whipping cream, whipped

GANACHE
6 ounces of chocolate chips
6 ounces of heavy whipping cream
2 tablespoons unsalted butter
1 tablespoon corn syrup

FONDANT PIGS
Pink fondant from craft store

For the Crust: Mix ingredients and press into a pie plate.

For Filling One: Mix softened cream cheese with sugar, then add egg, sour cream, vanilla, cocoa, and chocolate. Pour into Oreo crust and bake at 325°F for 25 to 30 minutes. Set in fridge and allow to cool.

For the Brownies: Melt butter, sugar, and water in a saucepan. Add chocolate chips. Stir until melted well. Mix together eggs and vanilla. Add to saucepan. In a separate bowl mix together flour, baking soda, and salt. Add to chocolate mixture and pour into a greased 9 x 13 pan. Bake at 350°F for 25 minutes. Cut into small squares till you have 1 cup of brownie bits. Save rest for another use.

For Filling Two—Mousse: Heat milk and add gelatin, let gelatin bloom for 5 minutes, then add chocolate chips and sugar. Add extracts and marshmallow cream. Fold whipped cream into cooled mixture. Spread half onto filling one and sprinkle brownie bits, follow with remainder of mousse.

For the Ganache: Heat cream in microwave, add chocolate chips. Stir in rest of ingredients and, using a sieve, pour over cooled pie.

For the Fondant Pigs: Create fondant pigs with pink fondant available from local craft stores.

Happy Pigs in Chocolate Pie

YUMMY CHOCOANNA PIE

Alberta F. Dunbar, San Diego, CA
2013 American Pie Council Crisco National Pie Championships
Amateur Division 1st Place Crisco Classic Chocolate

CRUST
1½ cups all-purpose flour
½ teaspoon salt
½ cup Crisco shortening
3 to 4 tablespoons ice water

FILLING ONE
6 ounces cream cheese, softened
¼ cup half-and-half dairy creamer
1 teaspoon coffee extract
6 ounces semisweet chocolate, melted and cooled
¾ cup heavy cream (whip before adding to mixture)

FILLING TWO
2 large bananas (or 3 medium)
½ cup honey glazed almonds, sliced
¾ cup caramel ice cream topping

FILLING THREE
6 ounces cream cheese softened
1 teaspoon banana extract
6 ounces milk chocolate, melted and cooled
¾ cup heavy cream (whip before adding to mixture)

TOPPING
2½ cups heavy cream
¼ cup powdered sugar, sifted
1 teaspoon vanilla extract

GARNISH
½ cup honey almonds, sliced
Chocolate curls or flakes

For the Crust: Preheat oven to 450°F. Mix flour and salt together, cut in shortening using pastry blender or 2 knives, until flour is blended and forms pea-size chunks. Sprinkle with 1 tablespoon of water at a time. Toss lightly with a fork until dough forms a ball. Roll on a lightly floured surface until pastry is large enough to fit a 9-inch deep dish pie pan, with ½-inch overlap. Transfer pastry to pie pan, fold edges under, and flute using fingers. Prick bottom with fork and bake for 10 to 12 minutes or until golden brown. Cool completely before adding filling.

For Filling One: In a medium bowl, beat cream cheese and half-and-half together until smooth. Add coffee extract and cooled semisweet chocolate, blend well. Fold in whipped cream. Spread evenly into the pie crust then chill in refrigerator for 20 minutes or until set.

For Filling Two: Place sliced bananas over chilled layer. Sprinkle with almonds and drizzle caramel over filling. Chill in refrigerator until ready to add top layer.

For Filling Three: Repeat directions for filling one. Carefully spread mixture over banana slices. Chill until set.

For the Topping: Combine ingredients and beat on high until smooth. Reserve ⅓ of mixture for piping border of pie. Frost pie with remaining cream. Pipe border around pie.

For the Garnish: Sprinkle almonds over center of pie and chocolate curls (or flakes) over piped border.

Yummy Chocoanna Pie

TUXEDO BROWNIE PIE

Patricia Lapiezo, La Mesa, CA
2013 American Pie Council Crisco National Pie Championships
Amateur Division 2nd Place Crisco Classic Chocolate

CRUST
3 cups all-purpose flour
5 tablespoon ice water
1 teaspoon salt
1 tablespoon vinegar
1¼ cups butter-flavored Crisco
    shortening
1 egg, lightly beaten

FILLING
1 cup semisweet chocolate chips
½ cup biscuit baking mix
¼ cup butter
2 eggs
1 (14-ounce) can sweetened
    condensed milk
1 teaspoon vanilla
¾ cup chopped semisweet chocolate

TOPPING ONE
10 ounces frozen raspberries,
    thawed
½ cup granulated sugar
1 tablespoon cornstarch

TOPPING TWO
1 (8-ounce) package cream cheese,
    softened
¼ teaspoon white chocolate flavoring
⅓ cup powdered sugar
1½ cups heavy whipping cream,
    stiffly beaten
1 cup chopped white chocolate,
    melted and cooled
1 to 2 teaspoons cocoa powder
Fresh raspberries

For the Crust: Combine flour and salt in large bowl. Cut in shortening. In a small bowl, combine water, vinegar, and egg. Stir into flour mixture until dough comes together. Shape dough into two disks and refrigerate at least 1 hour. Roll out 1 disk to fit a 10-inch pie dish. Crimp edges and prick bottom and sides of crust. Bake at 400°F for 10 minutes. Turn oven down to 325°F and prepare filling.

For the Filling: In a small saucepan melt chocolate chips with butter. In a large mixing bowl, beat the chocolate mixture with the milk, baking mix, eggs, and vanilla until smooth. Stir in chopped chocolate. Pour into prepared pie crust and bake 35 to 40 minutes or until center is set. Cool and prepare raspberry topping.

For Topping One: In a blender, puree the thawed raspberries. In a medium saucepan combine the puree with the sugar and cornstarch. Cook over medium heat until thickened. Pour over brownie filling. Cool completely before preparing white chocolate topping.

For Topping Two: In a medium bowl, beat the cream cheese and sugar until fluffy. Beat in flavoring and fold in whipped cream. Separate ½ cup of the topping and stir the cocoa powder into it. Stripe a pastry bag with the chocolate whipped cream first, and then fill with the white chocolate topping. Pipe decoratively over top of pie and decorate with fresh raspberries. Refrigerate.

Tuxedo Brownie Pie

ZHAHN-DOO-YUH BANANA PANNA COTTA PIE

Grace Thatcher, Delta, OH
2013 American Pie Council Crisco National Pie Championships
Amateur Division 3rd Place Crisco Classic Chocolate

CRUST
2 cups flour
½ teaspoon salt
10 tablespoons Crisco shortening
3 to 4 tablespoons cold water

FILLING
⅓ cup hazelnuts (toasted and reserved)
8½ ounces Nutella
5 ounces mascarpone
4 teaspoons whole milk
3 bananas

CARMELIZED BANANAS
1 tablespoon butter
1 tablespoon brown sugar
1 sliced banana
(Makes 3¼ ounces of banana after cooking)

BANANA PANNA COTTA
2 tablespoons water
1 teaspoon gelatin
1 cup cream
⅓ cup sugar
¼ teaspoon vanilla
¼ teaspoon banana extract
Dash salt

TOPPING
1½ cups whipping cream
¾ cup Nutella

For the Crust: Preheat the oven to 425°F. Into a large mixing bowl, sift together the flour and salt, then add all of the Crisco shortening. Cut the shortening into the flour with a pastry blender until the mixture develops a course texture. Sprinkle the water over the mixture a spoonful at a time and toss until the dough begins to cohere. Gather the dough into a ball and press together with your hands, cover with plastic wrap, and refrigerate for at least one hour before using. Prepare pie crust in a 9-inch pie pan and prebake for 10 to15 minutes.

For the Filling: Place all ingredients except hazelnuts in a bowl and mix with a hand mixer until the mixture lightens, about 1 minute. Spread ⅓ of filling on bottom of crust, then sprinkle with the hazelnuts. Spread another ⅓ of the filling on top of nuts. Slice bananas into ¼-inch slices. Place two layers of bananas over the filling. Cover with the remaining filling.

For the Caramelized Bananas: Place butter and sugar in a medium-sized skillet over medium heat until butter has melted and add bananas that have been sliced into ¼-inch thick slices. Cook on one side until caramelized, then turn over and do the second side. Bananas should be cooked through. Set aside.

Zhahn-DOO-Yuh Banana Panna Cotta Pie

For the Panna Cotta: Bloom 1 teaspoon of gelatin in 2 tablespoons water for about 5 minutes; set aside. Heat cream, sugar, and salt to 175°F. Remove from heat and add softened gelatin mixture. Stir until dissolved. Place mixture in an ice water bath and continue to stir until the temperature of the mixture drops to 50°F. Stir in the vanilla and banana extracts. Puree in the caramelized banana with a stick blender. Pour Panna Cotta on top of the filling.

For the Topping: In a large bowl, beat whipping cream with an electric mixer on medium speed until soft peaks form, then beat in Nutella until incorporated but not over mixed. Refrigerate until ready to use. Pipe whipped cream decoratively over top of pie.

CITRUS

SOUR CREAM LEMON PIE

Adriel Hong, Chandler, AZ
2004 American Pie Council Crisco National Pie Championships
Amateur Division 2nd Place Citrus

CRUST
3 cups all-purpose flour
1 teaspoon salt
2½ tablespoons sugar
1 cup Crisco all-vegetable shortening
1 egg
1 teaspoon vinegar
4 tablespoons water

FILLING
1 cup sugar
3½ tablespoons cornstarch

1 tablespoon grated lemon peel
½ cup fresh lemon juice
3 egg yolks, slightly beaten
1 cup milk
¼ cup butter
1 cup sour cream

TOPPING
Fresh whipped cream, sweetened
Lemon rind twists for garnish

For the Crust: Preheat oven to 450°F. In a large bowl, combine flour, salt, and sugar. Mix well. Cut in shortening until mixture resembles coarse meal. In a small bowl, combine egg, vinegar, and 4 tablespoons water. Whisk together and gradually add to flour mixture, stirring with a fork. Mix until ingredients are well incorporated. Add one more tablespoon of water if necessary. Form into a ball with hands. Recipe makes enough dough for 2 crusts. Cut ball in half and freeze one half for future use.

If dough seems too soft, place in refrigerator for 5 to 10 minutes. Otherwise, roll out on a lightly floured surface to the size of a 9-inch pie pan. Place crust in pie pan. Trim crust to ½ inch beyond edge of pie plate. Fold under and crimp edge as desired. Prick bottom and sides of crust several times to prevent bubbling, and line with a double layer of aluminum foil. Bake for 8 minutes. Remove foil and bake for 5 to 6 minutes longer or until golden brown. Cool on a wire rack.

For the Filling: In a medium-sized heavy saucepan, combine sugar, cornstarch, lemon peel, lemon juice, egg yolks, and milk. Cook over medium heat until mixture is thick. Stir in butter and cool mixture to room temperature.

After filling has cooled, stir in sour cream and pour into pie shell. Chill for at least 4 hours.

Before serving, top pie with sweetened whipped cream and lemon rind twists.

AFTERNOON DELIGHT PIE

John Sunvold, Winter Springs, FL
2009 American Pie Council Crisco National Pie Championships
Amateur Division 1st Place Citrus

CRUST
1¼ cups Keebler Sandies (or any shortbread cookie)
¼ cup sugar

LIME LAYER
14-ounce can sweetened condensed milk
1 egg
½ cup lime juice
Few drops of green food coloring (optional)

SYLT HALLON & BLÅBÄR LAYER
¾ cup Sylt Hallon & Blåbär—can be purchased in the food marketplace at Ikea stores (substitute ¼ cup blueberry preserves and ¾ cup raspberry preserves if unavailable).

LEMON LAYER
14-ounce can sweetened condensed milk
1 egg
½ cup lemon juice
Few drops yellow food coloring (optional)

TOPPING
1 cup heavy cream
3 ounces cream cheese, softened
3 ounces white chocolate, melted

GARNISH
Fresh raspberries
Grated lemon or lime peel

For the Crust: Preheat oven to 375°F. Mix ingredients together and press mixture into a 9-inch pie pan. Bake for 8 to 10 minutes or until brown. Allow to cool to room temperature.

For Lime Layer: Mix all ingredients and pour mixture into cooled crust.

For Sylt Hallon & Blåbär Layer: Gently drop ¾ to 1 cup of Sylt Hallon and Blåbär on top of the unbaked lime mixture. Work to cover the lime mixture completely.

For Lemon Layer: Preheat oven to 375°F. Mix all ingredients together and pour the lemon mixture on top of the Sylt Hallon & Blåbär layer. Spread lemon mixture to cover completely and reach edge of crust. Bake pie for 18 minutes, remove from oven, and cool. Chill.

For the Topping: Combine cream cheese and white chocolate. Beat the cream until stiff peaks appear. Fold cream cheese mixture into the whipped cream. Top the pie.

Garnish with fresh raspberries and grated lemon or lime peel.

Chill for 2 hours before serving.

BERRY GOOD LEMON PIE

John Sunvold, Winter Springs, FL
2011 American Pie Council Crisco National Pie Championships
Amateur Division 3rd Place Citrus

CRUST
25 vanilla sandwich cookies (Vanilla Oreos)
4 to 5 tablespoons butter

FILLING ONE
2 (14-ounce) cans sweetened condensed milk
1 cup lemon juice
2 eggs and one egg yolk (beaten together)

FILLING TWO
1 cup Smucker's Orchard's Finest triple berry preserves

TOPPING
2 cups heavy cream
5-ounce white chocolate bar (broken into small pieces)
Fresh berries in season and lemon zest for garnish

For the Crust: Preheat oven to 375°F. Place whole cookies in food processor and pulse until cookies resemble wet sand. Melt butter and pour over cookie crumbs and mix until butter is evenly distributed. Press crumbs evenly into pie pan. Bake for 8 minutes. Let cool completely to room temperature.

For Filling One: Preheat oven to 375°F. Empty sweetened condensed milk in a medium mixing bowl and blend in 1 cup of the lemon juice. Add the eggs to the mix and blend thoroughly. Pour into crust and bake for 15 to 20 minutes. Remove from oven and cool on a cooling rack. Chill.

For Filling Two: Cover chilled pie with preserves.

For the Topping: Bring one cup of cream to a boil over medium heat. Add white chocolate and stir constantly until the chocolate is melted and mixture is combined. Remove from heat and let cool to room temperature. Refrigerate for at least four hours.

In a large bowl, beat the rest of the cream with an electric mixer set on high speed. Beat until soft peaks form. Slowly add the white chocolate mixture and continue to beat until stiff. Cover and refrigerate for 2 hours. Pipe on top of pie. Top with fresh berries, in season. Garnish as desired. Add lemon zest for color (optional).

Berry Good Lemon Pie

CELEBRATION KEY LIME PIE

Beth Campbell, Belleville, WI
2002 American Pie Council National Pie Championships
Amateur Division 3rd Place Citrus

CRUST
1 cup flour
½ teaspoon salt
½ cup shortening
¼ cup water

FILLING
8-ounce package cream cheese, softened
14-ounce can sweetened condensed milk

1 teaspoon vanilla
½ teaspoon grated lime rind
⅓ cup freshly squeezed lime juice

TOPPING
1 quart fresh strawberries
1 pint whipped cream
2 tablespoons strawberry Kool Aid
4 tablespoons powdered sugar
½ teaspoon grated lime rind

For the Crust: Preheat oven to 475°F. Put flour and salt in mixing bowl. With a pastry blender, cut shortening into flour and salt until pea-size pieces form. Then add ¼ cup water. Form dough into a ball. Roll out crust on a floured board and place in a 9-inch pie pan. Flute the edges. Bake for 8 to10 minutes or until golden brown. Cool.

For the Filling: Blend cream cheese until smooth. Add sweetened condensed milk, vanilla, and lime rind. Blend thoroughly. Add lime juice and mix until blended. Pour into cooled shell.

For the Topping: Remove stems from strawberries and place berries pointing up with flat side down, covering entire pie. Beat cream with powdered sugar and Kool Aid. Mound whipped cream mixture over berries. Sprinkle grated lime rind over whipped cream mixture. Chill before serving.

KEY LIME MOUSSE DREAM PIE

Emily Lewis, Mt. Dora, FL
2003 American Pie Council Crisco National Pie Championships
Amateur Division 2nd Place Citrus

CRUST
8 graham crackers (full sheets),
   crushed
½ stick butter, softened

FILLING
2¼ teaspoon Knox Gelatine (not
   whole package)
¼ cup water
⅓ cup plus 1 tablespoon key lime
   juice

1 teaspoon zest from key limes
   (use Persian lime for zest if using
   bottled juice)
1 cup sugar
4 egg yolks
1 egg
1 stick butter, cut up
¾ cup heavy whipping cream,
   whipped to soft peaks

For the Crust: Preheat oven to 275°F. Mix together crumbs and butter. Press into 9-inch pie pan and up sides, forming crust. Bake 1 hour. Cool on wire rack.

For the Filling: In the top of a double boiler, sprinkle the gelatin over cold water. Stir and allow to sit for 2 minutes. Set pan over hot water on medium heat and stir until gelatin dissolves; do not boil. Remove from heat.

Prepare a large bowl of ice, large enough to fit a smaller metal bowl that you will strain hot lime mixture into. Set aside. In a large heavy bottomed saucepan, combine key lime juice, sugar, yolks, egg, and butter. Over medium heat, whisk the mixture until it begins to thicken. Add gelatin mixture. Continue whisking a few more minutes. Do not let boil. Strain into prepared bowl. Stir to cool. Fold in the whipped cream and zest and pour mixture into cooled crust. Refrigerate for at least 3 hours. Decorate top with ½ slices of key limes and more whipped cream before serving, if desired. Keep refrigerated until just before serving.

KUMQUAT TROPICAL DELIGHT PIE

Phyllis Szymanek, Toledo, OH
2011 American Pie Council Crisco National Pie Championships
Amateur Division 2nd Place Citrus

CRUST
1⅓ cups finely crushed vanilla wafers
2 tablespoons sugar
½ teaspoon vanilla
⅓ cup butter, melted

FILLING
14-ounce can condensed milk
12 ounces Cool Whip (8 ounces for filling, 4 ounces for garnish)
½ cup lemon juice
1 teaspoon vanilla
½ cup pureed kumquats (cut in half and remove seeds)
½ cup crushed pineapple (well drained)
1 cup flaked coconut, toasted

GARNISH
Red and yellow food coloring
Remaining coconut
Remaining Cool Whip
½ teaspoon vanilla
⅓ cup well-drained crushed pineapple
1 small can mandarin oranges (drained and pat dried)
1 kumquat

For the Crust: Preheat oven to 350°F. Mix all ingredients in bowl until blended. Pour into 9-inch pie dish sprayed with butter-flavored non-stick spray. Press into bottom and sides of dish. Bake for 8 to 12 minutes or until lightly browned. Let cool.

For the Filling: Beat together condensed milk and Cool Whip. Add lemon juice and vanilla. Mix well. Add kumquats and pineapples. Mix. Fold in ⅔ cup coconut. Pour into cooled pie crust. Chill 5 to 6 hours or overnight.

For the Garnish: Add 2 drops of red and 2 drops yellow food coloring to remaining Cool Whip. Mix in ½ teaspoon vanilla and ⅓ cup drained pineapple. Spoon Cool Whip into 1-quart storage bag, cut one corner, and squeeze around edge of pie. Sprinkle with remaining ⅓ cup coconut. Arrange mandarin oranges around center of pie. Place one kumquat in center of pie.

Kumquat Tropical Delight Pie

LEMON LOVER'S FAVORITE CHESS PIE

Emily Lewis, Mt. Dora, FL
2002 American Pie Council National Pie Championships
Amateur Division 1st Place Citrus

CRUST
²/₃ cup Crisco shortening
4 tablespoons butter
3 tablespoons ice water
1 teaspoon salt
2 cups all-purpose flour

FILLING
2 cups sugar
1 tablespoon flour
1 tablespoon cornmeal
4 eggs
¼ cup butter, melted
¼ cup milk
2½ teaspoon grated lemon peel
¼ cup fresh squeezed lemon juice
Powdered sugar for garnish

For the Crust: In a tall, narrow bowl, combine flour, salt, and shortening. Using two knives scissors-style, cut fat into flour until only small pea-size bits of shortening remain. Sprinkle water over flour mixture as you toss with a fork. Turn only about 8 to 10 times. Do not over mix. Use more water if dry crumbs remain. Pour out of bowl onto plastic wrap. Divide into 2 parts. Create two 5-inch disks and flatten. Refrigerate. At this point, save one disk for another use in a freezer bag. It can be stored in the freezer for weeks. After about 15 minutes in the refrigerator, remove remaining disk. Place a piece of plastic wrap or parchment paper on the counter. Flour it. Cover disk with another piece of wrap or parchment. Roll out from the center until disk is about 11 inches in diameter. Remove top wrap, flour the surface lightly, and drape crust over rolling pin. Center over 9-inch pie plate and place crust gently. Smooth into pan. Remove wrap. Trim edge to about ½ inch around outside of pan. Fold edge under and flute using thumb and forefingers to make a stand up edge. Refrigerate until ready to fill.

For the Filling: Preheat oven to 350°F. Combine sugar, flour, and cornmeal in a large mixer bowl. Toss with a fork to mix. Add eggs, butter, milk, lemon peel, and juice. Blend with mixer until smooth and blended. Pour into pie shell. If using a disposable aluminum pan (8¾ inches), put on a cookie sheet to assure even baking and for easier handling. Bake until top is slightly golden and center test comes out clean, approximately 40 to 45 minutes.

Sprinkle with powdered sugar on top of cooled pie to decorate.

SITTIN' ON THE SANDBAR KEY LIME PIE

Amy Freeze, Avon Park, FL
2013 American Pie Council Crisco National Pie Championships
Amateur Division Best of Show and 1st Place Citrus

CRUST
2 cups crushed vanilla wafers
2 tablespoons granulated sugar
5 tablespoons melted butter

FILLING
8 ounces Philadelphia cream cheese, softened
2 whole eggs
2 egg yolks
1 (15-ounce) can Eagle Brand condensed milk

¾ cup Coco Lopez (Cream of Coconut)
¾ cup key lime juice

TOPPING
1 cup heavy whipping cream
1 cup powdered sugar

GARNISH
Lime slices and white chocolate seashells

For the Crust: In a bowl, combine vanilla wafer crumbs, sugar, and melted butter. Press into a 9-inch deep dish pie plate. Bake at 350°F for 10 minutes. Allow to cool to the touch before filling.

For the Filling: In a medium bowl, beat cream cheese until smooth. Add eggs and egg yolks, one at a time, beating well after each addition. Add condensed milk and beat well. Add key lime juice and Coco Lopez and beat well. Pour into crust. Bake at 325°F for 30 minutes or until center is set to the touch. Allow to cool before refrigerating.

For the Topping: In a cold bowl, beat whipping cream and powdered sugar until stiff. Pipe large rosettes around edges.

For the Garnish: To make white chocolate seashells: Melt white chocolate almond bark or white chocolate pieces in microwave. Pour into seashell molds. Chill until set.

Sittin' On the Sandbar Key Lime Pie

LUSCIOUS LEMON LIME RIBBON PIE

Karen Hall, Elm Creek, NE
2005 American Pie Council Crisco National Pie Championships
Amateur Division 2nd Place Citrus

CRUST
2 cups all-purpose flour
½ teaspoon salt
¾ cup butter-flavored Crisco
  shortening
5 to 7 tablespoons cold water

LIME FILLING
1¼ cups sugar
3 tablespoons cornstarch
1 cup milk
3 egg yolks, beaten
⅓ cup key lime juice

2 tablespoons butter
¾ cup sour cream

LEMON FILLING
½ cup sugar
2 tablespoons cornstarch
¾ cup water
3 egg yolks, beaten
¼ cup lemon juice
1 tablespoon butter

GARNISH
Whipped topping, as desired

For the Crust: Preheat oven to 375°F. Mix flour and salt in a bowl. With pastry blender, cut in Crisco shortening until mixture resembles pea-sized chunks. Sprinkle cold water over mixture one tablespoon at a time, tossing with fork until dough will form a ball. Divide dough into two equal parts; press between hands to form two 5-inch disks. Wrap each disk in plastic wrap. Refrigerate until needed. Only one of the disks will be used for this pie.

When ready, roll out dough to fit a 9-inch pie pan. Place crust in pan. Bake until golden brown, about 10 minutes. Cover edges of crust with foil to prevent excessive browning.

For the Lime Filling: Combine sugar, cornstarch, milk, beaten egg yolks, and key lime juice in a saucepan and cook over medium heat until thick. Stir in butter, then whip in sour cream until well blended. Set aside.

For the Lemon Filling: Combine sugar, cornstarch, water, beaten egg yolks, and lemon juice in a saucepan and cook over medium heat until thick. Stir in butter. Set aside.

Spread ½ of the lime filling into the baked 9-inch pie crust, spread all the lemon filling over this layer, and top with remaining lime mixture. Refrigerate pie. When cool, top with whipped topping as desired.

SPACE COAST CITRUS PIE

Evette Rahman, Orlando, FL
2013 American Pie Council Crisco National Pie Championships
Professional Division 1st Place Citrus

CRUST
1½ cups ground graham cracker
   crumbs
¼ cup sugar
½ cup unsalted butter, melted

FILLING
2 (14-ounce) cans sweetened
   condensed milk
½ cup orange flavored powdered
   drink mix

$2/3$ cup sour cream
½ cup Persian lime juice

TOPPING
1 cup heavy cream
3 tablespoons powdered sugar
¼ teaspoon vanilla extract
Fresh raspberries

For the Crust: Preheat oven to 350°F. Mix together crust ingredients and press into bottom and sides of deep dish pie plate. Bake for 8 minutes. Cool.

For the Filling: Beat filling ingredients together and pour into pie shell. Bake for 10 minutes. Cool completely in refrigerator.

For the Topping: Beat together topping ingredients until firm peaks form. Garnish pie with the whipped cream and raspberries.

Space Coast Citrus Pie

ORANGE MERINGUE

Phyllis Bartholomew, Columbus, NE
2002 American Pie Council National Pie Championships
Amateur Division 2nd Place Citrus

CRUST
2 cups flour
1 cup cake flour
1 cup shortening
2 tablespoons Super-Rich butter powder
1 egg
1 tablespoon vinegar
½ teaspoon salt
⅓ cup ice water

FILLING
¾ cup sugar
3 tablespoons flour
3 tablespoons cornstarch
2 cups reconstituted orange juice (made from orange juice concentrate)

3 egg yolks
2 tablespoons butter
1 teaspoon grated orange peel (optional)
1 teaspoon pure orange oil flavoring

NEVER FAIL MERINGUE
1 tablespoon cornstarch
½ cup water
3 egg whites
⅛ teaspoon salt
¾ teaspoon cream of tartar
6 tablespoons extra-fine sugar

For the Crust: Mix the flours, shortening, and butter powder together. Using a pastry blender, cut in the shortening until it resembles coarse crumbs. Beat egg, vinegar, salt, and ice water together and add to the flours. Mix lightly. Form into a disk and wrap in plastic. Chill for several hours or overnight.

Preheat oven to 350°F. Roll out between 2 sheets of plastic wrap. Place in pie dish. Bake for 20 minutes until golden brown.

For the Filling: Combine the sugar, flour, and cornstarch in a heavy saucepan. Add the orange juice and stir. Bring to a boil and cook for about 1 minute. Add a small amount of this to the beaten egg yolks. Stir quickly until well blended. Return the egg mixture to the sugar mixture remaining in the saucepan. Return to the heat and continue cooking for 2 more minutes. Remove from the heat and add the butter, grated peel, and flavoring. Pour through a fine strainer into a pre-baked pie shell.

For the Meringue: Cook the cornstarch and the water in a saucepan until it forms a clear, thick paste. Set aside to cool. Beat the egg whites until frothy, then add the cream of tartar and salt. Continue to beat on high until it forms soft peaks and then add the cornstarch mixture. Add the sugar, one tablespoon at a time. Beat until it forms stiff peaks. Do not over beat. Add the meringue to the top of the pie filling, making sure that the meringue touches the crust so it won't shrink while baking. Swirl the top into soft swirls and peaks. Bake in a 350°F oven for 12 to 15 minutes, or until golden brown.

SONOMA VALLEY SUNDOWNER PIE

John Sunvold, Winter Springs, FL
2010 American Pie Council Crisco National Pie Championships
Amateur Division 3rd Place Citrus

CRUST
26 vanilla sandwich cookies (Famous
  Amos or vanilla Oreos)
5 tablespoons butter

FILLING
2 (14-ounce) cans sweetened
  condensed milk
1⅓ cups Meyer lemon juice
3 egg yolks and 1 whole egg (beaten
  together)

TOPPING ONE
1 cup boysenberry preserves

TOPPING TWO
2½ cups heavy cream
6 ounces white chocolate (broken
  into small pieces)

For the Crust: Preheat oven to 375°F. Place whole cookies in food processor and pulse until cookies resemble wet sand. Melt butter and pour over cookie crumbs. Mix until butter is evenly distributed. Press crumbs evenly into pie pan. Bake for 10 minutes. Let cool.

For the Filling: Pour sweetened condensed milk into a medium mixing bowl and blend in 1 cup of the lemon juice. Add the eggs to the mixture and blend thoroughly. Pour into crust and bake for 20 minutes. Remove from oven and cool on a cooling rack. Chill.

For Topping One: Cover chilled pie with boysenberry preserves.

For Topping Two: In a saucepan, bring one cup of cream to a boil over medium heat. Add white chocolate and stir constantly until the chocolate is melted and mixture is combined. Remove from heat and let cool to room temperature. Refrigerate for at least four hours.

In a large bowl, beat the rest of the cream with an electric mixer set on high speed. Beat until soft peaks form. Slowly add the white chocolate mixture and continue to beat until stiff. Cover and refrigerate for 2 hours.

Garnish pie with the cream and chocolate mixture before serving.

TWISTED CITRUS BLACKBERRY PIE

Michele Stuart, Norwalk, CT
2010 American Pie Council Crisco National Pie Championships
Professional Division 1st Place Citrus

CRUST
1 cup finely chopped graham cracker pieces
1 tablespoon sugar
6 tablespoons unsalted butter, melted.

BLACKBERRY GLACÉ
1 cup mashed blackberries
1 cup sugar
3 tablespoons cornstarch
½ cup water

FILLING
2 tablespoons warm water
1 teaspoon gelatin
14-ounce can sweetened condensed milk, refrigerated for 30 minutes
1 cup heavy cream
¾ cup fresh lime juice
¾ cup fresh lemon juice
1½ tablespoons lime zest
1½ tablespoons lemon zest

GARNISH
Whipped cream
Lemon and lime zest
Blackberries

For the Crust: Preheat oven to 350°F. Combine all ingredients until moist. Spread evenly in pie dish making sure there are no gaps. Bake until golden brown, about 5 minutes. Cool pie shell before using.

For the Glacé: Combine all ingredients in a medium size saucepan over high heat. Stir glaze continuously until it thickens, about 8 minutes. Strain the glacé to eliminate any seeds if desired. Let glaze cool and thicken in refrigerator for at least 6 hours before using.

For the Filling: Place gelatin and warm water in a saucepan and let soften for about 5 minutes. Place on low heat for about 30 seconds to dissolve gelatin. In a mixing bowl, combine heavy cream, condensed milk, lemon juice, lime juice, lemon zest, and lime zest on high speed until filling thickens. Add the gelatin to the cream mixture. Continue to mix on high speed until the filling is thick and creamy.

Spread the blackberry glacé evenly on the bottom of the graham cracker pie shell. Pour the pie filling over the blackberry glacé. Spread evenly. Refrigerate pie overnight before serving.

Garnish with whipped cream, lemon and lime zest, and blackberries as desired.

Twisted Citrus Blackberry Pie

KEY LIME PIE

Risa Wight, Celebration, FL
2004 American Pie Council Crisco National Pie Championships
Amateur Division 2nd Place Celebration

CRUST
1 package graham crackers, crushed
¼ cup sugar
⅓ cup melted butter

FILLING
½ cup key lime juice (either 12 key limes juiced with seeds and pulp removed or Nellie & Joe's key lime juice)
8 ounces Cool Whip
1 can sweetened condensed milk

For the Crust: Preheat oven to 375°F. Combine all ingredients and press into pie plate. Bake for 6 minutes; cool before filling.

For the Filling: Combine all ingredients and pour into cooled pie crust. Freeze at least 2 hours. Top with more Cool Whip if desired. Take out of freezer 10 minutes before serving.

MILE HIGH KEY LIME PIE

Nikki Penley, Tipton, IN
2013 American Pie Council Crisco National Pie Championships
Amateur Division, 2nd Place Citrus

CRUST
2½ cups crushed graham crackers
5 tablespoons butter, melted

FILLING
9 ounces cream cheese, softened
1 can sweetened condensed milk

½ cup key lime juice
1¼ cup sour cream

For the Crust: Preheat oven to 375°F. Mix together graham crackers and butter and press into a 9-inch pie pan. Bake for 15 to 20 minutes. Cool.

For the Filling: Mix cream cheese and sweetened condensed milk until smooth.

Add key lime juice and sour cream. Pour into cooled pie crust, let set, and refrigerate pie.

Garnish with whipped cream.

Mile High Key Lime Pie

ON THE BEACH KEY LIME CHOCOLATE HEAVEN

Francine Bryson, Pickens, SC
2013 American Pie Council Crisco National Pie Championships
Amateur Division 3rd Place Citrus

CRUST
1 package Oreo cookies, finely
  ground
¼ cup sugar
⅓ cup butter, melted

FILLING
1 cup whipping cream
11 ounces white chocolate chips

1 tablespoon sour cream
1 teaspoon lime zest
⅓ cup lime juice

TOPPING
1 cup bittersweet chocolate, chopped
3 tablespoons heavy cream

For the Crust: Mix ingredients together in a 9-inch pie plate until evenly combined. Press evenly onto the bottom and up the sides of the pie plate. Refrigerate for 30 minutes before filling.

For the Filling: Melt together cream and chocolate chips in a small saucepan, setting over low heat. Remove from heat, stir in sour cream, lime zest, and juice. Pour into prepared pie crust. Let chill 30 minutes.

For the Topping: Melt bittersweet chocolate and heavy cream, stir till smooth. Pour over pie crust and refrigerate for 2 hours or overnight if possible. Top as desired

On the Beach Key Lime Chocolate Heaven

CLEM 'N MELLOW PIE

Caroline Imig, Oconto, WI
2013 American Pie Council Crisco National Pie Championships
Professional Division Honorable Mention, Citrus

CRUST
1 premade, prebaked crust

FILLING
1 teaspoon clementine zest
2 large eggs
4 large egg yolks
1 cup clementine juice
2 tablespoon and 1 teaspoon lemon
    juice
2 teaspoon cornstarch

1 cup granulated sugar
½ cup cold butter

TOPPING
½ cup milk
8 ounces marshmallows
4 ounces Cool Whip
½ cup whipping cream (whipped)
1 can mandarin oranges
Clementine pieces for decoration

For the Filling: In small saucepan, whisk clementine juice, lemon juice, cornstarch, and sugar over medium heat until warm. Slowly add beaten eggs, whisking constantly. Add butter, 1 tablespoon at a time. Add zest and continue whisking until mixture is thick and translucent 10 to 12 minutes more. Pour into baked crust, set aside to cool.

For the Topping: Heat the milk and add the marshmallows and melt. Cool and fold in Cool Whip, whipped cream, and drained mandarin oranges. Spread over clementine curd layer. Decorate with whipped cream and extra clementines. Refrigerate until serving.

Clem 'n Mellow Pie

CREAM CHEESE

HEAVENLY HAWAIIAN CHEESE PIE

Patricia Lapiezo, La Mesa, CA
2010 American Pie Council Crisco National Pie Championships
Amateur Division 3rd Place Cream Cheese

CRUST
1½ cups graham cracker crumbs
2 tablespoons sugar
6 tablespoons butter, melted

FILLING
4-ounce bar Lindt white coconut chocolate, melted
¼ cup heavy whipping cream
2 (8-ounce) packages cream cheese, softened
¾ cup granulated sugar
2 large eggs
½ teaspoon vanilla
1 cup finely chopped macadamia nuts

PINEAPPLE TOPPING
20-ounce can crushed pineapple, drained, reserving juice
¼ teaspoon piña colada flavor or ½ teaspoon vanilla extract
½ cup sugar
1 tablespoon butter
3 tablespoons cornstarch

GARNISH
Whipped cream
Toasted coconut

For the Crust: Preheat oven to 350°F. Combine the crumbs, sugar, and melted butter. Press into bottom and up sides of a 9-inch pie dish. Bake for 8 minutes. Remove from oven and cool while preparing filling.

For the Filling: In a large mixing bowl, beat the cream cheese and sugar until fluffy. Gradually beat in cooled chocolate. Beat in eggs, one at a time, blending well after each. Stir in whipping cream and piña colada or vanilla extract. Pour into prepared crust and bake at 350°F for 30 minutes. Remove from oven and cool. Sprinkle macadamia nuts over the cream cheese layer.

For the Topping: Stir together the pineapple and sugar in a medium saucepan over low heat until the sugar is dissolved. Combine the pineapple juice and cornstarch and stir into the pineapple. Bring the mixture to a boil, stirring constantly until thickened. Remove from heat and stir in the flavoring and butter. Cool slightly and spread over top of pie. Chill pie 2 to 4 hours. Garnish with a border of sweetened whipped cream and toasted coconut.

RUTH'S RASPBERRY CHEESY PIE

Mary Weihman, Orlando FL
2013 American Pie Council Crisco National Pie Championships
Amateur Division 1st Place Cream Cheese

CRUST
1½ cups crushed graham crackers
6 tablespoons stick margarine or
   butter, melted
3 tablespoons sugar

FILLING
2 (8-ounce) packages of cream
   cheese, softened
½ cup sugar
½ teaspoon vanilla
2 eggs
⅓ cup raspberry chips
⅓ cup white chocolate chips
1 can Comstock Wilderness Raspberry Pie Filling, divided

GARNISH
Whipped cream
Fresh raspberries

For the Crust: Preheat oven to 350°F. Lightly grease a 9-inch pie plate with Crisco. Mix graham cracker crumbs, melted butter, and sugar. Press mixture firmly against bottom and sides of pie plate. Chill in refrigerator while preparing filling.

For the Filling: Blend softened cream cheese and sugar in a large bowl with electric mixer on medium speed. Add vanilla, then eggs, one at a time until just blended. Remove 1 cup of mixture from the bowl. Melt the raspberry chips in the microwave and stir into the removed 1 cup of cream cheese mixture until well blended. Pour into prepared crust. Top with a portion of the raspberry pie filling, as much as you desire, but save some for garnish. Melt the white chocolate chips and add to the remainder of the cream cheese mixture. Pour on top of pie. Bake at 350°F for 40 minutes or until center is done. Cool and refrigerate for 3 hours or overnight.

Garnish with whipped cream, the remainder of the pie filling, or some fresh raspberries.

Ruth's Raspberry Cheesy Pie

MEYER LEMON CHEESE PIE

Patricia Lapiezo, La Mesa, CA
2009 American Pie Council Crisco National Pie Championships
Amateur Division 1st Place Cream Cheese

CRUST
3 cups all-purpose flour
1 teaspoon salt
1¼ cups Crisco shortening
5 tablespoons ice water
1 tablespoon vinegar
1 egg, lightly beaten
¾ cup finely ground vanilla cream-filled cookies
1 tablespoon melted butter
¼ teaspoon finely grated lemon peel

LEMON CHEESECAKE FILLING
4 ounces white chocolate, melted
¼ cup heavy whipping cream
2 (8-ounce) packages cream cheese, softened
¾ cup granulated sugar

2 large eggs
2 tablespoons freshly squeezed Meyer lemon juice
1½ teaspoons finely grated lemon peel
½ teaspoon vanilla

MEYER LEMON CURD
4 large egg yolks
¾ cup granulated sugar
3 ounces fresh Meyer lemon juice
¼ cup unsalted butter
Pinch of salt
1 teaspoon finely grated lemon peel

GARNISH
Whipped cream
White chocolate, shaved

For the Crust: Preheat oven to 400°F. Combine flour and salt in large bowl. Cut in shortening. In a small bowl, combine the water, vinegar, and egg. Stir into flour mixture until dough comes together. Shape dough into two disks and refrigerate 1 hour. Use 1 disk for a 10-inch pie dish. Roll out crust on lightly floured work surface. Transfer to pie pan, flute edges. Prick bottom and sides of crust. Bake for 10 minutes; remove from oven. Combine cookie crumbs, butter, and lemon peel in a small bowl. Press firmly over bottom of crust and bake an additional 8 minutes. Remove from oven and turn oven down to 350°F. Prepare cheesecake filling.

For the Lemon Cheesecake Filling: In a large mixing bowl, beat the cream cheese and sugar until fluffy. Gradually beat in cooled chocolate. Beat in eggs, one at a time, blending well after each. Stir in whipping cream, lemon juice, vanilla, and lemon peel. Pour into prepared crust and bake at 350°F for 30 minutes. Remove from oven and cool. Prepare lemon curd.

For the Lemon Curd: In a large saucepan, beat the yolks and sugar together until well blended. Stir in the remaining ingredients. Cook over medium-low heat, stirring constantly, until thickened and resembling a thin hollandaise sauce. Do not bring to a boil. When thickened, pour at once into a strainer. Discard residue. Pour over prepared pie. Refrigerate until well chilled.

For the Garnish: Garnish edge of pie with sweetened whipped cream and shaved white chocolate, if desired.

SURPRISE CHERRY CHEESE PIE

Karen Hall, Elm Creek, NE
2008 American Pie Council Crisco National Pie Championships
Amateur Division 3rd Place Cream Cheese

CRUST
3 cups unbleached flour
1 cup plus 1 tablespoon butter-flavored Crisco, cold
½ teaspoon baking powder
1 egg
1 teaspoon sea salt
¼ cup plus 1 tablespoon ice cold water
1 tablespoon sugar
1 tablespoon rice vinegar

CHERRY FILLING
2 (14.5-ounce) cans sour pitted cherries, drained and reserving ¾ cup cherry juice
1¼ cups sugar
1 tablespoon tapioca
2 tablespoons cornstarch
½ teaspoon almond flavoring
¼ teaspoon red food coloring
2 tablespoons butter

BOTTOM CREAM CHEESE LAYER
8-ounce package Philadelphia cream cheese, softened
¼ cup plus 1 tablespoon sugar
2 egg whites
½ teaspoon almond flavoring
3 sheets of frozen phyllo (filo) dough, thawed

GLAZE
1 egg white, beaten
1 tablespoon sugar

For the Crust: In a large bowl, combine flour, baking powder, salt, and sugar. With a pastry blender, cut in Crisco until mixture resembles coarse crumbs. In a small bowl, beat egg, water, and vinegar together. Add egg mixture slowly to flour mixture, tossing with a fork until mixture is moistened. Do not over mix. Divide dough and shape into 2 balls, flatten each to form a disk. Wrap each disk with plastic wrap and refrigerate for at least 30 minutes before using. Makes enough pastry for one double crust 10-inch deep dish pie.

For the Cherry Filling: In a medium saucepan, combine sugar, tapioca, and cornstarch. Add reserved cherry juice, almond flavoring, red food coloring, and butter; cook and stir over medium-high heat for 8 to 10 minutes or until mixture bubbles and begins to thicken. Stir in cherries, simmer for 5 minutes. Refrigerate until completely cooled or overnight.

For the Bottom Cream Cheese Layer: Preheat oven to 425°F. In a medium mixing bowl, beat cream cheese, sugar, egg whites, and almond flavoring until smooth. Set aside.

To Assemble: Roll out bottom crust and line a 10-inch deep dish pie pan. Spread cream cheese filling into bottom of pie shell. Cut a 10-inch circle from phyllo dough, place on top of cream cheese layer, and gently press down. Spoon chilled cherry pie filling over phyllo dough. Roll out top crust, make pretty pie vents, place onto top of pie, adjust, trim, and flute edge. Brush top with slightly beaten egg white and sprinkle with sugar for the glaze. Protect edge of pie with foil. Bake at 425°F for 10 minutes. Reduce oven to 375°F and bake 30 to 35 minutes or until golden.

Surprise Cherry Cheese Pie

CARAMEL MACAROON PIE

Tammi Carlock, Chickamauga, GA
2013 American Pie Council Crisco National Pie Championships
Amateur Division 2nd Place Cream Cheese

CRUST
2 cups shortbread cookies, crushed
  fine
1 cup coconut
5 tablespoons butter, melted

MACAROON TOPPING ONE
4 tablespoons butter
2 cups coconut
½ cup sliced almonds

CARAMEL TOPPING TWO
20 caramels
2 tablespoons half-and-half

FILLING
1 (8-ounce) package cream cheese,
  softened
1 (14-ounce) can sweetened
  condensed milk
2 cups heavy cream, whipped

GARNISH
1 cup heavy cream, whipped
2 tablespoons sugar
1 tablespoon vanilla

For the Crust: Mix together the cookie crumbs with the coconut and butter and press into a 10-inch pie plate. Bake in a 350°F oven for 10 to 12 minutes or until golden brown. Cool on wire rack.

For the Macaroon Topping One: Place the 4 tablespoons butter into small bowl and microwave until melted. Toss with coconut and almonds to coat. Place on cookie sheet and toast in 350°F oven until golden brown. Set aside to cool.

For the Caramel Topping Two: Unwrap the caramels and put in a small bowl with the half-and-half and microwave until melted, stopping and stirring often.

For the Filling: Mix the cream cheese and sweetened condensed milk with an electric mixer until creamy. Fold in the whipped cream. Divide in half. Place half of the cream cheese mixture in the pie plate and then drizzle the caramel mixture on top, saving some for the top of the pie. Pour the remaining cream cheese mixture on top and sprinkle the macaroon mixture over top of pie.

For the Garnish: Whip the heavy cream with sugar and vanilla and pipe onto top of pie. Drizzle with remaining caramel. Refrigerate.

Caramel Macaroon Pie

SPLITSVILLE SUMMER SUNDAE PIE

Carol Socier, Bay City, MI
2013 American Pie Council Crisco National Pie Championships
Amateur Division 3rd Place Cream Cheese

CRUST
2 cups finely ground vanilla wafers
1 tablespoon sugar
6 tablespoons unsalted butter, melted and cooled
1 teaspoon pineapple extract
¼ cup white chocolate chips
2 teaspoons light cream

FILLING
1 (8-ounce) can crushed pineapple in its own juice
2 bananas
8 ounces cream cheese

1 teaspoon vanilla
1½ cups pineapple sherbet, softened
1 small box instant vanilla pudding mix
1 cup heavy whipping cream, whipped and divided

TOPPING
½ cup Maraschino cherries
⅓ cup pineapple sundae topping
Chocolate sundae topping
Caramel sundae topping
Chopped macadamia nuts
Whipped Cream

For the Crust: Preheat oven to 350°F. Combine crumbs, sugar, butter, and pineapple extract in bowl, stirring until crumbs are moist. Press evenly into a 9-inch pie plate. Bake in preheated oven 6 to 8 minutes or until golden and crisp. Cool. Melt chips and cream. Brush bottom and sides of cooled crust.

For the Filling: Drain pineapple, reserving juice. In a small bowl, combine sliced bananas with reserved juice. Let set for 5 minutes. Drain bananas. Arrange over bottom of crust.

In a large bowl, beat cream cheese and leftover pineapple juice. Beat in pineapple sherbet and vanilla. Gradually beat in pudding mix until well blended. Fold in drained crushed pineapple and half of whipped cream. Spread mixture evenly over banana slices. Cover and refrigerate until set.

For the Topping: Remove pie from refrigerator. Chop all but one of the cherries into quarters. Arrange chopped cherries around edge of pie. Drizzle with chocolate, pineapple, and caramel topping. Place large dollop whipped cream onto center of pie. Sprinkle with nuts. Top with remaining cherry. Drizzle with syrups. Refrigerate until ready to serve.

Splitsville Summer Sundae Pie

RAZZLE DAZZLE RASPBERRY CHEESE PIE

Evette Rahman, Orlando, FL
2013 American Pie Council Crisco National Pie Championships
Professional Division 1st Place Fruit/Berry

CRUST
2 cups coconut cookie
   crumbs
2 tablespoons sugar
½ cup unsalted butter, melted

FILLING ONE
3 cups fresh raspberries, divided
½ cup sugar
2 tablespoons cornstarch
1 tablespoon water

FILLING TWO
8-ounce package cream cheese,
   softened
1 cup powdered sugar
2 tablespoons lime juice
8-ounce container of frozen whipped
   topping, thawed

GARNISH
Sweetened whipped cream
Fresh raspberries

For the Crust: Preheat oven to 350°F. Mix together crust ingredients and press into bottom and sides of deep dish pie plate. Bake for 8 minutes. Cool.

For the Filling One: In saucepan over medium heat mix 1 cup of raspberries, ½ cup sugar, cornstarch, and water. Cook until very thick, stirring constantly. Remove from heat and stir in remaining 2 cups of raspberries. Cool in refrigerator.

For the Filling Two: Beat together cream cheese, powdered sugar, and lime juice until smooth. Fold in whipped topping. Spread half of cheese mixture into pie shell. Spread half of raspberry mixture on top. Repeat with remaining fillings.

For the Garnish: Garnish pie with whipped cream and raspberries.

Razzle Dazzle Raspberry Cheese Pie

BLUEBERRY BUCKLE PIE

Matt Zagorski, Arlington Heights, IL
2013 American Pie Council Crisco National Pie Championships
Professional Division Honorable Mention Fruit/Berry

CRUST
2 cups all-purpose flour
½ cup cake flour
1 tablespoon powdered sugar
½ teaspoon salt
½ cup butter-flavored Crisco, cold
½ cup whole butter, salted, cold
¼ cup sour cream
½ cup water

FILLING
16 ounces cream cheese
2 packages of Wilde Thyme Food's
  Blueberry Buckle Dip mix

2 tablespoons of fresh lemon juice
1 cup fresh blueberries
1 cup Cool Whip

TOPPING
4 tablespoon sugar
4 teaspoons cornstarch
½ cup water
2 cups blueberries
2 tablespoons fresh lemon juice

GARNISH
2 cups whipping cream
5 tablespoons sugar

For the Crust: Cut the Crisco and butter into ¼-inch pieces. Once cut, place them in the freezer to harden. Combine the flours, powdered sugar, and salt in a food processor and combine for about 30 seconds. Once the dry ingredients are combined, scatter the very cold Crisco and butter pieces over the flour mixture and process thoroughly using 10 one-second pulses on the food processor. Make sure the mixture has no fat bits larger than small peas. If so, pulse one or two more times. Remove to a large bowl. Combine the sour cream and water in a glass or bowl and stir to combine. Sprinkle 4 tablespoons of the sour cream mixture over the flour mixture and with a fork use a folding motion to incorporate. Add enough additional water so that the dough just comes together. It should be slightly damp, cold, and hold together when squeezed. Divide the dough into 2 piles, shape into balls and flatten each into a 6 to 8-inch disk. Wrap each in plastic wrap and refrigerate at least 2 hours—best if overnight. Before rolling out, let the dough come to just below room temperature. This should take 6 to 7 minutes. The dough should be slightly cool to the touch. Roll to desired thickness and place in pie pan. Place the pan with the rolled out dough in the refrigerator to chill for at least 40 minutes. After 40 minutes in the refrigerator, place the dough and pie pan in the freezer for 20 minutes. While the dough is in the freezer, pre-heat the oven to 400°F.

After 20 minutes in the freezer, take the dough and pie pan out of the freezer, line the bottom of the pie shell with a parchment circle, and then add about 1 to 1.5 pounds of ceramic pie weights. Place the pie shell on a cookie sheet and bake on

Blueberry Buckle Pie

the floor of the oven for 20 minutes. After 20 minutes, remove the weights and parchment paper. Dock or prick the dough with a fork to let air escape, and return the shell to the middle rack of the oven to cook for another 6 to 8 minutes or until the bottom of the crust is golden brown. If the crust starts to bubble, prick it again with a fork. When the pie crust is golden brown, remove it from the oven and let cool completely before filling.

For the Filling: Place the first 3 ingredients in a stand mixer and combine. Fold in the Cool Whip and blueberries. Fill the cooled pie crust with blueberry cream cheese filling. Smooth over with an offset spatula and set aside.

For the Topping: In a small saucepan, mix the sugar, cornstarch, water, blueberries, and lemon juice. Cook and stir until thickened. Cool down in an ice bath. Spread over the blueberry cream cheese filling.

For the Garnish: In a stand mixer, whip the whipping cream and sugar to stiff peaks. Pipe around edges of pie. Chill 2 hours.

UP, UP, AND AWAY

Raine Gottess, Coconut Creek, FL
2013 American Pie Council Crisco National Pie Championships
Professional Division Honorable Mention Open

CRUST
2 (8.8-ounce) packages Lotus
   Biscoff cookies,* (airline cookies
   found at Publix)
1 cup graham cracker crumbs
½ cup plus up to 3 tablespoons
   butter, melted

FILLING ONE
3 ounces melted Lindt Milk Hazelnut
   Grandeur chocolate, melted
8 ounces Philadelphia cream cheese,
   softened
1½ cups powdered sugar
1½ teaspoons pure vanilla

1 tablespoon milk
6 ounces Cool Whip

FILLING TWO
8 ounces Philadelphia cream cheese,
   softened
1¼ cup powdered sugar
1 teaspoon pure vanilla
1 cup Lotus Biscoff
   crunchy spread,
   (found in Publix)
6 ounces Cool Whip

GARNISH
8 ounces Cool Whip

For the Crust: Process cookies with graham crumbs in a food processor until fine. Place into a bowl and toss with melted butter until moist. Press into a 10-inch deep dish pie pan to form a crust. Freeze.

For Filling One: In a mixing bowl, beat well cream cheese with melted chocolate, sugar, vanilla, and milk. Add in Cool Whip and blend well. Spread over crust and freeze.

For Filling Two: In a mixing bowl beat well cream cheese with sugar, vanilla and Biscoff spread. Add in Cool Whip and blend well. Spread over filling one.

For the Garnish: Pipe with the Cool Whip and refrigerate overnight.

*Biscoff is the official airline cookie. I dedicate this pie to my son Tye who will be an officer with the Air Force in the Drones 2013.

Up, Up, and Away Pie

DROP DEAD GORGEOUS STRAWBERRY PIE

Grace Thatcher, Delta, OH
2012 American Pie Council Crisco National Pie Championships
Amateur Division 1st Place Cream Cheese

STRAWBERRY GLAZE

Note: Start glaze 1 day before making pie!
1 pound (3 cups) frozen strawberries
½ cup sugar
1 tablespoon Clearjel (available from King Arthur's baking catalog)

CRUST

10 tablespoons butter
2 cups all-purpose flour (available from King Arthur's baking catalog)
½ teaspoon salt
1 tablespoon sugar
6 to 7 tablespoons ice water
3 ounces white chocolate

WHITE CHOCOLATE FILLING

3 ounces white chocolate
4 ounces cream cheese at room temperature
2 tablespoons sour cream

STRAWBERRY LAYER

20 to 25 fresh strawberries, washed, dried, and stemmed

WHIPPED CREAM FILLING

8 ounces cream cheese, room temperature
¼ cup heavy cream
¾ cup confectioners' sugar
3 ounces white chocolate
1¼ cups heavy cream

For the Crust: Cut butter into ¾-inch cubes and refrigerate for at least 30 minutes. In a food processor with a metal blade, mix flour, salt, and sugar for a few seconds then add ⅓ of the butter and pulse for 10 seconds. The mixture should look like coarse meal. Add the remaining butter and pulse until butter is the size of peas, then add six tablespoons of water and pulse 5 to 7 times. Pinch some dough together, and if it doesn't hold together, pulse in the last tablespoon of water. Take dough out of processor, press into a disk, wrap in plastic wrap, and refrigerate for 20 to 40 minutes. Take dough out of plastic and roll out on a lightly floured surface to a 14-inch round. Ease into a deep dish pie pan and flute edges decoratively. Bake in a 425°F oven until browned, about 10 to 12 minutes. Cool about 20 minutes. Melt 3 ounces of white chocolate in the microwave and brush over bottom and sides of pie shell.

For the Glaze: Pour frozen strawberries into a bowl. Cut larger berries in half. Pour ½ cup sugar over berries and stir the mixture. This mixture can be left out to thaw for around 5 hours, then must be placed in the refrigerator overnight. Remove bowl from refrigerator when ready to make glaze. Pour the strawberry mixture through a colander lined with cheese cloth, reserving juice. This should yield ¾ cup of intensely flavored, clear ruby red juice. Do not press berries against colander; it will cause the juice to become cloudy. Pour the liquid into a saucier, reserving ¼ cup of juice. In a small bowl, make a slurry with Clear-Jel and ¼ cup of reserved juice. Add this to the saucier and cook, stirring over medium heat until the glaze comes to a boil. Simmer 2 minutes to cook ClearJel completely, and set aside to cool.

Drop Dead Gorgeous Strawberry Pie

For the White Chocolate Filling: In a small bowl, melt 3 ounces white chocolate in microwave and set aside to cool. In a medium bowl, beat cream cheese at high speed with hand mixer until light and smooth, about 2 to 3 minutes. Mix in lightly cooled white chocolate and beat for another minute. Add the sour cream and beat until well blended. Transfer mixture to pie shell and spread evenly.

For the Strawberry Layer: To make strawberry layer, arrange strawberries with points facing up on top of white chocolate mixture.

For the Whipped Cream Filling: Place 8 ounces of cream cheese in medium bowl and beat on high speed with a hand mixer until light and fluffy, 2 to 3 minutes. Add heavy cream, confectioners' sugar, and white chocolate to the whipped cream cheese and whip again. In a second bowl, whip heavy cream to soft peaks, then stir ⅓ of the whipped cream into cream cheese mixture. Fold in the remaining whipped cream. Place ⅔ of this mixture into pie shell covering strawberries and level the surface. Place leftover ⅓ of mixture in a pastry bag; reserve. Pour strawberry glaze over pie and carefully pipe remaining ⅓ cream cheese mixture over glaze. Refrigerate until ready to serve.

CREAM

AMISH CREAM PIE

Terri Fiez, Verona, WI
2003 American Pie Council Crisco National Pie Championships
Amateur Division 3rd Place Cream

CRUST
1 cup flour
$\frac{1}{8}$ teaspoon salt
½ cup butter-flavored Crisco
¼ cup cold water

FILLING
¾ cup white sugar
¼ cup cornstarch

¼ teaspoon salt
2½ cups light cream or half-and-half
(or 1 pint half-and-half plus ½ cup
milk for liquid)
½ cup butter, softened
¼ cup brown sugar
1 teaspoon vanilla
1 teaspoon cinnamon (to sprinkle as
a garnish)

For the Crust: Preheat oven to 475°F. Cut shortening into dry ingredients with pastry blender until pea-size pieces form. Then add water and cut until dough forms a ball. Roll out and place in pan. Prick bottom and sides of crust with a fork and bake for 8 to 10 minutes. Cool crust.

For the Filling: Preheat oven to 325°F. In medium saucepan, combine white sugar, cornstarch, and salt. Whisk in cream and cook over medium heat until thickened and bubbly, stirring constantly. Remove from heat, add butter, brown sugar, and vanilla and stir well. Pour into baked pie shell and sprinkle lightly with cinnamon. Bake for 30 minutes. Watch carefully as filling will bubble over the edge if cooked too long. Cool completely before serving. Store in refrigerator.

BANANA COCONUT PECAN DELIGHT

Michele Stuart, Norwalk, CT
2011 American Pie Council Crisco National Pie Championships
Professional Division 1st Place Cream

CRUST
2 cups flour
1 teaspoon salt
¾ cup Crisco
5 tablespoons very cold water
Cream for brushing pie crust

VANILLA CREAM FILLING
3 egg yolks, beaten
½ cup sugar
¼ teaspoon salt
⅓ cup flour
1⅓ cups whole milk
¾ cup water
1 teaspoon vanilla
1 cup bananas, thinly sliced

COCONUT CREAM FILLING
½ cup sugar
¼ teaspoon salt
⅓ cup flour
1⅓ cups milk
¾ cup water
¼ cup cream
   of coconut
3 egg yolks, beaten
½ teaspoon vanilla
½ teaspoon coconut
   extract
½ cup sweetened
   coconut

PECAN WHIPPED CREAM
2 cups heavy cream
¼ cup confectioners' sugar
1 teaspoon vanilla
¼ cup coconut
¼ cup toasted pecans

For the Crust: Preheat oven to 425°F. Mix dry ingredients, then cut in shortening. Add water one tablespoon at a time until dough comes together. Form into a ball, wrap in plastic, and chill for at least 30 minutes. Roll out and put in a 9-inch pan. Brush edge of crust with cream. Blind bake the pie shell for 15 to 20 minutes or until golden brown. Let crust cool before filling.

For the Vanilla Cream Filling: Place the egg yolks in a mixing bowl, beat well, and set them aside. In a medium-sized saucepan, whisk together the sugar, salt, and flour. Add the milk and water to the whisked dry ingredients and heat the saucepan over medium heat, constantly whisking and scraping the sides of the pan. Monitor the mixture carefully; when it begins to simmer and becomes thick and bubbly after approximately 4 minutes, let it cook for 1 more minute. Add 2 tablespoons of the heated mixture to the egg yolks and mix them together well. Pour the egg yolks into the cream in the saucepan and let the cream simmer for 2 minutes, stirring and scraping the sides constantly to prevent burning. Add the vanilla.

Place the bananas on the bottom of the pie shell. Pour the vanilla filling over the sliced bananas.

For the Coconut Cream Filling: In a small bowl, beat egg yolks. Set aside. In a medium saucepan, combine the sugar, salt, and flour and whisk well. Add the milk, water, and cream of co-

Banana Coconut Pecan Delight

conut to dry ingredients and place the saucepan over medium heat. Once the mixture begins to simmer and thicken, stir 1 tablespoon of the heated mixture into the egg yolks. Pour the egg yolks into the cream mixture and let it simmer for 3 to 4 minutes, stirring constantly. Stir in the vanilla and coconut extract. Add the sweetened coconut and mix it in evenly. Pour the coconut cream filling over the banana cream.

Refrigerate the pie and allow to cool for at least 2 hours.

For the Pecan Whipped Cream: Combine the heavy cream, confectioners' sugar, and vanilla in a mixer on high speed. Continue mixing for about a minute or until a creamy consistency is achieved. Fold in toasted pecans. Garnish the pie with whipped cream and coconut.

BANANA SPLIT PIE

Jill Jones, Palm Bay, FL
2006 American Pie Council Crisco National Pie Championships
Amateur Division 3rd Place Cream

CRUST
1 cup flour
6 tablespoons shortening
½ teaspoon salt
3½ tablespoons cold water

FILLING
1 large banana
2 tablespoons lemon juice
3 cups milk
8 ounces cream cheese
8 ounces Cool Whip

1 small package (3.4 ounces) instant vanilla pudding
1 small package (3.4 ounces) instant chocolate pudding
4 ounces strawberry cream cheese
4 ounces pineapple, crushed

GARNISH
½ cup Hershey syrup
½ cup chopped peanuts
8 maraschino cherries

For the Crust: Preheat oven to 425°F. Blend ingredients together in a bowl until dough forms. Roll out dough and place in pie pan. Bake for 9 to 12 minutes.

For the Filling: Slice banana and soak the slices in the lemon juice. Set aside. Mix strawberry cream cheese with pineapple, set aside. Mix ½ regular cream cheese with 1½ cups of milk and vanilla pudding mix until thick and blended, set aside. Mix remaining cream cheese and milk with the chocolate pudding mix until thick and blended. Drain bananas and place on the bottom and sides of the prepared pie crust. Spread out the strawberry cream cheese and pineapple mixture on top of the bananas. Then add the chocolate pudding on top. Layer the vanilla pudding on top of the chocolate pudding.

Garnish with 8 ounces Cool Whip, nuts, cherries, and chocolate syrup. Let stand in the refrigerator for 1 hour before serving.

BLUEBERRY MOUSSE PIE

Jeanne Ely, Mulberry, FL
2008 American Pie Council Crisco National Pie Championships
Amateur Division 1st Place Cream

CRUST
3 cups flour
1 teaspoon salt
¼ cup Crisco shortening
1 cup Crisco butter-flavored
   shortening
1 egg
5 tablespoons cold water
1 tablespoons vinegar
½ teaspoon almond flavoring

FILLING
1 stick butter
½ cup sugar

1 (10-ounce) jar blueberry fruit
   spread
3 squares almond bark, melted
2 eggs
11 ounces extra creamy Cool Whip
   topping

TOPPING
3 cups fresh
   blueberries
⅓ cup orange juice
⅓ cup sugar
⅓ cup water
3 tablespoons cornstarch

For the Crust: Preheat oven to 350°F. Cut together flour, salt, and shortening until oatmeal-like consistency. Beat egg in cup, then add water, vinegar, and almond flavoring. Beat all and pour into flour mixture. Blend well. Roll out dough and place in a 9-inch pie plate. Bake until golden brown. Cool.

For the Filling: Beat butter and sugar until creamy. Add fruit spread and melted almond bark to butter and sugar mixture. Add eggs one at a time, beating for 5 minutes for each egg. Fold in Cool Whip. Add to baked pie shell and cool in refrigerator.

For the Topping: In medium saucepan, combine all ingredients. Cook over medium heat until thickened. Allow to cool. Place topping on top of mousse filling. Garnish as desired.

Blueberry Mousse Pie

CARIBBEAN SUNSET COCONUT PIE

Naylet LaRochelle, Miami, FL
2010 American Pie Council Crisco National Pie Championships
Amateur Division 3rd Place Cream

CRUST

1¾ cups finely chopped shortbread
  cookies
1 tablespoon sugar
½ cup flour
¼ cup butter, melted

FILLING

½ cup heavy whipping cream, cold
1 teaspoon unflavored gelatin
½ cup sugar
3 tablespoons cornstarch
Pinch of salt
1½ cups coconut milk
4 egg yolks
4 ounces cream cheese
1 teaspoon vanilla extract, preferably
  Mexican vanilla extract
⅔ cup chopped macadamia nuts

TOPPING

1½ cups heavy whipping cream
2 tablespoons powdered sugar
17-ounce can grated coconut in
  heavy syrup, very well drained
¼ cup toffee chips
Macadamia nuts, for garnish

For the Crust: Preheat oven to 375°F. Combine all crust ingredients in a large bowl, mixing with a fork. Press the crumb mixture onto bottom and up the sides of a 9-inch pie plate. Bake for 20 to 22 minutes, until crust is light golden brown. Remove from oven and let cool while preparing filling.

For the Filling: Pour ½ cup whipping cream into a small bowl. Sprinkle gelatin over cream and let sit for 5 minutes. In a large saucepan, whisk together sugar, cornstarch, salt, and coconut milk. Cook over medium heat. Add the egg yolks one at a time, whisking between each addition. Whisk in the cream cheese. Cook until mixture begins to boil; let boil for 1 minute. Reduce heat to low. Add the gelatin mixture. Continue to whisk until coconut filling is smooth. Remove from heat; stir in the vanilla extract. Mix until well combined.

Sprinkle macadamia nuts over bottom of pie crust. Pour coconut filling over nuts. Refrigerate for 3 to 4 hours.

For the Topping: Remove pie from refrigerator; carefully layer the grated coconut over filling, making sure to not touch the edges of the pie. In a medium bowl, beat 1½ cups whipping cream until soft peaks form. Add sugar and beat until stiff peaks form. Carefully spread the whipped cream over grated coconut. Pipe rosettes around perimeter of pie. Sprinkle macadamia nuts on top of rosettes. Sprinkle all the toffee chips in the center of pie.

Pie holds well in the refrigerator and can be refrigerated for storage. The whipped cream/nut/toffee topping can be added right before serving, if necessary.

TRES LECHES CARAMEL CREAM PIE

Christine Montalvo, Windsor Heights, IA
2009 American Pie Council Crisco National Pie Championships
Amateur Division 1st Place

CRUST
- 1 cup unsalted butter, room temperature
- ½ cup granulated sugar
- 1 cup all-purpose flour
- 1 cup finely ground shortbread cookies

FILLING
- 12-ounce can dulce de leche caramel, divided
- 12-ounce can sweetened condensed milk
- 1 can evaporated milk
- 1 cup whole milk
- 3 egg yolks
- 3 tablespoons cornstarch
- 2 tablespoons sugar
- 2 whole cinnamon sticks
- 2 teaspoons vanilla extract

TOPPING
- 1 cup heavy whipping cream
- 4 tablespoons powdered sugar
- Remaining dulce de leche
- ½ cup toffee chips

For the Crust: Preheat oven to 350°F. Using an electric mixer, cream the butter and sugar together on medium high speed for 3 to 4 minutes. Add flour and ground shortbread cookies to the mixture and blend for 3 to 4 seconds until fully incorporated. Press the mixture evenly into the bottom of a 9-inch pie pan. Bake the crust for 20 to 25 minutes, or until golden brown. Allow the crust to cool completely.

For the Filling: Spread ½ of the can of dulce de leche caramel evenly over bottom of cooled pie crust. Set aside while you make the filling. In a medium saucepan, stir the sweetened condensed milk, evaporated milk, and whole milk until well blended. Add cinnamon sticks. In a bowl, beat egg yolks. In another bowl, mix the cornstarch and sugar together. Stir the cornstarch mixture into the eggs. Heat milk mixture over low heat, stirring until hot. Whisk some of the hot milk into the egg mixture, whisking constantly to temper the eggs. Pour the egg milk mixture into the milk mixture in the saucepan and heat until very thick and bubbling, stirring constantly. Remove from the heat and stir in vanilla extract. Remove cinnamon sticks and pour into prepared pie crust and cover with plastic wrap. Refrigerate for at least 3 hours or overnight.

For the Topping: Whip cream with powdered sugar. Warm remaining dulce de leche in a microwave until smooth and easily pourable. Drizzle dulce de leche over top of pie. Pipe whipped cream around edges of pie. Sprinkle with toffee chips.

Tres Leches Cream Pie

PEANUT BUTTER–BANANA CREAM PIE

Veselina Iovanovici
2010 American Pie Council Crisco National Pie Championships
Amateur Division 3rd Place Cream

CRUST
12 ounces oatmeal cookies, crumbled
½ cup chopped roasted unsalted
 peanuts
½ teaspoon cinnamon
½ cup butter, melted

PEANUT BUTTER FILLING
2 cups confectioners' sugar
1½ cups creamy peanut butter
8 ounces cream cheese
1 teaspoon vanilla
1½ cups peanut butter cups, cut into
 ¼ inch cubes
⅔ cup chopped roasted unsalted
 peanuts

BANANA CREAM FILLING
4.6-ounce box Jell-O Cook & Serve
 banana pudding
2 tablespoons cornstarch
3 cups milk
16 ounces whipping cream or 2
 (8-ounce) containers whipped
 topping
4 bananas
1 cup peanut butter cups for
 decorating

TOPPING
½ cup confectioners' sugar
½ teaspoon vanilla
Reserved cream from banana filling

For the Crust: Preheat oven to 375°F. Mix together cookie crumbs, peanuts, cinnamon, and butter. Press mixture on bottom and sides of two 9-or 10-inch pie dishes. Bake for 7 to 8 minutes. Remove from oven and let cool on a wire rack.

For the Peanut Butter Filling: With a mixer, beat cream cheese, gradually adding the sugar and vanilla until mixture is nice and smooth. Add peanut butter to cream cheese mixture and beat until incorporated. Spread mixture over the crust, sprinkle with chopped peanuts and peanut butter cups and press gently.

For the Banana Cream Filling: In a medium size saucepan, add banana pudding mix and cornstarch, slowly whisking in the milk. Cook over a medium heat until bubbly. Remove from heat and chill in refrigerator. Meanwhile beat cream. Reserve 1/3 of the cream for decorating. Fold the remaining cream into the chilled banana pudding. Slice bananas, arrange over the peanut butter mixture, top with banana cream.

For the Topping: Mix remaining cream from banana filling with ½ cup confectioners' sugar and ½ teaspoon vanilla. Pipe over the pie. Sprinkle with peanuts and peanut butter cups. Chill before serving.

TRIPLE DECADENCE

Patricia Lapiezo, La Mesa, CA
2005 American Pie Council Crisco National Pie Championships
Amateur Division 2nd Place Cream

CRUST
3 cups unbleached flour
1 cup plus 2 tablespoons Crisco
1 teaspoon salt
5 tablespoons ice water
1 tablespoon vinegar
1 egg, slightly beaten
2 ounces semisweet chocolate, melted

CHOCOLATE NUT LAYER
½ cup semisweet chocolate chips
½ cup heavy whipping cream
½ cup finely chopped toasted pecans

MILK CHOCOLATE COFFEE-TOFFEE LAYER
8 ounces milk chocolate, chopped
1½ cups heavy whipping cream

2 teaspoons instant espresso powder
½ cup toffee bits

WHITE CHOCOLATE TOPPING
8-ounce package cream cheese, softened
⅓ cup powdered sugar
2 tablespoons crème de cacao
6 ounces white chocolate, melted
1 cup heavy whipping cream, stiffly beaten

GARNISH
1 cup heavy whipping cream
1 to 2 tablespoons powdered sugar
⅓ cup grated semisweet chocolate
Melted milk chocolate

For the Crust: Preheat oven to 400°F. Combine flour and salt in a large bowl. Cut in shortening. In a small bowl, combine egg, water, and vinegar. Gradually add liquid to flour mixture until dough comes together. Refrigerate 1 hour. Prepare enough dough for a 10-inch pie. Roll out and place in pie pan. Bake for approximately 20 minutes, or until browned. When crust comes out from oven, brush bottom with 2 ounces melted semisweet chocolate. Cool completely.

For the Chocolate Nut Layer: In a small saucepan, heat the whipping cream to simmer. Stir in chocolate chips and stir until smooth; stir in nuts. Spread over bottom of prepared crust. Chill while preparing remaining fillings.

For the Milk Chocolate Coffee Toffee Layer: In a small saucepan, heat ½ cup whipping cream with the espresso powder to a simmer. Place chopped chocolate in a medium bowl. Pour hot cream over chocolate. Let stand 5 minutes. Stir until smooth. In a large mixing bowl, beat the remaining whipping cream until soft peaks form. Fold ½ into chocolate chip mixture. Beat remaining cream until slightly stiffer. Fold into the chocolate mixture. Fold in toffee bits. Spread over first layer.

Triple Decadence Pie

For the White Chocolate Topping: In a medium mixing bowl, beat the cream cheese and sugar until fluffy. Blend in liqueur. Add melted chocolate, beating on low speed until blended. Fold in whipped cream. Spread over second layer.

For the Garnish: Drizzle milk chocolate over top of pie. Beat whipping cream and powdered sugar until stiff. Stir in grated chocolate. Pipe a border around edge of pie. Refrigerate until set.

STRAWBERRY CREAM DELIGHT

Carole Socier, Bay City, MI
2007 American Pie Council Crisco National Pie Championships
Amateur Division 1st Place Cream and Best of Show

CRUST
1 cup all-purpose flour
¼ cup crushed vanilla wafers
½ teaspoon salt
⅓ cup Crisco shortening
3 to 4 tablespoons cold water

STRAWBERRY LAYER
¾ cup sugar
¼ cup cornstarch
⅛ teaspoon salt
1½ cups water

3-ounce package strawberry
  Jell-O
2 cups frozen unsweetened
  strawberries

CREAM LAYER
3-ounce package cream cheese,
  softened
⅓ cup powdered sugar
1 teaspoon vanilla
⅛ teaspoon salt
1 cup whipping cream, whipped

For the Crust: Preheat oven to 350°F. In mixing bowl, combine flour, crushed wafers, and salt. Cut in Crisco shortening until pieces are the size of small peas. Sprinkle 1 tablespoon of water over mix. Gently toss with fork. Repeat with remaining water until all is moistened. Form dough into ball. On lightly floured surface, flatten dough with hands. Roll into a 12-inch circle. Transfer into a 9-inch pie plate. Trim, flute, and prick bottom and sides of pie crust with a fork. Bake for 10 to 12 minutes or until golden brown. Cool.

For the Strawberry Layer: Combine sugar, cornstarch, and salt in medium saucepan. Gradually stir in water. Cook and stir until mixture comes to a boil and is thick and clear. Add Jell-O and stir until dissolved. Add frozen strawberries and refrigerate until slightly thickened.

For the Cream Layer: Combine cream cheese, powdered sugar, vanilla, and salt in medium-sized bowl. Beat until smooth. Add whipped cream. Spoon half of mixture into prepared crust. Top with half of strawberry mixture. Repeat layers. Garnish with more whipped cream and fresh strawberries.

OLD TIME BUTTERSCOTCH CREAM PIE

Christine Montalvo, Windsor Heights, IA
2013 American Pie Council Crisco National Pie Championships
Amateur Division 1st Place Cream

CRUST
2 cups all-purpose flour
1 cup cake flour
1 cup Crisco
1 whole egg, beaten
1 tablespoon apple cider vinegar
1/3 cup ice water

FILLING
1 cup dark brown sugar
1/4 cup butter
1 tablespoon corn syrup
1/4 cup water
3 tablespoons all-purpose flour
3 tablespoons cornstarch
1 3/4 cups milk
3 egg yolks
1/2 cup sugar
3/4 teaspoon salt
1 teaspoon vanilla extract

GARNISH
Whipped cream

For the Crust: In food processor, blend flours together. Cut the Crisco into small pieces and add to processor. Pulse until mixture resembles small peas. Transfer mixture to a large mixing bowl. In a separate small bowl, mix the egg, vinegar, and ice water. Mix well. Pour over flour mixture in the bowl. Using a fork, combine just until the dough comes together. Do not over mix. Form dough into a disk, wrap in plastic, and chill for several hours or overnight. Makes 2 9-inch crusts. Roll out bottom crust and place in pie dish. Bake at 375°F for 15 to 20 minutes or until golden brown. Cool.

For the Filling: Mix together brown sugar, butter, corn syrup, and water in a heavy-bottomed medium saucepan. Cook, stirring constantly, over medium heat until mixture reaches 250°F on a candy thermometer, about 15 minutes. Immediately lower heat to keep the temperature at 250°F, keeping butterscotch warm over low heat. Mix together flour and cornstarch in a medium bowl. Add ½ cup milk, whisking until smooth. Whisk in egg yolks, then set aside. Combine sugar, salt, and remaining 1¼ cups milk in a heavy saucepan and bring just to a boil over medium heat, about 10 minutes. Whisk ½ cup hot milk mixture into yolk mixture, then whisk yolk mixture into remaining hot milk. Cook over low heat, whisking constantly, until thick and boiling, about 1 minute. Boil for 1 minute more, remove from heat, and stir in vanilla. Immediately mix together warm butterscotch and custard mixture. Pour into baked pie shell. Allow cooling to room temperature, then refrigerating until set, about 2 hours.

For the Garnish: Just before serving, top pie with whipped cream, leaving butterscotch exposed in center.

Old Time Butterscotch Cream Pie

SUB-LIME BLUEBERRY COCONUT TRUFFLE PIE

Julie DeMatteo, Clementon, NJ
2004 American Pie Council Crisco National Pie Championships
Amateur Division 1st Place

CRUST
1⅓ cups flour
½ teaspoon salt
½ cup Crisco shortening
3 tablespoons ice water
1 egg white, lightly beaten

FILLING
1 packet unflavored gelatin
2 tablespoons cold water

1½ cups heavy cream
14-ounce can cream of coconut
¼ cup lime juice
2 teaspoons grated lime zest
6 ounces white baking chocolate, chopped
20-ounce can blueberry pie filling
6 tablespoons toasted coconut
Lime slices for garnish

For the Crust: Preheat oven to 400°F. Combine the flour and salt in a medium bowl. Cut in Crisco until mixture forms crumbs. Sprinkle with water, 1 tablespoon at a time, until dough forms a ball. Flatten to make a pancake of dough. Lightly flour work surface and roll dough to a 10-inch circle. Place into a 9-inch pie plate and flute edges, then prick all over with a fork to prevent shrinkage. Brush egg white over pie crust. Bake until golden brown, 10 to 12 minutes.

For the Filling: In a cup, sprinkle gelatin over the cold water. In a medium saucepan, combine the heavy cream, cream of coconut, lime juice, and lime zest and bring to a boil. Remove from heat and stir in the gelatin and white baking chocolate, whisking until melted and smooth. Pour into cooled crust and refrigerate until set. Once set, spread blueberry pie filling over top. Sprinkle toasted coconut around edge of pie and garnish with lime slices.

PAMMIE'S BANOFFEE CREAM PIE

John Sunvold, Orlando, FL
2013 American Pie Council Crisco National Pie Championships
Amateur Division 2nd Place Cream

CRUST
1½ cups graham cracker crumbs
3 tablespoons sugar
5 tablespoons melted butter

FILLING ONE
1 can dulce de leche (caramel)
3 to 5 bananas (ripe, but not over-ripe)

FILLING TWO
½ cup plus 2 tablespoons sugar
¼ teaspoon salt
¼ cup cornstarch
½ cup heavy cream
5 egg yolks
2 cups milk
1 tablespoon vanilla extract
2 tablespoons butter

TOPPING
2¼ cups heavy cream
6 ounces white chocolate (broken into small pieces)

GARNISH
1 milk chocolate bar

For the Crust: Mix all ingredients together and press mixture into pie plate. Bake in a 375°F oven for 10 minutes, or until brown. Allow to cool down to room temperature.

For Filling One: Spread ⅓- to ½-inch layer of dulce de leche on cooled baked crust. Slice bananas and place on caramel. Drizzle more dulce de leche on banana, if desired. Chill.

For Filling Two: Mix sugar, salt, and starch in a pot. In a bowl, whisk egg yolks, milk, and cream slightly. Slowly add the milk, egg yolk, and cream mixture. Heat over medium heat, whisking frequently, until thick and bubbling (but not rapidly boiling). Once the cream is bubbling, continue to cook and whisk for 30 to 60 seconds more. Finally, add the butter and vanilla and mix until the cream is smooth. Set aside until just warmer than room temperature. Place as much of the cream on top of the caramel/banana as your pan allows. It is unlikely that all of this cream will be used. Chill.

For the Topping: Bring one cup of cream to a boil over medium heat. Add white chocolate and stir constantly until the chocolate is melted and mixture is combined. Remove from heat and let cool to room temperature. Refrigerate for at least four hours. In a large bowl, beat the rest of the cream with an electric mixer set on high speed. Beat until soft peaks form. Slowly add the white chocolate mixture and continue to beat until stiff. Top pie and refrigerate for 4 hours.

For the Garnish: Top with milk chocolate curls made by drawing a vegetable peeler or knife down the side of a chocolate bar. Be generous with the chocolate.

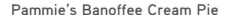

Pammie's Banoffee Cream Pie

GERMAN CHOCOLATE PIE

Jennifer Nystrom, Morrow, OH
2013 American Pie Council Crisco National Pie Championships
Amateur Division 3rd Place Cream

CRUST
1 tablespoon granulated sugar
½ teaspoon salt
⅓ cup ice cold water
1 tablespoon cider vinegar
8 tablespoons (½ cup) Crisco vegetable shortening, cold, cut into ½ inch cubes
8 tablespoons (1 stick) very cold butter, cut into ½ inch cubes
2¾ cups all-purpose flour
½ cup canned coconut pecan frosting

FILLING ONE
¾ granulated sugar
3 tablespoons cornstarch
pinch of salt
2 cups whole milk
3 large egg yolks
2 tablespoons butter
1 teaspoon vanilla extract
½ cup semisweet chocolate chips
2 tablespoons toasted coconut

2 tablespoons toasted and chopped pecans

FILLING TWO
½ cup granulated sugar
3 tablespoons cornstarch
pinch of salt
1 (13.5-ounce) can coconut milk
½ cup whole milk
3 large egg yolks
2 tablespoons butter
1 teaspoon coconut extract
1 teaspoon vanilla extract

TOPPING
1½ cups heavy whipping cream
1 teaspoon vanilla
2 tablespoons granulated sugar
¼ cup chocolate syrup
2 tablespoons toasted coconut
2 tablespoons toasted and chopped pecans
Chocolate curls

For the Crust: Preheat oven to 375°F. Place the paddle of your stand mixer in the freezer for at least an hour. While your paddle is in the freezer, mix the sugar, salt, water, and vinegar together in a glass measuring cup until salt and sugar are dissolved. Refrigerate until very cold. Put the flour into the bowl of your stand mixer. With the paddle that has been in the freezer, on low speed mix in the cold, cubed shortening. When that is incorporated, add the butter and continue to mix on low speed until about the consistency of small peas. Do not over mix. Add the cold water/vinegar mixture and mix just until incorporated. You may need to mix in 1 to 2 tablespoons more of ice cold water depending on the humidity of the day. When the dough is just coming together, remove the bowl from the mixer and carefully make two balls out of the dough. Form both balls into disks and cover tightly with plastic wrap. Refrigerate dough for at least 2 hours. Remove one disk of dough and roll out to fit a 9-inch deep dish pie plate. (Reserve second disk for another use.) Place a piece of parchment paper over dough and fill the plate with pie weights or dried beans. Blind bake the crust for 20 minutes. Remove parchment paper and weights and continue baking another 5 to 10 minutes or until crust is just beginning to turn golden brown. Place foil around the edges to prevent overbrowning. Cool crust completely. When crust is completely cooled, spread the coconut pecan frosting evenly over the bottom of the pie shell.

For Filling One: Whisk the sugar, cornstarch, and pinch of salt in a large, heavy bottomed saucepan. Whisk in the milk and egg yolks. Place pan over medium-high heat and bring mixture to a boil, stirring constantly. This will take about 5 minutes. Continue cooking and stirring for another 1½ minutes. Remove mixture from heat and whisk in the butter, vanilla, and the chocolate chips. Whisk until the butter and chocolate chips are completely melted and well incorporated. Put mixture in a medium-sized bowl, cover the top with plastic wrap, and place in the refrigerator until cool. Once cooled, evenly spread the cooled chocolate filling over the frosting in the pie pan. Sprinkle 2 tablespoons toasted coconut and 2 tablespoons toasted pecans over the chocolate filling.

For Filling Two: Whisk the sugar, cornstarch, and pinch of salt in a large, heavy bottomed saucepan. Whisk in the coconut milk, whole milk, and egg yolks. Place pan over medium-high heat and stirring constantly, bring mixture to a boil. This will take about 5 minutes. Continue cooking and stirring for another 1½ minutes. Remove mixture from the heat and add the coconut extract, vanilla extract, and butter and whisk until butter is completely melted and well incorporated. Put mixture in a medium-sized bowl and cover the top with plastic wrap and place in the refrigerator for about 30 minutes. Once cooled, carefully and evenly spread the cooled coconut filling over the chocolate filling. Place a piece of plastic wrap directly over the top of this. Refrigerate for at least 30 minutes.

For the Topping:

When ready to serve the pie, make the topping by placing the whipping cream, vanilla, and

German Chocolate Cream Pie

granulated sugar in a large mixing bowl. Beat at high speed until soft peaks form. Add the chocolate syrup and continue whipping until desired consistency. Remove the plastic wrap from the top of the pie. Either pipe or spread the whipped cream mixture over the top of the pie. Sprinkle the remaining toasted coconut and pecans over the top. Shave chocolate curls over the top if desired.

I'D ÉCLAIR SOME MORE CREAM PIE

Kathryn Hanson, Orlando, FL
2013 American Pie Council Crisco National Pie Championships
Professional Division Honorable Mention Cream

CRUST
1½ cups Nilla Wafers, crushed
2 tablespoons sugar
Pinch of salt
½ cup unsalted butter, melted

FILLING
¾ cup sugar
¼ cup cornstarch
¼ teaspoon salt
1 vanilla bean, scraped

1½ cups milk
1½ cups heavy cream
3 egg yolks, slightly beaten
2 tablespoons butter
1 (8-ounce) package cream cheese, softened

TOPPING
1 cup heavy cream
1 tablespoon powdered sugar
Hot fudge sauce

For the Crust: Preheat oven to 400°F. Mix the crushed Nilla Wafers, sugar, and salt together. Melt the butter and add to the Nilla Wafer mix. Press into pie plate and bake until set.

For the Filling: In medium saucepan, combine sugar, cornstarch, and salt. Stir in vanilla bean, heavy cream, and milk, blending until smooth. Cook over medium heat until mixture boils and thickens, stirring constantly. Remove vanilla bean. Boil 2 minutes. Remove from heat. Blend a small amount of hot mixture into egg yolks. Return to saucepan, blending well. Cook until mixture just begins to bubble, stirring constantly. Remove from heat; stir in butter. Refrigerate until set. In separate bowl whip the cream cheese. Slowly add the vanilla filling to cream cheese, mixing until there are no lumps. Pour into the cooled cookie pie crust. Refrigerate until set.

For the Topping: Whip cream with powdered sugar. Top with a layer of whipped cream and drizzle chocolate syrup.

I'd Éclair Some More Cream Pie

FRUIT & BERRY

BERRY RHUBARB PIE

Susan Gills, Boulder, CO
2000 American Pie Council National Pie Championships
Amateur Division 1st Place Fruit/Berry

CRUST

⅔ cup shortening

1 teaspoon salt

4 tablespoons ice cold water

2 tablespoons butter

2 cups flour

Half-and-half

Sugar

FILLING

1 cup blackberries

2 cups rhubarb, cut into
   ½ inch pieces

¼ cup flour

1 teaspoon lemon juice

1 cup raspberries

1 cup sugar

1 tablespoon butter, melted

For the Crust: Mix flour and salt. Add butter and shortening, mixing until texture is like corn-meal. Place 1/3 of the mixture in a separate bowl. Add water and form a paste. Add this paste to the remaining flour mixture and mix thoroughly. Form a ball. Let sit at least 20 minutes before rolling. Divide in half. Roll out bottom crust and place in pie pan. Reserve remaining half for a top crust.

For the Filling: Preheat oven to 400°F. Mix sugar and flour. Add to fruits. Refrigerate overnight. Just before adding to pie shell, stir in melted butter and lemon juice. Pour filling into prepared pie shell. Roll out remaining crust and place on top. Crimp edges. Brush lightly with half-and-half. Sprinkle with sugar. Bake at 400°F for 10 minutes, then reduce temperature to 350°F. Bake for 40 to 50 minutes or until crust is golden brown.

BLACKBERRY APRICOT RIBBON PIE

Phyllis Szymanek, Toledo, Ohio
2008 American Pie Council Crisco National Pie Championships
Amateur Division 2nd Place Fruit/Berry

CRUST
1⅓ cups flour
½ cup Crisco shortening
3 tablespoons cold water
½ teaspoon salt
1 beaten egg plus 1 teaspoon water
  for egg wash

FILLING
8-ounce package Philadelphia cream
  cheese, softened
¼ cup sour cream
½ cup Smucker's Simply Fruit
  apricot spread

1 cup fresh blackberries (set aside
  3 berries for garnish)
15-ounce can apricots (quartered;
  set aside ½ apricot for garnish)

GLAZE
1 cup sugar
2 tablespoons cornstarch
3-ounce box Blackberry Fusion
  Jell-O
1 cup 7UP soda

GARNISH
Cool Whip (optional for garnish)

For the Crust: Preheat oven to 425°F. Mix flour and salt in mixing bowl. Add Crisco shortening. With pastry cutter, cut shortening into flour mixture until pea-sized chunks form. Add water, one tablespoon at a time, until it forms into a ball. Roll out on floured surface one inch larger than 9-inch pie pan. Place into pie plate and flute edges. Mix beaten egg with 1 teaspoon water; brush bottom and side of pie with egg wash. Prick bottom and sides of pie crust. Bake for 12 to 15 minutes. Remove from oven and cool on a wire rack.

For the Filling: In a medium bowl, beat cream cheese until creamy; mix in sour cream, and fold in Smucker's Simply Fruit apricot. Set aside. Reserving 3 blackberries and ½ apricot for garnish, combine blackberries and apricots in another bowl. Set aside.

For the Glaze: Combine sugar and cornstarch in a saucepan; slowly add 7UP. Cook over medium heat until thick. Remove from heat and add Jell-O. Place in refrigerator for 15 minutes.

Pour one half of cheese filling into bottom of pie shell and top with one half fruit. Pour one half glaze over the top, then place in the freezer for 15 minutes. Top with the rest of the filling, then the other half of the fruit, then top with remainder of glaze.

Garnish with 3 berries, ½ apricot, and Cool Whip topping. Refrigerate for 2 hours before serving.

Blackberry Apricot Ribbon Pie

PEACH/BLACKBERRY/ STRAWBERRY (A PBS SPECIAL)

Beth Campbell, Belleville, WI
2004 American Pie Council Crisco National Pie Championships
Amateur Division 3rd Place Fruit/Berry

CRUST
1 cup flour
½ cup Crisco shortening
Pinch of salt
¼ cup water

FILLING
¼ cup cornstarch
4 tablespoons strawberry Jell-O
1 can frozen apple juice, thawed

2 tablespoons frozen orange juice, thawed
1 cup fresh blackberries
1 cup fresh strawberries
5 medium peaches, peeled and coarsely chopped or frozen and thawed if not in season

GARNISH
Whipped cream

For the Crust: Preheat oven to 375°F. Cut shortening into flour and salt until pea-sized pieces form. Mix in cold water. Refrigerate until chilled. Roll out crust on a floured board. Place into pie pan and prick the crust with a fork so it doesn't bubble. Bake 8 to 10 minutes or until golden brown.

For the Filling: In a saucepan, combine cornstarch, strawberry Jell-O, and apple and orange juice concentrates until smooth. Bring to a boil. Add ½ cup blackberries, cook and stir for 2 minutes or until thickened. Toss together the chopped peaches, strawberries, and remaining blackberries. Place into prepared crust. Pour orange juice mixture over the fruit—crust will be full. Cover and refrigerate for 8 hours or overnight.

Garnish with whipped cream.

OLD-TIME BLACKBERRY PIE

Carol Socier, Bay City, MI
2008 American Pie Council Crisco National Pie Championships
Amateur Division 1st Place Fruit/Berry

CRUST
2 cups flour
½ teaspoon salt
⅔ cup Crisco shortening
1 egg yolk
1 teaspoon white vinegar
5 tablespoons ice water

FILLING
6 cups frozen unsweetened blackberries
1 cup granulated sugar
½ cup brown sugar
3 tablespoons cornstarch

1 tablespoons tapioca
½ teaspoon cinnamon
⅛ teaspoon nutmeg
⅛ teaspoon ginger
¾ cup blackberry syrup
   (Blackberry Patch)
1 teaspoon vanilla

TOPPING
½ cup flour
½ cup sugar
¼ cup butter
½ cup flaked coconut

For the Crust: Preheat oven to 400°F. In a large bowl, mix together flour and salt. Using a pastry blender, cut in shortening until pieces are pea-sized. Whisk egg yolk, then add ice water and vinegar. Sprinkle liquid one tablespoon at a time, as much as needed, over dry mixture, tossing with a fork until all is moistened. Form into a ball, and roll out on a floured board to fit a 9-inch deep dish pie pan. Prick bottom and sides, flute edges as desired and partially bake crust for 10 minutes.

For the Filling: In a large saucepan, stir together sugars, cornstarch, tapioca, and spices. Toss in frozen blackberries and blackberry syrup. Cook and stir over medium heat until thick and bubbly. Stir in vanilla. Pour filling into partially baked crust.

For the Topping: Mix four topping ingredients. Top pie with crumb mixture. Bake in 400°F oven for 20 to 25 minutes.

Old-Time Blackberry Pie

BLUEBERRY PIE

Susan Boyle, DeBary, FL
2006 American Pie Council Crisco National Pie Championships
Amateur Division 2nd Place Fruit/Berry

CRUST
3 cups all-purpose flour
1 tablespoon sugar
1 teaspoon salt
1¼ cups shortening
1 egg, whipped
1 tablespoon distilled white vinegar
4 tablespoons cold water
1 egg, whisked
Coarse sugar for topping

FILLING
1½ cup sugar
2 cups frozen blueberries
1 cup dried blueberries
½ teaspoon nutmeg
⅛ teaspoon cinnamon
2 tablespoons cornstarch
6 tablespoons cold water
⅓ cup butter
Pinch of salt

For the Crust: Preheat oven to 425°F. In large bowl, mix flour, sugar, and salt; cut in shortening with pastry cutter. In a second bowl, mix egg, vinegar, and cold water; pour liquid in small amounts around dry mixture, cutting it in. Knead dough briefly until smooth, allow to rest about 8 minutes. Roll out dough, line pie pan, bake for 10 to 12 minutes, depending on oven. Reserve some dough for a top crust. Use egg wash for top crust and sprinkle with sugar.

For the Filling: Preheat oven to 425°F. Mix sugar, cinnamon, nutmeg, salt, cornstarch, and water together. Add berries and toss to mix well.

Pour into prepared crust, dot with butter, and cover with top crust. Cut slits or decorations for steam to escape. Use egg wash for top of crust before applying coarse sugar. Bake at 425°F for 15 minutes. Lower heat to 350°F and bake for 40 more minutes, with edges covered with foil to prevent burning. Remove foil last 6 minutes of baking. Cool before slicing.

BURGUNDY CHERRY BERRY PIE

Marles Riessland, Riverdale, NE
2007 American Pie Council Crisco National Pie Championships
Amateur Division 2nd Place Fruit/Berry

CRUST
3 cups all-purpose flour
1 teaspoon salt
1 teaspoon sugar
½ teaspoon baking powder
1 cup plus1 teaspoon butter-flavored
 shortening, chilled
⅓ cup water
1 tablespoon vinegar
1 egg, beaten
1 egg white, slightly beaten
1 tablespoon sugar

FILLING
12-ounce package frozen dark sweet
 cherries, thawed and halved
12-ounce bag frozen raspberries,
 thawed
1 cup sugar
3 tablespoons tapioca
¼ teaspoon salt
½ teaspoon almond extract

For the Crust: In a large bowl, combine the flour, salt, sugar, and baking powder. Cut in shortening with a pastry blender until texture resembles cornmeal. In a small bowl, mix water and vinegar with beaten egg. Add the liquid mixture, one tablespoon at a time, to the flour mixture, tossing with a fork to form soft dough. Shape in three disks. Wrap in plastic wrap and chill in refrigerator. Use two disks when making this pie. Freeze remaining dough for later use. Roll out one disk and place bottom crust into a 9-inch pie pan. Roll out another disk for the top crust. Use beaten egg white to brush on top crust and sprinkle with sugar

For the Filling: Preheat oven to 450°F. In a medium bowl, combine sugar, tapioca, and salt. Add cherries, raspberries with all the juices and almond extract; mix well. Let stand 15 minutes to soften tapioca. Spoon mixture into prepared pie shell. Dot with butter, adjust top crust; seal, flute edge, and vent top. Brush top with slightly beaten egg white and sprinkle with sugar. Bake at 450°F for 15 minutes. Reduce oven temperature to 350°F and bake 35 to 45 minutes longer, or until golden. Cool on rack.

Burgundy Cherry Berry Pie

CONCORD GRAPE PIE

Susan Gills, Boulder, CO
2002 American Pie Council National Pie Championships
Amateur Division 2nd Place Fruit/Berry

CRUST
2 cups flour
1 teaspoon salt
2/3 cup Crisco
2 tablespoons butter
¼ cup cold water
1 tablespoon half-and-half
1 teaspoon sugar

FILLING
3½ cups seedless grapes (all kinds)
½ cup sugar
3 to 4 tablespoons flour
Dash of cinnamon
1 tablespoon butter

For the Crust: Mix flour and salt. Cut in shortening and butter until texture is like cornmeal. Add cold water and form a ball. Let rest 20 minutes. Divide dough in two. Roll out one half and place in pie pan. Roll out the other for a top crust. Add filling. Cover with top crust. Use pastry brush to lightly brush on half-and-half. Sprinkle with sugar.

For the Filling: Preheat oven to 400°F. Slip skins off fresh grapes and add pulp to a saucepan. Bring pulp to a boil. Separate the seeds by pressing pulp through a sieve. Mix skins and pulp together.

Mix sugar, flour, and cinnamon together. Add to grapes. Place pats of butter on top.

Bake at 400°F for 10 minutes. Turn oven down to 350°F and continue baking for 30 to 40 minutes until crust is golden brown.

FRESH STRAWBERRY PEACH PIE

Evette Rahman, Orlando, FL
2008 American Pie Council Crisco National Pie Championships
Amateur Division 3rd Place Fruit/Berry

CRUST

2 cups flour
2 tablespoons sugar
1 teaspoon salt
½ teaspoon baking powder
⅓ cup vegetable shortening
⅓ cup unsalted butter, very cold, cubed
1 tablespoon oil
1 tablespoon vinegar
⅓ cup heavy cream
1 egg plus 1 teaspoon water for egg wash
2 tablespoons sugar

FILLING

16 ounces fresh or frozen sliced peaches, thawed
16 ounces fresh or frozen whole strawberries, thawed
1½ tablespoons butter
1 cup sugar
¼ teaspoon ground cinnamon
2 tablespoons cornstarch
2 tablespoons tapioca

For the Crust: Mix flour, sugar, salt, and baking powder. Cut in shortening and butter. Stir together oil, vinegar, and cream. Mix liquid into flour. Form into two disks. Wrap in plastic. Refrigerate for one hour. Roll out one disk on lightly floured surface and place in deep dish pie plate. Reserve second disk for top crust.

For the Filling: Preheat oven to 400°F. Mix together filling ingredients. Fill pie shell. Roll out top crust and place on filling or cut out strips to form a lattice top. Cut off excess dough and crimp edges as desired. Make slits for ventilation.

Make egg wash by mixing egg with 1 teaspoon water. Brush over top of crust and sprinkle with sugar. Bake in 400°F oven for 20 minutes; then reduce temperature to 375°F and bake another 35 minutes until golden brown and bubbly. Cover pie edges with shield to prevent excess browning during baking. Cool completely.

Fresh Strawberry Peach Pie

ULTIMATE STRAWBERRY PIE

Jeanne Ely, Mulberry, FL
2005 American Pie Council Crisco National Pie Championships
Amateur Division 3rd Place Fruit/Berry

CRUST
3 cups flour
1 teaspoon salt
1¼ cups shortening
1 egg
5 tablespoons cold water
1 tablespoon vinegar

LAYER ONE
¾ cup chocolate chips
2 tablespoons heavy whipping cream

LAYER TWO
1½ quarts strawberries, sliced

FILLING
1 cup sugar
2 tablespoons cornstarch
1 cup water
1 teaspoon lemon juice
1 package strawberry gelatin powder

For the Crust: Preheat oven to 375°F. Cut together flour, salt, and shortening until oatmeal-like in consistency. Beat egg in cup. Add water and vinegar to beaten egg and beat together. Pour egg mixture into flour mixture. Blend well. Form dough into a ball and roll out. Place in a 9-inch pie pan. Bake until golden brown, about 15 minutes.

For Layer One: Melt chocolate chips and heavy cream together. Spread over top of baked pie shell.

For Layer Two: Place strawberries on top of chocolate mixture.

For the Filling: Combine the sugar, cornstarch, and water in a small saucepan. Cook over medium heat until thickened and clear, stirring constantly. Remove from heat, then stir in lemon juice and gelatin powder. Chill until mixture begins to thicken.

Spoon slightly thickened gelatin mixture over the top of the strawberries. Chill at least 4 hours. Garnish as desired.

Ultimate Strawberry Pie

AMERICAN FREEDOM G. I. JOE PIE

Phyllis Szymanek, Toledo, OH
2013 American Pie Council Crisco National Pie Championships
Amateur Division 2nd Place Fruit/Berry

CRUST
1½ cups Pillsbury all-purpose flour
½ teaspoon salt
1 tablespoon sugar
1 teaspoon vinegar
½ cups Crisco shortening, chilled
3 tablespoons butter, chilled
3 to 4 tablespoons ice water
1 egg plus 1 teaspoon water
   (egg wash)

FILLING ONE
2 ounces cream cheese
2 tablespoons powdered sugar
2 ounces white chocolate chips
   (melted, then cooled)
¼ cup whipped topping

FILLING TWO
3 cups fresh blackberries
1 cup white chocolate chips

8 ounces softened cream cheese
2 teaspoons vanilla
1 cup powdered sugar
⅓ cup malted milk powder
8 ounces whipped topping
½ cup English toffee bits

TOPPING
4 ounces cream cheese
¼ cup powdered sugar
2 teaspoons vanilla
½ cup white chocolate chips
   (melted)
8 ounces whipped topping
2 tablespoons Smucker's Blackberry
   Jam
¼ cup toffee bits

For the Crust: In a mixing bowl, combine flour, salt, and sugar. Cut in shortening and butter until crumbly. Add vinegar to ice water. Add vinegar/ice water mixture one tablespoon at a time until dough forms into a ball. Shape dough into a disk shape, wrap in plastic, and chill for one hour. Roll out on floured surface to fit a 9-inch pie dish. Trim crust and flute edges. Brush with egg wash. Prick bottom and sides with fork. Bake at 425°F for about 12 to 15 minutes. Cool on wire rack.

For Filling One: Whip cream cheese, add powdered sugar and melted chocolate chips, and mix until smooth. Mix in whipped topping. Spread on bottom of cooled crust.

For Filling Two: Place 2½ cups fresh blackberries in blender, cover and puree, then set aside.

In a small microwave safe bowl, melt chocolate chips for about 1 minute or until melted; cool slightly. Beat cream cheese until smooth. Add vanilla, powdered sugar, and malted milk powder until well blended. Fold in melted chocolate; beat in blackberries, then add whipped topping.

Fold in toffee bits. Pour mixture into pie crust and chill for 4 hours or overnight.

For the Topping: Beat cream cheese; add powdered sugar and vanilla until smooth. Add cooled melted chocolate; mix in whipped topping until well blended. Place in a pastry bag with a star tip. Pipe around edge of pie. Mix jam and remaining ½ cup blackberries. Arrange in center of pie. Sprinkle with toffee bits.

Garnish as desired.

American Freedom G. I. Joe Pie

RASPBERRY DEVOTION PIE

John Sunvold, Orlando, FL
2013 American Pie Council Crisco National Pie Championships
Amateur Division 3rd Place Fruit/Berry

CRUST
2 cups shortbread or pecan
   shortbread cookies
¼ cup melted butter
¼ cup flour

FILLING ONE
3 tablespoons butter
2 tablespoons corn syrup
2 tablespoons milk
2 ounces dark chocolate, chopped
   into pieces
1 cup powdered sugar

FILLING TWO
6 ounces cream cheese
⅓ cup powdered sugar

6 ounces Cool Whip
¼ to ⅓ cup raspberry pie layer
   (made below)

TOPPING
3 cups frozen raspberries, thawed
6 to 8 teaspoons sugar (depending
   on your raspberries)
1 to 2 tablespoons cornstarch

GARNISH
Whipped cream

For the Crust: Mix flour and shortbread crumbs, then add melted butter until mixture looks like wet sand. Press into deep pie pan and bake at 350°F for around 10 minutes or until golden brown. Place on cooling rack and bring to room temperature.

For Filling One: Mix butter, corn syrup, and milk and heat over medium heat until boiling. Stir constantly. Add chocolate chips and stir until melted. Once fully combined, slowly add powdered sugar. Mix completely, then carefully spread the chocolate onto the bottom of the crust (may include a thin layer around the sides of the crust in order to hold the crust together). It cools quickly, so you must spread immediately.

For Filling Two: Beat cream cheese and powdered sugar until smooth. Fold in the Cool Whip and reserved raspberry layer filling. Spread onto cooled chocolate layer and chill in refrigerator.

For the Topping: Whisk sugar and starch together and place in a pot. Add thawed raspberries (including the juice) and cook over medium heat. Bring to a boil and boil for 2 minutes, stirring constantly. Cool for 20 minutes, then spread onto pie. Chill.

For the Garnish: Pipe whipping cream on top of pie. You can also add raspberries and chocolate shavings.

Raspberry Devotion Pie

BLUEBERRY PARFAIT

Pat Smith, Deltona, FL
2013 American Pie Council Crisco National Pie Championships
Amateur Division 1st Place Comstock Blueberry

CRUST
2 cups graham cracker crumbs
⅓ cup sugar
¼ cup melted butter

FILLING
1 cup cream cheese
1¾ cup condensed milk
⅓ cup lemon juice
1 teaspoon vanilla

TOPPING
2 cans Comstock Blueberry
   Pie Filling
2 cups fresh blueberries

4 tablespoons cornstarch
¼ cup water
½ cup sugar
¼ teaspoon cinnamon

GARNISH
Whipped cream
Fresh blueberries
Coconut flakes, optional

For the Crust: Mix all above ingredients, press into pie pan and bake on 350°F for 7 minutes. Cool before filling.

For the Filling: Whip cream cheese until fluffy, add condensed milk and continue whipping until smooth. Stir in lemon and vanilla. Spoon into prepared crust and chill for a few hours.

For the Topping: In a saucepan mix ¼ cup cold water, 4 tablespoons cornstarch, and ½ cup sugar and cook on low until mixture begins to thicken. Remove from heat. Slowly add Comstock Blueberry Pie Filling, stirring well but gently. Add fresh blueberries and spoon on top of the prepared crust with cream cheese filling.

For the Garnish: Pipe whipped cream and decorate with blueberries. Add coconut flakes, if desired.

Blueberry Parfait

PEACH MELBA CREAM PIE

Patricia Lapiezo, La Mesa, CA
2013 American Pie Council Crisco National Pie Championships
Amateur Division 1st Place Comstock Peach

CRUST
3 cups all-purpose flour
5 tablespoons ice water
1 teaspoon salt
1 tablespoon vinegar
1¼ cups Crisco butter-flavored
    shortening
1 egg, lightly beaten

FILLING BASE
1 can sweetened condensed milk
⅓ cup lemon juice
1 (8-ounce) package cream cheese
6 ounces white chocolate chips,
    melted

FILLING ONE
1½ cups frozen raspberries, thawed,
    not drained
¼ cup granulated sugar

1 tablespoon cornstarch
1½ cups heavy cream, beaten stiffly
    with 2 tablespoons powdered
    sugar

FILLING TWO
1 can Comstock Peach Pie filling
1 teaspoon peach flavoring

GARNISH
Fresh or canned peach slices
Fresh raspberries
1 cup heavy cream, stiffly beaten
2 tablespoons powdered sugar,
    divided
1 teaspoon vanilla

For the Crust: Combine flour and salt in large bowl. Cut in shortening. In a small bowl, combine water, vinegar, and egg. Stir into flour mixture until dough comes together. Shape dough into two disks and refrigerate at least 1 hour. Roll out 1 disk to fit a 9-inch pie dish. Crimp edges and prick bottom and sides with fork. Bake blind in a preheated 400°F degree oven for 15 minutes. Remove pie weights and bake an additional 10 minutes or until crust is golden brown. Cool completely.

For Filling Base: In a large bowl, beat the cream cheese and sweetened condensed milk until creamy. Blend in melted white chocolate. Beat in lemon juice until well blended. Divide mixture in half. Set aside.

For Filling One: Puree raspberries in blender. Strain to remove seeds. Place puree and sugar in small saucepan. Whisk in the cornstarch. Cook over medium heat until mixture thickens and just comes to a boil. Remove from heat and cool completely. Fold puree into ½ of the cream cheese mixture. Divide whipped cream in half. Fold ½ of the whipped cream into the raspberry mixture. Spread over bottom of prepared crust.

For Filling Two: Remove ⅔ cup of the gel filling from 1 can of the Comstock Peach Pie Filling and set aside. Chop the peaches from the pie filling into smaller pieces (about ½-inch pieces). To ½ of the mixture, add chopped peach pie filling, 1 teaspoon peach flavoring, and ½ of the whipped cream. Spread over raspberry filling, smoothing top. Spread reserved peach gel over center of pie to within 1-inch of sides.

For the Garnish: Whip heavy cream with sugar and vanilla. Place a pinwheel of peach slices onto center of pie with a raspberry or raspberry cluster in the middle. Pipe the vanilla whipped cream around edge of pie. Refrigerate 2 hours, or until firm.

Peach Melba Pie

NUTTY STRAWBERRY RHUBARB PIE

Laurie Wilson, Bern, KS
2013 American Pie Council Crisco National Pie Championships
Amateur Division 1ˢᵗ Place Comstock Wilderness Strawberry

CRUST
2 cups all-purpose flour
1 teaspoon salt
½ cup Crisco shortening plus ¼ cup
   cold butter
4 to 5 tablespoons cold water

FILLING
1 (21-ounce) can Comstock/Wilderness
   Strawberry pie filling
2 cups rhubarb, cut in ½ pieces

3 tablespoons Minute Tapioca
½ cup sugar
⅓ cup chopped pecans

For the Crust: Preheat oven to 400°F. Measure the salt and flour into a bowl. Cut in shortening and butter until pea-size pieces form. Add cold water 1 tablespoon at a time until dough ball forms. Divide the dough in half. Store one half covered with a damp cloth in the refrigerator. Roll the other half of the dough on floured surface to fit 9-inch pie plate. Trim and dampen edge with water.

For the Filling: Place nuts in empty shell and press lightly into pastry. Mix rhubarb, tapioca, and sugar thoroughly and place in shell. Then place strawberry pie filling into pastry shell. Dot with about a tablespoon of butter. Remove stored dough and roll out top crust. Place on filled pastry. Trim and flute edges with fingers. Add a sprinkle of sugar and add vent holes to top.

Protect edges if wanted and place pie in preheated oven. Bake 45 minutes, remove edge protection, and bake about 15 more minutes or until evenly browned and beginning to bubble out.

Nutty Strawberry Rhubarb Pie

NUT

CARAMEL CHOCOLATE PECAN PIE

Lisa Sparks, Atlanta, IN
2010 American Pie Council Crisco National Pie Championships
Professional Division 1st Place Nut

CRUST
1 cup butter-flavored Crisco
2 cups flour
3 tablespoons sugar
½ cup cold water

FILLING
½ cup sugar
2 tablespoons flour
1⅓ cups light corn syrup

1 teaspoon vanilla
3 tablespoons butter
3 eggs
1 cup pecan pieces
2 squares semisweet chocolate
Caramel syrup

GARNISH
Pecan halves

For the Crust: Combine Crisco, flour, and sugar until crumbly. Add cold water and mix lightly. Don't over mix. Cover and refrigerate. Roll out and turn into a 9-inch pie dish. Use extra dough to make decorative shapes for top of pie.

For the Filling: Preheat oven to 350°F. Combine dry ingredients and mix well. Add corn syrup and mix. Add vanilla and butter and mix. Add eggs and mix. Add pecans and mix. Melt semi-sweet chocolate. Cover bottom of pie shell with melted chocolate followed by a layer of caramel syrup. Pour pecan mixture into shell and bake for 15 minutes. Cover and bake for an additional 45 minutes or until center is almost set.

Garnish as desired with pecan halves.

Caramel Chocolate Pecan

CAPPUCCINO MACADAMIA CRUNCH PIE

Nikki Norman, Milton, TN
2004 American Pie Council Crisco National Pie Championships
Amateur Division 3rd Place Nut

CRUST
1 cup flour plus 2 tablespoons
¼ teaspoon sea salt
½ teaspoon ground nutmeg
4 tablespoons unsalted butter, cubed
3 tablespoons Crisco shortening
½ cup sour cream

FILLING
1 stick unsalted butter, softened
½ cup brown sugar
1 cup granulated sugar

3 eggs, slightly beaten
¼ teaspoon salt
¼ cup heavy whipping cream
½ cup very strong black coffee
1½ cups macadamia nut pieces
2 tablespoons vanilla extract

For the Crust: Preheat oven to 400°F. In a medium bowl, combine flour, salt, nutmeg, butter, and shortening; cutting until pieces are small—about the size of small peas—with 2 knives or pastry blender. Freeze 15 minutes. Remove from freezer and stir in sour cream. Shape dough into a ball. Cover with plastic wrap and refrigerate 30 minutes. Roll out dough on a lightly floured surface. Place in a 9-inch pie plate. Bake for 15 minutes. Lightly cover edges with aluminum foil if browning too quickly and bake an additional 5 minutes.

For the Filling: Preheat oven to 350°F. In a mixing bowl, cream butter, brown sugar, and granulated sugar. Add eggs, beating well. Add salt, cream, vanilla, and coffee and mix well. Stir in 1 cup macadamia pieces (reserving ½ cup for next step). Pour into prebaked pie shell. Protect edges with aluminum foil to keep from overbrowning. Bake for 55 minutes to an hour. Remove from oven and cover with reserved ½ cup macadamia pieces. Return to oven and bake 5 minutes. Remove from oven and cool.

CHOCOLATE CHIP PECAN PIE

Sarah Spaugh, Winston Salem, NC
2005 American Pie Council Crisco National Pie Championships
Amateur Division 1st Place Nut

CRUST
2 cups all-purpose flour
1 teaspoon salt
¾ cup Crisco shortening
5 tablespoons cold water

FILLING
4 eggs
½ cup light brown sugar
½ cup granulated sugar
1 cup light corn syrup

3 tablespoons butter, melted
2 teaspoon vanilla, divided
¼ teaspoon salt
1¼ cups chopped pecans
½ cup semisweet chocolate chips

TOPPING
1½ cups pecan halves
1 cup Heath Toffee bits
8 tablespoons water

For the Crust: Spoon flour into measuring cup and level. Combine flour and salt in a medium bowl. Cut in Crisco until all flour is blended to form pea-size chunks. Sprinkle with water, 1 tablespoon at a time. Toss lightly with fork until dough will form a ball. Roll dough into a circle. Trim 1 inch larger than upside down pie plate. Place crust into 9-inch pie plate.

For the Filling: Preheat oven to 350°F. Beat eggs in large bowl at low speed until blended. Stir in sugars, corn syrup, butter, 1 teaspoon vanilla, and salt with spoon until blended.

Stir in nuts, chocolate chips, and remaining vanilla. Pour into unbaked pie crust.

For the Topping: Toast pecans for 6 to 8 minutes in 350°F oven. Melt toffee bits in water and barely bring to boil. Stir until mixture becomes a glaze. Remove from heat and dip pecans.

Bake pie for 35 minutes. Remove from oven and add topping. Return to oven and bake 10 to 20 minutes more or until topping is bubbly. Cool to room temperature before serving.

Chocolate Chip Pecan Pie

CARAMEL NUT PIE

Christine Montalvo, Windsor Heights, IA
2007 American Pie Council Crisco National Pie Championships
Amateur Division 2nd Place Nut

CRUST

1½ cups all-purpose flour
2 tablespoons sugar
½ teaspoon ground cinnamon
¼ teaspoon ground nutmeg
¼ teaspoon salt
1 stick chilled unsalted butter, cut
   into ½ inch pieces
1 teaspoon vanilla extract
3 tablespoons ice water

FILLING

1¼ cups sugar
¼ cup water

⅔ cup whipping cream
¼ stick unsalted butter, cut into
   small pieces
1 tablespoon honey
1 teaspoon vanilla extract
1 cup walnuts, coarsely chopped
½ cup pecans, coarsely chopped
½ cup slivered blanched almonds

GARNISH

1 ounce white chocolate, chopped
Whipped cream (optional)

For the Crust: Preheat oven to 375°F. Mix flour, sugar, cinnamon, nutmeg, and salt in processor. Add butter. Using on/off turns, process until mixture resembles coarse meal. Mix in vanilla and enough ice water, one tablespoon at a time, to form moist clumps. Gather dough into a ball; flatten into a disk. Wrap in plastic and refrigerate until firm, about 2 hours.

Roll dough out flat on floured surface and place dough into a 9-inch pie plate. Trim and flute pie edges. Pierce dough all over with fork. Freeze 15 minutes.

Bake crust about 20 minutes until set but still pale in color, piercing with fork if crust bubbles. Transfer to rack; cool.

For the Filling: Preheat oven to 400°F. Combine sugar and water in heavy medium saucepan. Stir over medium-low heat until sugar dissolves. Increase heat. Boil without stirring until caramel is a deep amber color, occasionally brushing down sides of pan with wet pastry brush and swirling pan, about 9 minutes. Reduce heat to medium. Gradually whisk in cream (mixture will bubble). Stir until caramel is smooth. Add butter, honey, and vanilla. Stir until well blended. Mix in all nuts.

Pour caramel mixture into crust. Bake at 400°F for about 20 minutes, or until filling bubbles all over. Cool completely on rack.

For the Garnish: Stir white chocolate in top of double boiler set over hot water just until melted and smooth. Drizzle chocolate over pie. Let stand until chocolate is set, about 30 minutes. Garnish with whipped cream if desired.

PECAN PIE

Grace Thatcher, Delta, OH
2010 American Pie Council Crisco National Pie Championships
Amateur Division 3rd Place Nut

CRUST
2 cups flour
½ teaspoon salt
10 tablespoons shortening
3 to 4 tablespoons cold water

FILLING
4 extra-large eggs, room temperature
1 cup sugar
½ cup plus 1 tablespoon light brown
   sugar

¼ teaspoon salt
8 tablespoons butter, melted
1⅓ cups chopped pecans

TOPPING
⅓ cup packed brown sugar
3 tablespoons honey
3 tablespoons butter
1⅓ cups pecan halves

For the Crust: Preheat oven to 425°F. In a large mixing bowl, sift together the flour and salt, then add all of the shortening. Cut the shortening into the flour with a pastry blender until the mixture develops a coarse texture. Sprinkle the water over the mixture a spoonful at a time and toss until the dough begins to come together. Gather the dough into a ball and press together with your hands. Cover with plastic wrap and refrigerate for at least one hour before using. Prepare pie crust in a 9-inch pie pan and prebake for 10 to 15 minutes.

For the Filling: Preheat oven to 425°F. Beat eggs with a fork until well blended. Stir in sugar and brown sugar. Make sure there are no lumps. Stir in salt, butter, and pecan pieces. Pour mixture into prebaked pie shell, cover with foil, and bake for 10 minutes. Reduce temperature to 350°F, remove foil, and bake for 30 more minutes.

For the Topping: Combine brown sugar, butter, and honey in a saucepan. Cook 2 minutes or until sugar dissolves. Add pecan halves and stir until well coated. After pie has finished baking for 30 minutes, remove foil, spoon topping over pie, and continue baking 15 more minutes or until a knife inserted into the center of the pie comes out clean.

EXTREME PECAN PIE

Emily Lewis, Eustis, FL
2005 American Pie Council Crisco National Pie Championships
Amateur Division 2nd Place Nut

CRUST
1 cup Crisco shortening, cut up
6 tablespoons butter
6 tablespoons ice water
1½ teaspoon salt
3 cups all-purpose flour

FILLING
½ cup white sugar
¼ cup dark brown sugar (packed)
1 cup light corn syrup

2 eggs
3 tablespoons browned butter
2 teaspoons vanilla extract
½ teaspoon salt
2 cups toasted pecans, chopped
30 whole pecans for top of pie

GLAZE
1 tablespoon sugar
1 tablespoon water

For the Crust: Put flour and salt into work bowl of processor. Pulse. Add Crisco and pulse 6 times. Add butter and pulse 6 times. Add water 1 tablespoon at a time, pulsing after each addition. Pour out of bowl onto plastic wrap. Divide into 2 parts. Create two disks and flatten. Refrigerate. At this point, save one disk for another use. It can be stored in a freezer bag in the freezer for weeks. After about 30 minutes in the refrigerator, remove your disk. Place a piece of plastic wrap or parchment paper on the counter. Flour it. Cover your disk with another piece of wrap or parchment. Roll out from center, until disk is about 11 inches in diameter. Remove top wrap, flour the surface lightly, and drape crust over rolling pin. Center over pie plate and press crust into pie plate. Smooth into pan. Remove wrap. Trim crust edge to about ½ inch around outside of pan. Fold edge under and flute using thumb and forefingers to make a stand up edge. Refrigerate until ready to prebake. Preheat oven to 350°F. Layer 2 pieces of aluminum foil into chilled crust. Bake for 15 minutes. Remove foil and continue to bake another 5 minutes. Add filling as below and continue with baking.

For the Filling: Remove partially prebaked crust from oven. Toast pecans on a cookie sheet for 5 to 7 minutes, then place in a bowl. Set aside. In a large bowl, lightly beat eggs. Stir

Extreme Pecan Pie

in sugars, corn syrup, vanilla, and salt. Brown butter in a pan and pour over toasted chopped pecans. Stir together. Put chopped nuts into pie crust. Pour filling over nuts, being careful not to disturb the nuts too much. Take groups of 5 pecan halves and arrange in 6 five-pointed stars on top of pie. When pie is cut, each piece will have a complete star.

For the Glaze: Dissolve the sugar in the water. Brush over top of pecan halves. To keep crust edge from darkening too much, cover with foil. Bake 50 to 60 minutes at 350°F, watching for signs of bubbling. When center begins to bubble or when a knife inserted into the center of the pie comes out clean, remove pie from oven. Cool.

MACADAMIA MADNESS PIE

Evette Rahman, Orlando, FL
2008 American Pie Council Crisco National Pie Championships
Amateur Division 2nd Place Nut

CRUST
1 cup flour
1 tablespoon sugar
½ teaspoon salt
¼ teaspoon baking powder
3 tablespoons vegetable shortening
3 tablespoons unsalted butter
3 tablespoons heavy cream
½ tablespoon vinegar
½ tablespoon oil
1 egg plus 1 teaspoon water for egg wash

FILLING
⅓ cup unsalted butter, softened
½ cup dark brown sugar
¼ cup granulated white sugar
3 large eggs, slightly beaten
2 teaspoons pure vanilla extract
½ teaspoon salt
1 cup light corn syrup
1½ cups chopped macadamia nuts

GARNISH
1½ tablespoons melted white chocolate
1½ tablespoons melted semisweet chocolate

For the Crust: Mix flour, sugar, salt, and baking powder together. Cut in shortening and butter. Stir together oil, vinegar, and cream. Add to flour mixture. Wrap dough in plastic. Refrigerate one hour. Roll out dough on lightly floured surface and place in deep dish pie plate. Crimp edges as desired. Brush on egg wash.

For the Filling: Preheat oven to 400°F. Cream butter and sugars. Beat in eggs slowly, mixing until well combined. Beat in vanilla and salt. Mix in syrup and nuts. Pour into prepared pie shell. Bake for 20 minutes at 400°F, then reduce oven to 350°F. Bake for 30 minutes or until pie is almost completely set. Cool completely.

Garnish by drizzling melted chocolates on top of pie.

Macadamia Madness Pie

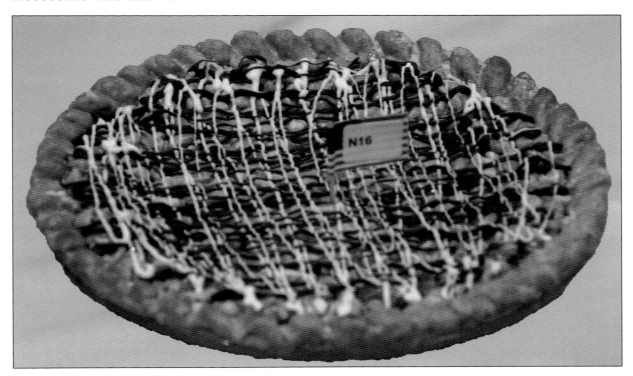

PECAN TOFFEE SUPREME

Alberta Dunbar, San Diego, CA
2010 American Pie Council Crisco National Pie Championships
Amateur Division 1st Place Nut

CRUST
1⅓ cups all-purpose flour
½ teaspoon salt
½ stick Crisco all vegetable shortening
3 tablespoons cold water

FILLING
12 ounces cream cheese, softened to
    room temperature
¼ cup heavy whipping cream
1½ teaspoon pecan extract
12-ounce package white chocolate
    chips, melted and cooled
¾ cup ground toasted pecans

¾ cup toffee baking bits
¾ cup heavy whipping cream,
    whipped

TOPPING
1½ cups heavy whipping cream
⅓ cup sifted powdered sugar
1 teaspoon pecan extract
Large rosette tip
Pastry bag
¼ cup ground toasted pecans
¼ cup toffee baking bits
Toasted pecan tips dipped in chocolate
    (optional)

For the Crust: Preheat oven to 450°F. Spoon flour into measuring cup and level. Mix flour and salt in medium bowl. Cut in shortening using pastry blender or 2 knives until flour is blended and forms pea-size chunks. Sprinkle mixture with 1 tablespoon of water at a time. Toss lightly with a fork until dough forms a ball. Shape into a flat round disk. Roll on lightly floured board to fit into deep-dish 9-inch pie plate. Turn into pie plate and crimp edges of pie. Pierce bottom and sides of pie crust with a fork. Bake for about 8 to 10 minutes until golden brown. Cool on rack and set aside. Make filling while crust is cooling.

For the Filling: In a large bowl, combine cream cheese and ¼ cup heavy whipping cream with an electric mixer on high until smooth. Beat in white chocolate and pecan extract. With a wooden spoon, fold in pecans and toffee bits. Gently fold in ¾ cup whipped cream. Turn into pie crust and smooth top of pie. Chill pie until set, about 45 minutes to an hour.

For the Topping: In a medium mixing bowl, combine the cream, sugar, and pecan extract and beat with an electric mixer until stiff. Reserve one third of mixture for piping border around edge of pie. Spread remaining mixture over top of pie. Pipe a border around pie with large rosettes on outer edge. Combine nuts and toffee bits in a small bowl. Sprinkle them evenly over center of pie. Chill until ready to serve.

Optional: Dip whole pecan halves in melted chocolate. Place on waxed paper and chill in the refrigerator to set up. When set, place pecans on rosettes.

PERFECT PECAN PIE

Deborah Gray, Winter Haven, FL
2007 American Pie Council Crisco National Pie Championships
Amateur Division 3rd Place Nut

CRUST
1¼ cups all-purpose unbleached
 flour
½ teaspoon salt
¼ teaspoon sugar
½ cup frozen Crisco, cut up
4 tablespoons ice water

FILLING
2 cups Karo light corn syrup
½ cup sugar

¼ cup butter
3 extra-large eggs
1 teaspoon vanilla
Pinch of salt
1½ cups pecans

For the Crust: In medium mixing bowl, combine flour, salt, and sugar. Cut in Crisco. Add water until dough forms a soft ball. Roll out on floured surface. Spray 9-inch pan with non-stick spray. Flute edges as desired.

For the Filling: Preheat oven to 350°F. In a 2 quart saucepan, combine corn syrup, sugar, and butter. Bring mixture to a boil. Reduce heat to medium and boil gently for 8 minutes, stirring occasionally. Cool slightly.

Whisk together eggs, vanilla, and salt in medium bowl. Slowly pour syrup mixture into eggs, whisking constantly. Place pecans in pie crust. Pour mixture over pecans. Bake at 350°F for 45 minutes.

Perfect Pecan Pie

VERMONT MAPLE PECAN PIE

Christine Montalvo, Windsor Heights, IA
2009 American Pie Council Crisco National Pie Championships
Amateur Division 3rd Place Nut

CRUST

2 cups all-purpose flour

1 cup cake flour

½ teaspoon salt

1 cup butter-flavored Crisco, cut into small pieces

⅓ cup ice water

1 egg, slightly beaten

1 tablespoon cider vinegar

FILLING

¾ cup dark corn syrup

¼ cup maple syrup

1 teaspoon maple extract

½ cup sugar

3 extra-large eggs

1 teaspoon vanilla

2 tablespoons unsalted butter, melted

2 cups pecan halves

½ teaspoon salt

For the Crust: Place flours and salt into food processor. Pulse to blend. Add Crisco pieces and pulse until mixture resembles coarse meal. Place flour mixture into a medium-sized bowl. Set aside. In another small bowl, mix water, egg, and vinegar until blended. Using a fork, gently toss flour while sprinkling with water/vinegar mixture. Add enough water until dough just comes together. Divide into 2 disks. Wrap each in plastic wrap and chill at least one hour or overnight. Roll out 1 disk into a 12-inch circle and place into a 9-inch pie plate. Flute edges.

For the Filling: Preheat oven to 350°F. Whisk together corn syrup, maple syrup, extract, sugar, eggs, and vanilla. Stir in the melted butter. Add pecans and salt. Pour into pie shell. Bake for 45 minutes. Cool completely.

Vermont Maple Pecan Pie

FRUITS OF THE FOREST PIE

Emily Lewis, Eustis, FL
2003 American Pie Council Crisco National Pie Championships
Amateur Division 1st Place Nut

CRUST
⅓ cup Crisco shortening
2 tablespoons butter
2 tablespoons ice water
1 cup all-purpose flour

FILLING
4 eggs, lightly beaten
¼ cup packed brown sugar
½ cup white sugar
1 teaspoon vanilla

1 cup light corn syrup
½ teaspoon salt
4 tablespoons butter, melted
2 cups lightly toasted nuts
(recommended: ½ cup pecan halves, ⅓ cup coarsely chopped macadamias, ⅓ cup slivered almonds, ½ cup cashew halves, split, ⅓ cup chopped hazelnuts)

For the Crust: In a narrow bowl, combine flour and salt. Using two knives scissor style, cut butter and shortening into flour until only small pea-size bites of shortening remain. Sprinkle water over flour mixture as you toss with a fork. Don't over mix. Turn only about 8 to 10 times. Pour out of bowl onto plastic wrap. Create a 5-inch disk and flatten. Refrigerate. After about 15 minutes in the refrigerator, remove disk. Place a piece of plastic wrap or parchment paper on the counter. Flour it. Cover your disk with another piece of wrap or parchment. Roll out from the center until disk is about 11 inches in diameter. Remove top wrap and flour the surface slightly. Drape crust over rolling pin. Center crust over pie pan, place hand under wrap and flip the crust into pan. Remove wrap. Trim edge to about ½ inch around outside of pan. Fold edge under and flute using thumb and forefingers to make a stand-up edge. Refrigerate until ready to fill.

For the Filling: Preheat oven to 350°F. Coarsely chop macadamias and almonds. Put all nuts (separate large nuts from chopped) on cookie sheet and toast 5 to 6 minutes. Cool. Put hazelnuts into a kitchen towel and rub together to remove skins. Chop hazelnuts. Combine filling ingredients. Mix well. Sprinkle chopped nuts on bottom of crust. Arrange pecan halves, slivered almonds, and cashews in attractive pattern on bottom of unfilled crust. Pour filling into crust, deflecting on back of spoon so as not to disturb nuts. Larger nuts will rise up to top. Cover edge of crust with foil. Bake for 45 to 50 minutes. Test with a stainless steel knife in center. When knife comes out clean, pie is done. Cool completely on wire rack. Serve after cooling or wrap in heavy foil and refrigerate until next day to serve.

AWARD WINNER'S CHOCOLATE PECAN PIE

Emily Lewis, Mt. Dora, FL
2002 American Pie Council National Pie Championships
Amateur Division 1st Place Nut

CRUST
⅔ cup Crisco shortening
4 tablespoons butter
4 tablespoons ice water
1 teaspoon salt
2 cups all-purpose flour

FILLING
4 eggs
1 cup sugar

1 cup light corn syrup
1 ounces unsweetened chocolate, melted
3 tablespoons butter, melted
2 teaspoons vanilla extract
¼ teaspoon salt
2 cups pecans, toasted, chop 1 cup
½ cup chocolate chips

For the Crust: In a tall, narrow bowl, combine flour and salt. Using two knives scissors-style, cut butter and shortening into flour until only small pea-size bits of shortening remain. Sprinkle water over flour mixture as you toss with a fork. Don't over mix. Turn only about 8 to 10 times. Add more water if dry crumbs remain. Pour out of bowl onto plastic wrap. Divide into two parts. Create two 5-inch disks and wrap in plastic. Refrigerate. At this point, freeze one disk for another use in a freezer bag. It can be stored in the freezer for weeks. After about 15 minutes in the refrigerator, remove the disk you are using. Place a piece of parchment paper or plastic wrap on the counter. Flour it and place dough on surface. Cover your disk with another piece of wrap or parchment. Roll out from the center until disk is about 11 inches in diameter. Remove top wrap, flour the surface lightly, and drape crust over rolling pin. Center crust over pie pan, place hand under wrap, and flip the crust into pan. Remove wrap. Trim edge to about ½-inch around outside of pan. Fold edge under and flute using thumb and forefingers to make a stand-up edge. Refrigerate until ready to fill.

For the Filling: Preheat oven to 350°F. Toast pecans on cookie sheet about 5 minutes. In a large bowl, lightly beat eggs. Stir in sugar, corn syrup, melted chocolate, butter, vanilla, and salt. Into prepared crust, layer chocolate chips and 1 cup chopped pecans. Then carefully arrange second cup of pecans on top of chopped pecans. Slowly pour egg mixture over pecans, deflecting with a spoon to prevent moving pecans. If using an 8¾-inch disposable pan, place on sturdy cookie sheet to assure even baking and easier handling. Bake for 15 minutes at 350°F. Remove from oven and cover edge with foil. Return to oven. Bake for another 40 minutes until knife inserted in center comes out clean.

CARAMELIZED PECAN CHESS PIE

Sarah Spaugh, Winston Salem, NC
2002 American Pie Council National Pie Championships
Amateur Division 2nd Place Nut

CRUST
2 cups all-purpose flour
½ teaspoon salt
½ cup butter flavored shortening
¼ cup plain shortening
6 to 7 tablespoons cold milk

CARAMELIZED TOASTED PECANS
1½ cups pecan halves
⅓ cup firmly packed brown sugar
3 tablespoons butter
2 tablespoons pure maple syrup

FILLING
2 cups white sugar
2 tablespoons white cornmeal
1 tablespoon all-purpose flour
¼ teaspoon salt
½ cup butter, melted
¼ cup whole milk
1 tablespoon white vinegar
½ teaspoon vanilla extract
4 large eggs, lightly beaten
Caramelized toasted pecans
   (recipe above)

For the Crust: Combine flour and salt in a bowl. Cut in shortening with pastry blender to form pea-size chunks. Sprinkle with ice cold milk, 1 tablespoon at a time. Toss lightly with fork until dough forms a ball. Roll out on waxed paper. Place in pie plate and flute edges.

For the Caramelized Toasted Pecans: Preheat oven to 350°F. Spread pecans on cookie sheet or other baking pan and toast 5 minutes, stirring often. Combine brown sugar, butter, and maple syrup in a medium saucepan over medium heat. Cook about 2 minutes, stirring often or until sugar dissolves. Add toasted nuts and stir until coated. Place on buttered foil for 1 to 2 minutes, or until sugar starts to bubble. Cool. Chop fine. (Remember to include half of nuts for chess pie filling and half for topping.)

For the Filling: Preheat oven to 350°F. Stir together sugar, cornmeal, flour, salt, butter, milk, vinegar, and vanilla. With an electric mixer, whip mixture on high speed until light-colored and creamy, scraping down sides occasionally, about 4 minutes. Add eggs and stir just until combined well. Add half of caramelized toasted pecans (about ½ cup). Pour mixture into pie crust. Bake 50 to 55 minutes, shielding edges of crust with aluminum foil after 10 minutes. (If rest of top starts to get too brown, cover entire top with foil.) Remove from oven and sprinkle with remaining caramelized toasted pecans. Cool completely on a wire rack.

DATE NIGHT CASHEW COCONUT PIE

Beth Campbell, Belleville, WI
2013 American Pie Council Crisco National Pie Championships
Amateur Division 1st Place Nut

CRUST
1½ cups crushed graham crackers
¼ cup sugar
1/3 cup butter, melted

FILLING
14-ounce can of sweetened condensed milk (caramelized)
2/3 cup chopped dates

1 cup coarsely chopped cashews
1 teaspoon maple flavoring
¾ cup whipping cream, whipped
½ cup coconut

For the Crust: In a small bowl, combine the crumbs and sugar; add butter, and blend well. Press into the bottom and up the sides of an ungreased 9-inch pie plate. Bake at 375°F for 7 minutes. Cool completely.

For the Filling: Caramelize the sweetened condensed milk.* Stir in dates, cashews, coconut, and maple flavoring and chill thoroughly. Fold in the whipping cream. Pour into graham cracker crust. Chill at least 3 hours or until set.

Garnish as desired. Refrigerate leftovers.

*Directions for Caramelizing the Condensed Milk: Preheat the oven to 425°F. Pour the condensed milk into an 8- or 9-inch pie plate. Cover with aluminum foil; place in shallow pan. Fill pan with hot water. Bake 1 to 1½ hours or until thick and light caramel color. Remove foil; cool. Chill completely.

An alternative method for caramelizing condensed milk, is to pour condensed milk into a double broiler; cover. Place over boiling water. Over low heat, simmer 1 to 1½ hours or until thick and light caramel color. Beat until smooth. Cool. Chill thoroughly.

Date Night Cashew Coconut Pie

SWEET SOUTHERN PECAN PIE

Savannah Kreinhagen, Palm Bay, FL
2012 American Pie Council Crisco National Pie Championships
Amateur Division 1st Place Nut

CRUST
1¼ cups flour
1 tablespoon sugar
½ teaspoon salt
½ cup unsalted butter, softened
4 tablespoons water

FILLING
½ cup unsalted butter
¼ cup sugar
¾ cup light brown sugar
¾ cup light corn syrup

4 eggs
2 teaspoons vanilla extract
1¼ cups crushed pecans
1 cup whole pecans (for top)
½ cup semisweet chocolate chips
½ cup semisweet white chocolate chips
2 tablespoons molasses

GARNISH
Whipped cream

For the Crust: Mix flour, sugar, and salt together. Cut in softened butter, mixing until texture is crumbly. Add in water, continuing to mix. Roll dough into a ball on a floured surface. Refrigerate for 1 hour. Roll crust out on a floured surface and drape in pie pan loosely.

For the Filling: Mix the butter, sugars, corn syrup, eggs, vanilla extract, and molasses together until frothy. Mix in the crushed pecans and chocolate chips. Pour mixture into prepared pie crust. You may have more filling than you need. Spread one cup of whole pecans over the top of the pie. Bake pie at 350°F for 50 to 60 minutes, or until set. Cool completely at room temperature. Serve with whip cream.

Sweet Southern Pecan Pie

SALTED CARAMEL NUT PIE

Matt Zagorski, Arlington Heights, IL
2012 American Pie Council Crisco National Pie Championships
Professional Division Honorable Mention Nut

CRUST
½ cup unsalted butter, melted
1 cup plus 1 tablespoon all-purpose flour
1 cup Planters peanut butter, finely chopped in a food processor
1 tablespoon superfine sugar

PEANUT BUTTER MOUSSE
1 cup powdered sugar
8 ounces cream cheese
¾ cup peanut butter, preferably Planters
1 cup Cool Whip

OTHER LAYERS
8 ounces Smucker's Hot Caramel Topping, divided
6 ounces Planter's Smooth Peanut Butter, divided
1½ cups crushed Planter's peanuts

GARNISH
2 cups whipping cream
5 tablespoons sugar

For the Crust: Preheat the oven to 375°F. In the bowl of a food processor, combine all of the ingredients until they look like a paste, approximately 1 minute. Press the dough evenly into the bottom of a deep dish pie pan with your hands. Bake for 18 to 20 minutes until the crust is no longer wet and the edges and center are lightly browned. Remove from oven and set aside to cool completely.

For the Peanut Butter Mousse: Place the first 3 ingredients in a stand mixer and combine. Fold in the Cool Whip. Set aside until crust is cooled. In the cooled peanut crust, place ½ of the Peanut Butter mousse.

For the Other Layers: On top of the mousse, pour 4 ounces of caramel. Place the pie into the refrigerator for a few minutes so that the caramel has a chance to harden. Once the caramel has hardened, pour 3 ounces of peanut butter over the caramel and top with half of the crushed peanuts. Place the pie back into the refrigerator to harden. Once the pie has firmed up, repeat all of the layers.

For the Garnish: In a stand mixer, whip the whipping cream and sugar to stiff peaks. Garnish the top of pie with the whipped cream.

Salted Caramel Nut Pie

PIE QUEEN'S HEATH TOFFEE PECAN PIE

Jaynie Buckingham, Austin, TX
American Pie Council Crisco National Pie Championships
Professional Division 1st Place Nut

CRUST
1¼ cup flour
½ teaspoon sugar
½ cup ice cold butter-flavored Crisco
  shortening
¼ cup ice cold water

FILLING
3 eggs
½ cup brown sugar

1 stick butter
3 tablespoons Karo syrup (light)
½ bag Health Toffee bits
1½ cup pecans

For the Crust: Preheat oven to 350°F. Mix flour and sugar together. Cut up shortening and mix with flour until it forms. Place ice water in freezer just until it begins to freeze and chips, then mix into flour and form a ball. Cover and flatten into a disk. Let chill an hour before rolling out. Makes one 9-inch pie.

For the Filling: Mix all ingredients together except for the butter. Melt butter and add to mixture. Pour into 9-inch pie pan and bake at 350°F for 30 minutes or until set and golden.

Pie Queen's Heath Toffee Pecan Pie

OPEN

BLACK FOREST CREAM PIE

Beth Campbell, Belleville, WI
2004 American Pie Council Crisco National Pie Championships
Amateur Division 2nd Place Open

CRUST
1 cup flour
½ cup shortening
¼ cup cold water
Pinch of salt

LAYER ONE
6-ounce package (1 cup) semisweet
   chocolate pieces
1 teaspoon butter
8-ounce package cream cheese,
   softened
¼ cup powdered sugar, sifted
⅓ cup whipping cream, whipped

LAYER TWO
4 ounces cream cheese, softened
¼ cup sugar
½ teaspoon vanilla extract
⅓ cup whipping cream, whipped

LAYER THREE
½ cup sugar
⅛ cup flour
2 cups fresh tart cherries (pitted)
½ teaspoon butter, softened
2 drops almond extract
Whipped cream for garnish (optional)

For the Crust: Preheat oven to 475°F. Combine flour and salt, then cut in shortening until mixture is pea-sized. Pour in water until mixture forms a ball. Wrap in plastic and refrigerate for several hours or overnight. Roll out on floured board and put into pie pan. Prick crust on bottom of pan with a fork. Bake for 8 to 10 minutes until light brown. Cool.

For Layer One: Melt the chocolate chips and butter in a saucepan over medium-low heat. Add cream cheese, heating and stirring until combined. Remove from heat. Stir in the powdered sugar. Cool mixture and fold in the whipped cream. Spread in the baked pastry shell.

For Layer Two: Combine ingredients and spread over the chocolate layer.

For Layer Three: Combine ingredients and spread over the second layer.

Garnish with whipped cream if desired.

CHOCOLATE MINT PARFAIT PIE

Patricia Lapiezo, La Mesa, CA
2011 American Pie Council Crisco National Pie Championships
Amateur Division 3rd Place Open

CRUST

10 Pepperidge Farm Milano mint cookies, finely ground
6 Oreo cookies, finely ground
2 tablespoons butter, melted

MINT FILLING

8-ounce package cream cheese, softened
¼ cup powdered sugar
4 ounces white chocolate
¼ cup heavy cream
1 cup heavy cream, stiffly beaten
1 drop green food coloring
½ cup Andes mint baking pieces

MINT GANACHE

4 ounces mint flavored chocolate, chopped
½ cup heavy whipping cream

CHOCOLATE FILLING

8-ounce package cream cheese, softened
½ cup powdered sugar
¼ cup heavy whipping cream
6 ounces semisweet chocolate, finely chopped
1 teaspoon vanilla
1 cup heavy whipping cream, stiffly beaten

GARNISH

Sweetened whipped cream
Additional mint pieces

For the Crust: Preheat oven to 350°F. Combine cookie crumbs and butter. Press onto bottom and up sides of a 9-inch pie dish. Bake for 8 minutes. Remove from oven and cool.

For the Mint Filling: Beat the cream cheese and powdered sugar together until light and fluffy. Heat the ¼ cup heavy cream in a saucepan and stir in white chocolate until melted. Blend into cream cheese mixture along with the food coloring. Fold in whipped cream. Add the Andes mint baking pieces. Spread into prepared crust, smoothing top.

For the Mint Ganache: In a saucepan, heat the whipping cream and chopped mint chocolate until melted. Chill while preparing chocolate filling. Set aside until needed. If necessary, heat slightly until of spreading consistency. Spread ½ of the mint ganache on top of mint filling.

For the Chocolate Filling: In a large mixing bowl, beat the cream cheese and powdered sugar until light and fluffy. Heat the ¼ cup whipping cream and stir in the semisweet chocolate until melted. Blend into cream cheese mixture along with vanilla. Fold in whipped cream. Spread over mint ganache layer, smoothing top. Spread remaining mint ganache over chocolate filling and chill until firm.

Decorate edge of pie with sweetened whipped cream and additional mint pieces.

Chocolate Mint Parfait Pie

CHOCOLATE DECADENCE PIE

Bobbie Allen, Canyon, TX
2004 American Pie Council Crisco National Pie Championships
Amateur Division 3rd Place Open

CRUST
1 cup flour, sifted
½ teaspoon salt
¼ cup salted peanuts, crushed
½ teaspoon baking powder
⅓ cup vegetable shortening
3 to 4 tablespoons cold water

FILLING
24 unwrapped caramels
¼ cup canned evaporated milk

1½ cups milk chocolate chips
1 cup heavy cream
3 tablespoons butter
½ cup chopped pecans

GARNISH
1 cup whipped cream

For the Crust: Preheat oven to 425°F. Sift flour, baking powder, and salt into mixing bowl. Cut in shortening with knives or blend with pastry blender until mixture resembles coarse cornmeal. Add peanuts. Sprinkle cold water over mixture, a little at a time, stirring with fork until dough is just moist enough to hold together and form a ball. Roll out on lightly floured surface to a circle 1½ inch larger than an 8-inch or 9-inch pie pan inverted over it. Fit loosely into pan and flute edges. Prick pastry surface all over with a 4-tined fork. Bake for 12 to 15 minutes. Cool.

For the Filling: Sprinkle pecans on cooled crust. Heat caramels and evaporated milk in a saucepan over medium-low heat, stirring often, until caramels melt and mixture is smooth. Pour caramel mixture over pecans. In another saucepan, heat chocolate chips, cream, and butter over low heat until chocolate melts and mixture is smooth. Pour over caramel layer and refrigerate for 4 hours, until set.

For the Garnish: Beat 1 cup whipping cream. Before serving pie, pipe whipped cream decoratively on top of pie.

GRANDMA AND MOMMY'S PUMPKIN CARAMEL APPLE PIE

Linda Hundt, DeWitt, MI
2011 American Pie Council Crisco National Pie Championships
Professional Division 1st Place Open

CRUST
1½ cups flour
¼ teaspoon baking powder
½ teaspoon salt
1 teaspoon sugar
¼ cup cold butter, cut in small pieces
½ cup refrigerated Crisco shortening

PUMPKIN FILLING
1¼ cups canned pumpkin
1 cup half-and-half
½ cup sugar
2 eggs, slightly beaten
1 tablespoon flour
2 teaspoons pumpkin pie spice
¼ teaspoon cloves
½ teaspoon orange zest
¼ teaspoon of salt
1 teaspoon cinnamon

HOMEMADE CARAMEL SAUCE
14-ounce can sweetened
    condensed milk
1 cup light corn syrup

1 cup sugar
½ cup brown sugar
½ stick butter
1 tablespoon real vanilla extract

APPLE FILLING
1 medium each, Michigan, Cortland,
    and Ida Red apples, peeled, thinly
    sliced, and diced
¼ cup sugar
2 tablespoons flour
1 tablespoon butter, melted
1 teaspoon cinnamon
½ teaspoon lemon juice
⅛ teaspoon salt
½ cup homemade caramel sauce
    (recipe above)

GARNISH
Whipped cream
Dried Apples
Caramel
Nutmeg

For the Crust: Mix all above ingredients in KitchenAid-style mixer on medium speed swiftly until pea-size pieces form. Carefully sprinkle water over crust mixture until it starts to become moistened and gathers together. Pat into a disk, then wrap and refrigerate for at least a half an hour. Roll out on a floured surface. Place into pie pan and crimp crust. Freeze until ready to use.

For the Pumpkin Filling: Combine ingredients in a bowl. Mix well. Set aside.

For the Caramel Sauce: In heavy 3-quart saucepan, combine all ingredients except the vanilla. Cook over medium heat, stirring constantly, covering all parts of bottom of pan with wire whisk to avoid scorching. Stir until mixture comes to a boil. Reduce heat to low, add vanilla, and cook, constantly stirring, until mixture comes to a boil. Reduce heat and continue stirring until caramel reaches 244°F on a candy thermometer or firm-ball stage. Pour in glass container. Cool before combining with apple filling.

For the Apple Filling: Preheat oven to 350°F. Mix all ingredients except apples and caramel sauce until blended. In a pan, cook apples and mixture until apples are almost cooked through. Add ½ cup of caramel sauce until melted. Remove from stove. Fill bottom ⅓ of pie with caramel apple mixture. Cover with pumpkin filling. Bake for 1 hour or until almost set in center of pie. Cool.

Garnish pie with real whipped cream, dried apples, and caramel. Dust with grated nutmeg.

Grandma and Mommy's Pumpkin Caramel Apple Pie

IRON CHEF LIME PIE

John Sunvold, Winter Springs, FL
2009 American Pie Council Crisco National Pie Championships
Amateur Division 1st Place Open

CRUST
1¼ cups graham cracker crumbs
¼ cup sugar
5 tablespoons butter

LIME LAYER
14-ounce can sweetened
   condensed milk
1 egg
½ cup lime juice

CHOCOLATE LAYER
2 tablespoons butter
2 tablespoons corn syrup

1 tablespoon heavy cream
1 tablespoon milk
⅓ cup chocolate chips (semisweet)
1 cup powdered sugar

TOPPING
2½ cups heavy cream
4 ounces white chocolate, broken
   into small pieces
Lime slices for garnish

For the Crust: Preheat oven to 375°F. Mix all ingredients and press mixture into 9-inch pie plate. Bake for 8 to10 minutes or until brown. Allow to cool to room temperature.

For the Lime Layer: Mix ingredients together well and pour into cooled pie shell. Bake for 15 minutes. Remove from oven and chill in refrigerator for 2 hours.

For the Chocolate Layer: Mix butter, corn syrup, cream, and milk together in a saucepan. Heat over medium heat until boiling. Stir constantly. Add chocolate chips and stir until melted. Once fully combined, slowly add powdered sugar. Mix completely, then carefully spread the chocolate onto the lime layer. It cools quickly, so you must spread immediately.

For the Topping: Bring ½ cup of cream to a boil over medium heat. Add white chocolate and stir constantly until chocolate is melted. Remove from heat and let cool to room temperature. Refrigerate for four hours. In large bowl, beat the remaining cream until soft peaks form. Slowly add the white chocolate mixture and continue to beat until stiff. Cover and refrigerate for 2 hours. Garnish with lime slices if desired.

JAPANESE GREEN TEA PIE

John Michael Lerma, St. Paul, MN
2011 American Pie Council Crisco National Pie Championships
Professional Division Honorable Mention Open

CRUST
1¾ cups graham cracker crumbs
2 tablespoons light brown sugar,
   firmly packed
½ teaspoon ground cinnamon or
   Garden County Cooking Apple Pie
   Spice
Pinch of salt
6 tablespoons unsalted butter, melted
Crisco butter-flavored cooking spray

SPREAD
2 cups pecans, soaked for 5 hours
½ cup raisins, soaked for 5 hours,
   reserving some of the soaking
   water

½ teaspoon cinnamon or Garden
   County Cooking Apple Pie Spice

FILLING
1½ cups coconut water
1 cup cashews, soaked for 5 hours
½ cup agave syrup
½ cup coconut oil
1½ teaspoon green tea powder
   (suggest: Matcha green tea)

For the Crust: Preheat oven to 350°F. Spray pie plate with cooking spray and set aside. Combine the graham cracker crumbs, brown sugar, cinnamon, and salt in a large mixing bowl. Using your fingers, mix together. Add the butter and incorporate well, mixing first with a fork, then with your hands, rubbing thoroughly to form evenly dampened crumbs. Spread the crumbs evenly and loosely in the pan, pressing them into the bottom and up the sides. Refrigerate for 10 minutes. Bake for 8 to 10 minutes. Cool on a rack. Refrigerate 15 minutes before filling. Makes one 9-inch graham cracker crust.

For the Spread: Mix all ingredients in the bowl of a food processor. Pour in some of the raisin soaked water until it makes a smooth paste. Gently spread inside cooled pie crust.

For the Filling: Mix all ingredients in a high speed blender or bowl of a food processor. Blend until well mixed. Pour into pie crust and chill overnight.

Japanese Green Tea Pie

MACADAMIA BERRY PIE

Raine Gottess, Coconut Creek, FL
2004 American Pie Council Crisco National Pie Championships
Amateur Division 1st Place Open

CRUST
1¼ package Nestle Toll House
  macadamia nut cookie dough

LAYER ONE
6 ounces raspberry cream cheese
  (strawberry can substitute)
1 cup powdered sugar
¾ teaspoon vanilla
1 tablespoon milk
6 ounces creamy Cool Whip

FILLING
Smucker's Boysenberry jam
  (raspberry can substitute)

LAYER TWO
8 ounces blueberry cream cheese
1¼ cups powdered sugar
1 teaspoon vanilla
1 tablespoon milk
8-ounce container Cool Whip

GARNISH
Blackberries
Raspberries
Strawberry Glaze
Cool Whip

For the Crust: Preheat oven to 325°F. Remove most of the white chips from the dough. Press dough into pie plate to form crust. Edge with foil and bake for 20 minutes. Remove from oven. Remove foil. Preheat oven to 350°F. Using a spatula, press dough against sides and bottom of pie plate and slightly down on the top edges to form thicker side crust. Flatten dough just slightly in the center. Place back in oven with foil edge for 10 to 12 minutes. Press again in the center slightly to flatten. Let cool completely.

For Layer One: In a mixing bowl beat all the ingredients well. Spread over a cooled cookie crust and freeze about 5 minutes.

For the Filling: Spread jam thinly and carefully over layer one, then freeze.

For Layer Two: In a mixing bowl, beat all the ingredients well and spread carefully over jam layer.

Decorate the top by arranging blackberries and raspberries. Drizzle with strawberry glaze and edge with Cool Whip. Refrigerate at least 6 hours to firm.

COFFEE TOFFEE SILK

David Harper, Richland Center, WI
2013 American Pie Council Crisco National Pie Championships
Amateur Division 3rd Place Open

CRUST
½ cup of butter-flavored Crisco
1 cup of flour
1 teaspoon salt
5 tablespoons ice cold water

FILLING ONE
8 ounces semisweet chocolate
¾ cup heavy cream
2 tablespoons light corn syrup
1 teaspoon vanilla

FILLING TWO
1¼ cup heavy cream, chilled
1 tablespoon instant coffee granules
4 eggs

1 cup sugar
3 tablespoons water
2 heaping teaspoons instant coffee
  granules
8 ounces semisweet chocolate,
  melted and cooled
1 tablespoon vanilla
8 tablespoons butter, softened
  to room temperature

TOPPING
1½ cup heavy cream
1 tablespoon coffee granules
¼ cup powdered sugar
Heath Toffee pieces

For the Crust: Preheat oven to 400°F. Place baking stone in oven to preheat. Whisk the flour and the salt together in a large bowl. Add the Crisco and mix with your fingers until combined. Add the ice water and use a fork to combine. Turn pie dough out onto a floured surface and gather into a circular disk. Roll out the dough big enough to fit into a pie plate. Flute edges for decoration. Place into the refrigerator for 20 minutes. After 20 minutes, place a piece of parchment paper in the pie shell and fill with pie weights or pennies. Bake crust until edges are golden brown and bottom is browned, about 15 to 20 minutes. Remove crust from oven and take out the parchment and pie weights. If bottom crust is not browned enough, place back in oven without parchment and pie weights and bake until bottom is browned, about 5 min. Cool on wire rack and set aside.

For Filling One: Place all ingredients in a microwaveable bowl and microwave, whisking often, until melted and smooth, about 1 to 2 minutes. Set aside to cool until thickened, about half an hour. Spread 1 cup over bottom of pie crust.

For Filling Two: Whip the heavy cream plus 1 tablespoon coffee granules together until stiff peaks form. Transfer to a bowl and chill. Place eggs, sugar, water, and 2 heaping teaspoons coffee granules in a large double boiler set over simmering water. Use a hand held mixer on high

Coffee Toffee Silk Pie

speed to beat the egg mixture until thickened, about 10 minutes. After 10 minutes, remove from heat and continue to beat until mixture is cooled, about 5 minutes. Add the cooled chocolate and vanilla to the egg mixture and beat until combined. Add the butter and beat until combined. Fold in the coffee-whipped cream until no white streaks remain. Pour chocolate-coffee filling over the chocolate into pie shell. Place in refrigerator for at least 3 hours or up to 24 hours.

For the Topping: Combine heavy cream and coffee granules together and place in refrigerator until pie is set up, 3 to 24 hours. When pie is set, whip the heavy cream-coffee mixture with the powdered sugar until stiff. Top pie immediately with coffee-whipped cream. Sprinkle ½ cup Heath pieces on top of pie. Serve immediately or chill until ready to eat.

STRAWBERRY BANANA NUT GOODIE PIE

Karen Hall, Elm Creek, NE
2007 American Pie Council Crisco National Pie Championships
Amateur Division 3rd Place Open

CRUST
1½ cups crushed Oreos
2 tablespoons brown sugar
⅓ cup plus 2 tablespoons butter, melted

FILLING
8 ounces cream cheese, softened
2 tablespoons milk
1 cup powdered sugar
4 ounces frozen whipped topping, thawed
2 tablespoons nut topping
1 banana, sliced

1 cup fresh strawberries, cut into ¼- to ½-inch pieces
⅓ cup strawberry jam
2 tablespoons chocolate fudge topping

TOPPING
8 ounces frozen whipped topping, thawed
2 tablespoons nut topping

GARNISH
Plain or chocolate covered strawberries

For the Crust: Preheat oven to 350°F. In a medium mixing bowl, combine chocolate cookie crumbs and brown sugar. Drizzle melted butter into crumb mixture, tossing to moisten crumbs. Mound mixture into a 9-inch pie dish and press into bottom and up sides of the dish. Bake for 6 to 8 minutes. Chill crumb crust until completely cooled.

For the Filling: In a large mixing bowl, beat together cream cheese, milk, and powdered sugar. Beat in whipped topping. Spoon half of the mixture into pie shell; sprinkle with nut topping. Layer sliced banana over nut topping. In a small bowl, stir together strawberries and jam; spread over banana layer. Top with remaining half of cream cheese mixture. Drizzle fudge topping over top of pie.

For the Topping: Pipe or dollop a ring of whipped topping around edge of pie; sprinkle with nut topping.

Garnish with strawberries as desired.

MRS. KELLY'S DATE PIE

Phyllis Bartholomew, Columbus, NE
2003 American Pie Council Crisco National Pie Championships
Amateur Division 2nd Place Open

CRUST
2 cups flour
1 cup cake flour
½ teaspoon salt
1 cup butter-flavored Crisco
1 egg
1 tablespoon cider vinegar
⅓ cup ice water

FILLING
⅔ cup sugar
3 eggs
1 cup milk
½ teaspoon salt
1 teaspoon cinnamon
1½ cups chopped dates

For the Crust: Mix dry ingredients together. Add Crisco and cut into flour with pastry blender until incorporated. Combine egg, vinegar, and water together. Sprinkle over flour mixture until dough forms a ball. Wrap dough in plastic and chill for several hours. Roll out and line pie dish.

For the Filling: Preheat oven to 325°F. Mix together sugar, eggs, milk, salt, and cinnamon. Separate the chopped dates, then add to mixture. Pour into 9-inch pie shell and bake for 40 to 45 minutes.

CANDY CANE EXPRESS

Susan Boyle, Debary, FL
2013 American Pie Council Crisco National Pie Championships
Professional Division 1st Place Open

CRUST
40 chocolate cream cookies
8 tablespoons butter-flavored
   Crisco, melted

FILLING ONE
2 cups whipping cream
3 teaspoons unsalted butter
2 cups of chocolate chips
1 teaspoon white corn syrup
¼ cup peppermint crunch baking
   chips

FILLING TWO
1 small box white chocolate instant
   pudding mix
½ teaspoon candy cane flavored oil

1 to 2 drops pink food coloring
½ cup milk
1 cup whipping cream
½ cup cream cheese
½ cup melted miniature
   marshmallows

GARNISH
½ cup peppermint crunch baking
   chips

For the Crust: Preheat oven to 350°F. In food processor, pulse cookies to a fine crumb stage; continue to pulse adding melted butter to incorporate. Press crumbs firmly into the bottom and sides of a 9-inch pie plate using a small glass. Bake 8 minutes. Cool to set crust before filling.

For Filling One: In a heavy saucepan, heat whipping cream and butter until butter has melted. Slowly add chocolate chips, stirring so it does not stick. Do not heat higher than 90°F. Remove from heat when mixture is smooth. Pour through a strainer into a clean bowl. Add corn syrup and stir slowly to prevent bubbles. Smooth a thin layer of ganache (filling one) on the bottom of cookie crust. Sprinkle peppermint crunch on top; set aside while filling is being prepared.

For Filling Two: In mixing bowl, whip cream cheese, pudding mix, candy cane flavoring, food coloring, and milk. Mix well. Add marshmallows and whipping cream. Continue to mix until light, creamy, and fluffy. Spoon into prepared cookie crust leaving ½ cup for garnish.

For the Garnish: Spread the remaining ½ of the ganache (filling one) on top of pie. Sprinkle peppermint crunch on edges of pie. Pipe the remaining ½ cup of filling two decoratively on top of pie.

Cool before serving

Candy Cane Express Pie

PEANUT BUTTERSCOTCH KRISPY TREAT PIE

Patricia Lapiezo, La Mesa, CA
2013 American Pie Council Crisco National Pie Championships
Amateur Division 1st Place Open

CRUST
2 tablespoons creamy peanut butter
¼ cup light corn syrup
1 cup semisweet chocolate chips
2 cups crispy rice cereal
2 tablespoons chopped peanuts

FILLING
⅔ cup semisweet chocolate chips
⅔ cup butterscotch chips
2 (8-ounce) packages cream cheese, softened

1⅓ cups powdered sugar
¾ cup creamy peanut butter
1 teaspoon vanilla
2½ cups heavy cream, whipped, divided

TOPPING
1 cup heavy whipping cream
2 tablespoons powdered sugar
1 tablespoon chopped peanuts

For the Crust: In a medium saucepan, combine the peanut butter, corn syrup, and chocolate chips until melted. Stir in rice cereal. Spray a 9-inch pie dish with nonstick spray. Press over bottom and up sides, pressing with the back of a spoon. Sprinkle chopped peanuts over bottom of crust.

For the Filling: Melt the chocolate chips and butterscotch chips together. Stir to combine. Set aside. In a large mixing bowl, beat the cream cheese, powdered sugar, and vanilla together until well blended. Divide in half. To one half, beat in melted chocolate/butterscotch mixture. Fold in half of the whipped cream. To the other half beat in the peanut butter until combined and then fold in remaining whipped cream. Alternately drop spoonfuls of each filling into the prepared crust, covering bottom of pie; run a knife through to marble. Repeat until all the filling is used.

For the Topping: Beat the whipping cream and powdered sugar until stiff. Decoratively pipe whipped cream around edge of pie and sprinkle with chopped peanuts.

Peanut Butterscotch Krispy Treat Pie

STRAWBERRY TWIST PIE

Raine Gottess, Fort Lauderdale, FL
2012 American Pie Council Crisco National Pie Championships
Professional Division Honorable Mention Open

CRUST
1 package Keebler chocolate covered
  graham cookies
10 Keebler mint cookies
5 tablespoons butter, melted

KEY LIME SQUARES LAYER
1½ cups graham cracker crumbs
¼ cup sugar
⅓ cup butter, melted
7 ounces sweetened condensed milk
2 small egg yolks
¼ cup key lime juice

CREAM CHEESE LAYER
6 ounces Philadelphia cream cheese,
  softened
¾ cup powdered sugar

1 tablespoon milk
1 teaspoon vanilla
3 ounces creamy Cool Whip

STRAWBERRY LAYER
6 ounces strawberry-flavored
  Philadelphia cream cheese
1½ cups powdered sugar
½ cup marshmallow cream
1 teaspoon vanilla
12 ounces Cool Whip, divided
3 large strawberries

For the Crust: Using a food processer, crush cookies finely and place into a bowl. Using a fork, add butter and toss to moisten. Put into a 9-inch deep dish pie pan. Using the back of a spoon, press to form a crust. Freeze.

For the Key Lime Squares: In a bowl, mix graham crumbs with sugar and butter, using a fork to toss and moisten. Press into the bottom of a small loaf pan. In a bowl, use a whisk to beat milk, egg yolks, and juice together. Pour over the graham cracker crust in the loaf pan. Bake 350°F for 15 minutes. Cool completely on a wire rack.

For the Cream Cheese Layer: Using a mixer, beat cream cheese, vanilla, and milk well. Add in powdered sugar and Cool Whip and beat until creamy. Pour half the mixture over the pie crust.

Freeze. Cut the cooled key lime loaf into squares and place them evenly over cream cheese layer. Leaving small spaces between the squares is fine. (You may have some key lime squares left to enjoy!) Spread remaining cream cheese mixture on top of the key lime layer and gently press down with a rubber spatula. Freeze.

For the Strawberry Layer: Using a mixer, beat cream cheese and marshmallow cream well. Add in vanilla, powdered sugar, and 3 ounces Cool Whip, beating until creamy. Spread evenly over the cream cheese layer. Cover with plastic wrap and refrigerate about 8 hours or overnight to firm. Using the remaining Cool Whip to decorate the pie and place the strawberries in the center for garnish.

Strawberry Twist Pie

MAIN STREET MALTED MILK-MARSHMALLOW PIE

Naylet LaRochelle, Miami, FL
2012 American Pie Council Crisco National Pie Championships
Amateur Division 3rd Place Open

CRUST

1¾ cups ground chocolate sandwich
   cookies (e.g., Oreo)
3 tablespoons butter, melted
¼ cup mini semisweet chocolate
   chips

FILLING ONE

1 teaspoon unflavored gelatin
¾ cup heavy whipping cream,
   divided
7-ounce container marshmallow
   crème
½ teaspoon vanilla extract
1¼ cups slightly crushed malted
   milk balls

FILLING TWO

1 cup milk chocolate chips
1½ cups heavy whipping cream,
   divided
¼ cup malted milk powder

TOPPING

Sweetened whipped cream
Toasted almonds
Malted milk balls

For the Crust: Preheat oven to 375°F. Lightly spray a 9-inch pie plate with nonstick cooking spray. In a medium bowl, combine the crust ingredients. Mix with a fork. Press onto bottom and up sides of pie plate. Bake for 8 to 10 minutes. Remove from oven; let cool completely before filling.

For Filling One: In a small bowl, sprinkle gelatin over ¼ cup whipping cream. Let sit 5 minutes. Microwave 20 to 30 seconds or until completely dissolved. Let cool 5 minutes. In a medium bowl, beat ½ cup whipping cream and cooled gelatin mixture until soft peaks form. Add marshmallow crème and vanilla extract; continue to beat until stiff peaks form. Carefully spread filling in pie crust. Refrigerate until set,

about 1 to 2 hours. Sprinkle with crushed malted milk balls.

For Filling Two: Microwave chocolate chips 20 seconds; stir until smooth and melted. (If needed, microwave in 10-second intervals to achieve melted and smooth consistency.) In a large bowl, beat whipping cream and malted milk powder until stiff peaks form. Stir in cooled chocolate. Carefully spread over marshmallow layer. Refrigerate until completely set, about 2 to 3 hours.

For the Topping: Before serving, top pie with sweetened whipped cream. Garnish with almonds and malted milk balls.

Main Street Malted Milk-Marshmallow Pie

SUPER GRANDE MOCHACHINO PIE

Rick Johnson, Belleville, IL
2012 American Pie Council Crisco National Pie Championships
Amateur Division 2nd Place Open

CRUST
1 large soup bowl with handle
2 cups flour
2 tablespoons sugar
½ cup butter
½ teaspoon salt
1 cup roasted chopped pecans
Cold water

FILLING
4 tablespoons butter
½ cup powdered sugar
1 ounce unsweetened chocolate
1 pouch Nescafe Classico instant
    coffee

1 teaspoon water
1 pasteurized egg
1 cup cream
2 tablespoons powdered sugar
2 tablespoons piping gel
1 teaspoon vanilla

TOPPING
1 cup cream
2 tablespoons powdered sugar
2 tablespoons piping gel
1 teaspoon vanilla
2 tablespoons caramel sauce
Optional: chocolate powder,
    cinnamon

For the Crust: Combine flour, salt, sugar, and butter in a food processor and process until gravely. Add pecans and water a little at a time until dough just starts coming together. Press into a disk and refrigerate for at least 1 hour. Roll into crust. Blind bake crust at 375°F for 20 minutes or until browned. Cool in refrigerator.

For the Filling: Combine coffee and water and set aside. Cream butter and powdered sugar until creamy and pale in color. Melt chocolate in microwave and add to the butter mixture along with the coffee. Blend on high for 5 minutes. Add egg and blend for another 5 minutes. Set mixture aside, then whip remaining ingredients to stiff peaks and fold into chocolate mixture. Fill pie and refrigerate.

For the Topping: Whip cream, powdered sugar, piping gel, and vanilla to stiff peaks. Pipe whipped cream on top of pie and decorate with caramel. Sprinkle with chocolate powder and cinnamon if desired.

Super Grande Mochachino Pie

PEANUT BUTTER

BUCKEYE PIE

Raine Gottess, Canton, OH
2008 American Pie Council Crisco National Pie Championships
Amateur Division 1st Place Peanut Butter

CRUST
18.3-ounce box Betty Crocker fudge
   brownies mix
2 whole eggs
¼ cup water
⅔ cup Crisco vegetable oil

LAYER ONE
8-ounce package Philadelphia cream
   cheese, softened
2 eggs
1 teaspoon vanilla
2 tablespoons flour
⅔ cup sugar
¼ cup sour cream

LAYER TWO
8-ounce package Philadelphia cream
   cheese, softened
1 tablespoon milk
1 teaspoon vanilla
1½ cups powdered sugar
1¼ cups creamy peanut butter
8-ounce creamy Cool Whip topping

BUCKEYES
¼ cup butter, softened
½ cup creamy peanut butter
¼ pound powdered sugar
3 tablespoons light corn syrup
Semisweet chocolate chips

For the Crust: Preheat oven to 350°F. Combine ingredients and bake as directed for 5 minutes less than suggested on brownie mix. Cool. Use a food processor to crumble well (will be moist). Press with fingers into a 10-inch deep dish pie pan to form the shape of a crust. Set aside while making layer one.

For Layer One: Preheat oven to 450°F. Using a mixer, beat softened cream cheese with eggs. Add remaining ingredients. Spread over brownie crust. Cover the edges with foil. Bake 8 minutes, then reduce oven temperature to 250°F and continue baking for 20 minutes. Turn off oven and leave in oven for 20 additional minutes. (Do not open oven during these steps). Remove and cool on a wire rack; uncover foil edges.

For Layer Two: Mix softened cream cheese with milk. Add powdered sugar (sifted) with vanilla. Mix in peanut butter, toss in Cool Whip. Spread over cooled layer one.

Refrigerate approximately 6 hours. Top with more Cool Whip and Buckeye candies (see below).

For Buckeyes: Beat butter, peanut butter, sugar, and corn syrup well in a mixer. Roll into small balls, refrigerate until firm for about 5 minutes. Melt semisweet chocolate chips (chocolate chips melt well in microwave on defrost setting for 2 to 3 minutes). Dip balls three-quarters way in melted chocolate. Place on top on pie.

Buckeye Pie

LIP SMACKIN' NO BAKEM' PEANUT BUTTER PIE

Jeanne Ely, Mulberry, FL
2009 American Pie Council Crisco National Pie Championships
Amateur Division 3rd Place Peanut Butter

CRUST
1 cup sugar
¼ cup milk
¼ cup cocoa
½ teaspoon vanilla
¼ cup butter
1½ cup quick oatmeal

FILLING
¾ cup firmly packed brown sugar
6 tablespoons butter, cut into chunks
1 package unflavored gelatin
⅓ cup milk
¾ cup smooth peanut butter
8 ounces frozen whipped topping,
    thawed

For the Crust: Mix sugar, milk, cocoa, vanilla, and butter together in saucepan. Bring to a boil, stirring constantly. Boil for 1 minute. Remove from heat and stir in oatmeal. Allow to cool until it can be worked with but is not completely cooled. Pour into pie plate and form into the crust. Allow to cool completely.

For the Filling: Place brown sugar and butter chunks in medium microwave-safe bowl and microwave at full power, stirring every 30 seconds, until butter melts and sugar dissolves, 1 to 2 minutes total. Mix in gelatin and cool approximately 10 minutes. Add milk and peanut butter to mixture and beat on medium speed until well blended. Add whipped topping and beat until well blended. Spoon the peanut butter mixture evenly into crust. Cover and chill at least 2 hours or up to 2 days. Garnish as desired.

P. B.'S PEANUT BUTTER AND JELLY PIE

Phyllis Bartholomew, Columbus, OH
2004 American Pie Council Crisco National Pie Championships
Amateur Division 1st Place Peanut Butter

CRUST
2 cups flour
1 cup cake flour
2 tablespoons super rich butter powder
1 cup Crisco shortening
1 whole egg
1 tablespoon cider vinegar
½ teaspoon salt
⅓ cup ice water

FILLING
¾ cup Jiff peanut butter
8-ounce package cream cheese, room temperature

½ cup milk
1 teaspoon vanilla
1¼ cups powdered sugar, sifted
8-ounce container whipped topping, thawed
12-ounce jar Smucker's strawberry jam
1 packet unflavored gelatin
⅛ cup warm water
A few whole peanuts (optional for garnish)

For the Crust: Preheat oven to 425°F. Mix the flours and butter powder together. Cut in the shortening until it resembles coarse crumbs. Beat together the other ingredients and stir into the flour. Mix just until incorporated. Form dough into a disk and wrap in plastic wrap. Refrigerate to chill. Roll out about one third of the dough between 2 sheets of plastic wrap. Place crust in a 9-inch pie dish. Bake for about 10 minutes or until golden. Cool.

Sprinkle the gelatin over ⅛ cup warm water and let stand to soften. In a small saucepan, combine the gelatin mixture and the strawberry jam over low heat to soften the gelatin. Set aside to cool.

For the Filling: Beat together the peanut butter, cream cheese, milk, vanilla, and powdered sugar until smooth and well blended. Stir the whipped topping until smooth and add the peanut butter mixture. Fold together gently.

Pour about one third of the jam into the cooled crust, then half of the peanut butter mixture. Top that layer with the second third of the jam mixture and then layer the rest of the peanut butter on top of that. Swirl the top of the layer in a decorative style. Then drizzle the remaining third of the jam mixture around the swirls on top. A few whole peanuts may be placed on top of the pie for garnish.

Chill well and keep refrigerated.

FABULOUS PEANUT BUTTER FLUFF PIE

Kathleen Costello, Tallmadge, OH
2011 American Pie Council Crisco National Pie Championships
Amateur Division 3rd Place Peanut Butter

CRUST
¾ cup Keebler Sandies Simply Shortbread cookies, finely crushed (food processor)
½ cup chocolate graham crackers, finely crushed (food processor)
3 tablespoons granulated sugar
5 tablespoons salted butter, melted

FILLING
12 ounces cream cheese, softened
1½ cups Jiff creamy peanut butter
2 cups powdered sugar
2 teaspoons vanilla
2 cups heavy whipping cream, divided
2 cups marshmallow fluff

TOPPING
2 tablespoons Smucker's chocolate fudge topping
2 tablespoons Fisher's ice cream toppers nut topping

For the Crust: In a small bowl, mix together the cookie crumbs and sugar. Make sure they are well blended. Add melted butter and continue to mix until ingredients are incorporated. Mixture will be moist. Prepare a 9-inch pie dish by spraying it with Baker's Joy baking spray with flour. Press cookie mixture into the pie dish being sure to spread the crust out evenly. Take another 9-inch pie dish and cover it with plastic wrap. With the bottom facing down, press the plastic covered dish firmly into the crust to even out and pack the crust mixture. Remove the pie dish covered in plastic wrap from the pressed pie crust. Place the pressed crust into the refrigerator for 30 minutes to set before filling.

For the Filling: In a large bowl with an electric mixer, mix cream cheese and peanut butter until well-blended. Add powdered sugar, vanilla, and ¼ cup whipping cream. Continue mixing ingredients until creamy. Add marshmallow fluff and ¼ cup whipping cream. Mix together until all ingredients are incorporated. In a chilled mixing bowl, add remaining 1½ cups whipping cream and whip with an electric mixer. Whip until cream is stiff. Add stiff cream to peanut butter mixture. Mix all ingredients together until incorporated. Spoon filling into prepared pie shell.

For the Topping: Microwave fudge topping in bowl for 10 seconds. Use a fork to drizzle melted

Fabulous Peanut Butter Fluff Pie

chocolate on top of pie. Next, sprinkle nut topping on top of the pie.

Optional Topping: For a more decorative look, fill the pie shell with half of the peanut butter fluff mixture and spread evenly into crust. Place the remaining half of the peanut butter fluff mixture into an icing bag with a large flower tip and pipe the mixture on top of the already half-filled pie crust. Next, drizzle the chocolate fudge topping and then add the nuts.

Chill for 8 hours or more before serving. Refrigerate leftovers.

PEANUT BUTTER BROWNIE PIE

Heidi CV Neidlinger-Givler, Schuylkill Haven, PA
2006 American Pie Council Crisco National Pie Championships
Amateur Division 2nd Place Peanut Butter

CRUST
1 cup plus 2 tablespoons all-purpose
  flour
1 tablespoon sugar
½ teaspoon salt
4 tablespoons cream cheese, chilled
  and cut into ½ inch cubes
4 tablespoons frozen butter
2 tablespoons frozen Crisco
  shortening
3 to 5 tablespoons ice-cold water

BROWNIE FILLING
2 ounces unsweetened chocolate
6 tablespoons butter
¾ cup sugar
½ teaspoon vanilla extract

2 eggs, room temperature
⅓ cup plus 1 tablespoon all-purpose
  flour

PEANUT BUTTER TOPPING
4 ounces cream cheese, softened
2 tablespoons whole milk ricotta
  cheese
1 cup confectioners' sugar (10x)
½ cup peanut butter chips, melted
2 tablespoons creamy peanut butter
1 teaspoon vanilla

GARNISH
½ cup white chocolate chips
½ teaspoon Crisco shortening

For the Crust: Mix flour, sugar, and salt in a medium bowl. Blend the cream cheese into the flour mixture until it resembles cornmeal. Using a cheese grater, grate the butter and shortening into the mixture. Mix again until it resembles cornmeal. Stir in the ice cold water a little at a time with a fork until the dough clumps and can be formed into a ball. Make a ball and cover with plastic wrap and refrigerate overnight. Then, remove dough from refrigerator and shape into a disk. Roll out on a floured board into a 14-inch circle and place into a deep dish pie plate. Fit sides and bottom of dish and crimp or flute lip of pie plate. Refrigerate until ready to use crust.

For the Brownie Filling: Preheat oven to 350°F. Melt chocolate and butter in the top of a double boiler placed over simmering water. Cool the mixture for 5 minutes. Place the sugar in a medium-sized bowl and pour the chocolate over the sugar. Using a mixer, beat until blended, about 2 minutes. Add the vanilla. With mixer on medium speed, add the eggs one at a time until mixed, about 10 seconds, scrape bowl and blend about 15 seconds more. Add the flour on slow speed for 20 seconds and finish mixing by hand until incorporated. Pour brownie filling into prepared crust and bake for about 30 to 35 minutes or until toothpick comes out clean when inserted into brownies and crust is golden brown. Take out and set aside to cool.

For the Peanut Butter Topping: Beat cream cheese and ricotta cheese in medium size mixing bowl until fluffy. Add sugar, peanut butter, melted chips, and vanilla. Spread evenly over top of cooled brown pie and refrigerate until ready to garnish.

For the Garnish: Mix white chocolate with Crisco and melt in microwave for about 20 to 40 seconds. Put into cake decorator's tubes and pipe out heart-shaped or other designs onto wax paper. Store in refrigerator to cool. Apply to cake for garnish.

PEANUT BUTTER CHIFFON PIE

Phyllis Bartholomew, Columbus, NE
2005 American Pie Council Crisco National Pie Championships
Amateur Division 3rd Place Peanut Butter

CRUST
2 cups all-purpose flour
1 cup cake flour
1 cup shortening
1 egg
1 tablespoon apple cider vinegar
½ teaspoon salt
⅓ cup ice water

FILLING
¾ cup peanut butter
8-ounce package cream cheese,
  room temperature

½ cup milk, warm
1 tablespoon gelatin
1¼ cups powdered sugar, sifted
1 teaspoon vanilla
4-ounce container of frozen whipped
  topping, thawed
½ cup meringue mix
½ cup water, warm
½ cup squeezable strawberry jelly
⅓ cup roasted peanuts for garnish

For the Crust: Preheat oven to 400°F. In a large bowl, cut the shortening into the flour until it resembles coarse crumbs. Beat the egg, vinegar, salt, and water together. Add the egg mixture to the flour and mix just until the dry ingredients are incorporated. Do not over mix. Form into a large ball and wrap in plastic. Chill for several hours or overnight. Roll out when ready. Place crust into a 9-inch pie pan. Bake until lightly browned, about 10 minutes. Set aside to cool.

For the Filling: Warm the milk in a saucepan and add the gelatin to soften. Gently warm it on low heat until gelatin dissolves. Do not boil. Combine meringue mix and water. Beat until you have stiff peaks. Set aside. Beat the peanut butter and cream cheese together until smooth. Add the milk mixture and the powdered sugar. Beat until smooth. Gently fold in the whipped topping, and then fold in the meringue.

Pour into the pie shell and swirl the top in a decorative fashion. Add drizzled jelly and small bunches of peanuts. Chill well.

Peanut Butter Chiffon Pie

PEANUT BUTTER CANDY BIT PIE

Beth Campbell, Belleville, WI
2004 American Pie Council Crisco National Pie Championships
Amateur Division 3rd Place Peanut Butter

CRUST
1 cup flour
½ cup Crisco shortening
Pinch of salt
¼ cup water

FILLING
10 ounces Heath toffee chips or
   chopped Heath bars
8 ounces cream cheese, softened

¾ cup powdered sugar
½ cup crunchy peanut butter
2 tablespoons milk
2 cups heavy whipping cream,
   whipped until thick
½ teaspoon vanilla

CHOCOLATE TOPPING
⅔ cup semisweet chocolate chips
4 tablespoons whipping cream

For the Crust: Preheat oven to 375°F. Combine flour and salt in a bowl. Cut shortening into flour and salt until pea size pieces form. Mix in cold water. Refrigerate until chilled. Roll out crust on floured board. Place into pie pan and prick the crust with a fork so it doesn't bubble. Bake until golden brown.

For the Filling: Put ¼ to ½ cup of Heath toffee chips in the bottom of the baked pie shell. Using an electric mixer, beat the cream cheese with the powdered sugar until creamy. Add the peanut butter and milk and beat well. Fold in the rest of the toffee chips into the cream cheese and peanut butter mixture. Fold the whipped cream and vanilla into the peanut butter mixture and spoon into the crust, smoothing the top. Refrigerate at least one hour until set.

For the Chocolate Topping: In a microwave or heavy saucepan, melt the chocolate chips with the cream over low heat until smooth. Drizzle over the peanut butter filling. Refrigerate for 2 hours or overnight. Cut with a warm knife.

PEANUT BUTTER EXPLOSION

Patricia Lapiezo, La Mesa, CA
2009 American Pie Council Crisco National Pie Championships
Amateur Division 2nd Place Peanut Butter

CRUST
12 Nutter Butter cookies
4 Nature Valley peanut butter granola bars
⅓ cup butter, melted.

FILLING
8-ounce package cream cheese, softened
⅔ cup powdered sugar
¾ cup creamy peanut butter
1 tablespoon butter
1 teaspoon vanilla
8-ounce container Cool Whip
2.1 ounces Butterfinger candy bar, crushed

CANDY TOPPING
Miniature peanut butter cups
Honey Roasted peanuts
Peanut butter chips
Any peanut butter candy bar of your choice
2 tablespoons caramel ice cream topping
2 tablespoons fudge topping
1 cup whipping cream
½ teaspoon sugar

For the Crust: In a food processor, finely grind the cookies and granola bars. Pulse in butter until blended. Press onto bottom and up sides of a 9-inch pie dish. Freeze at least 10 minutes while preparing filling.

For the Filling: In a large mixing bowl, beat the cream cheese and powdered sugar until fluffy. Add the peanut butter, butter, and vanilla and beat until well blended. Fold in the Cool Whip, then fold in the crushed candy bar. Spread filling in prepared crust. Smooth the top.

For the Candy Topping: Use any combination of the first four ingredients of candy topping to equal one cup. Mix well and sprinkle over top of pie to within 1-inch of crust. Drizzle with caramel and fudge toppings. Add sugar to cream and whip until peaks form. Pipe a border of sweetened whipped cream around edge of pie. Refrigerate about 2 hours or until firm. Keep refrigerated.

PEANUT BUTTER FUDGE PIE

Carolyn Blakemore, Fairmont, WV
2005 American Pie Council Crisco National Pie Championships
Amateur Division 2nd Place Peanut Butter

CHOCOLATE CRUST
1⅓ cups flour, sifted
¼ teaspoon salt
2 tablespoons sugar
1 tablespoon cocoa powder
½ stick margarine
3 tablespoons butter-flavored Crisco
3 to 4 tablespoons cold water

FILLING
3 tablespoons peanut butter, spread
   on crust bottom

2 tablespoons peanut butter chips,
   spread on inside edge of crust
10-ounce package peanut butter
   chips, melted
16-ounce can vanilla creamy frosting

TOPPING
1 cup confectioners' sugar
3 ounces cream cheese, softened
½ cup peanut butter
8-ounce container Cool Whip

For the Crust: Preheat oven to 325°F. In a bowl, sift together flour, salt, sugar, and cocoa. With a pastry blender, cut in margarine and Crisco until crumbly. Add water by tablespoons until crust forms a ball. Cover with wax paper. Chill until ready to use. Roll out on wax paper with floured rolling pin to fit a 9-inch pie pan. Place crust in pie pan, pricking bottom and sides with a fork. Cover crust rim with foil strips to bake. Bake in oven for 20 minutes. Remove from oven and let cool.

For the Filling: Spread 3 tablespoons peanut butter on the bottom of prepared pie crust.

Spread 2 tablespoons peanut butter chips on inside edge of prepared pie crust. In a saucepan on low heat, melt package of peanut butter chips. Remove from heat. Stir in frosting, mixing until smooth. Pour into crust to cover about ¼ inch and chill. Pour the remaining mix into a greased pan for some extra peanut butter fudge. Chill.

For the Topping: In large mixer bowl, cream sugar and cheese. Blend in peanut butter and add Cool Whip until thoroughly combined. Pour into peanut butter-filled pie crust. Chill until firm. Slice.

Peanut Butter Fudge

PEANUT BUTTER PIE

Nikki Norman, Milton, TN
2004 American Pie Council Crisco National Pie Championships
Amateur Division 2nd Place Peanut Butter

CRUST
1 cup plus 2 tablespoons flour
¼ teaspoon sea salt
½ teaspoon ground nutmeg
4 tablespoons unsalted butter, cubed
3 tablespoons Crisco shortening
½ cup sour cream

FILLING
⅓ cup creamy peanut butter
¾ cup confectioners' sugar, sifted
⅓ cup all-purpose flour
½ cup sugar
¼ teaspoon salt
2 cups half-and-half
3 egg yolks, beaten
2 tablespoons unsalted butter
1 tablespoon vanilla extract

MERINGUE
6 large egg whites
⅛ teaspoon sea salt
¾ teaspoon cream of tartar
¾ cup granulated sugar
1 teaspoon pure vanilla extract

For the Crust: In a medium bowl, combine flour, salt, nutmeg, butter, and shortening, cutting until pieces are small—about the size of small peas—with 2 knives or pastry blender. Freeze 15 minutes. Remove from freezer and stir in sour cream. Shape dough into a ball. Cover with plastic wrap and refrigerate 30 minutes. Preheat oven to 400°F. Roll out dough on a lightly floured surface. Place in a 9-inch pie plate. Bake for 15 minutes. Lightly cover edges with aluminum foil if browning too quickly and bake an additional 5 minutes.

For the Filling: Combine peanut butter and confectioners' sugar in a food processor. Pulse 6 to 8 times. Sprinkle 2/3 of mixture over prebaked pie shell. Set aside. In a medium saucepan, combine flour, sugar, salt, and half-and-half. Whisk until blended throughout. Cook over medium heat, stirring frequently until thickened. Gradually whisk in egg yolks. Cook, stirring constantly for 2 minutes. Remove from heat and whisk in butter and vanilla. Pour into pie crust.

For the Meringue: Preheat oven to 325°F. In a mixing bowl, combine egg whites, salt, and cream of tartar. Beat on high until foamy. Gradually add sugar, beating until soft peaks form. Beat in vanilla. Place meringue on hot pie filling. Sprinkle meringue with reserved peanut butter and sugar mixture. Bake on lowest shelf in oven for 30 minutes.

HONEY ROASTED PEANUT BUTTER PIE

George Yates, Dallas, TX
2013 American Pie Council Crisco National Pie Championships
Amateur Division 3rd Place Peanut Butter

CRUST
30 Nutter Butter cookies, crumbled
¾ cup vanilla wafer crumbs
¼ cup honey roasted peanuts, finely ground
3 tablespoons sugar
⅓ cup unsalted butter, melted
2 teaspoon vanilla extract
Crisco no-stick butter spray

FILLING
1 cup cold milk
1 package instant vanilla pudding mix
1 cup honey roasted creamy peanut butter

¼ cup honey
4 ounces cream cheese, softened
½ cup sweetened condensed milk
½ cup sour cream
2 teaspoon vanilla extract
1 cup heavy whipping cream
4 tablespoons powdered sugar

GARNISH
¼ cup honey roasted peanuts
¼ cup chopped Butterfinger
Chocolate curls
Mini Nutter Butter cookies

For the Crust: Preheat oven to 350°F. In a medium bowl, combine both crumbs, ground peanuts, and sugar. Stir vanilla into melted butter and add to the dry mixture. Mix until well combined. Lightly spray a 9- or 10-inch deep dish pie pan with Crisco cooking spray. Press into pan. Bake for 5 minutes or until lightly golden. Cool on wire rack.

For the Filling: In a small bowl, whisk milk and pudding mix for 2 minutes (mixture will be thick). Set aside. In a large bowl, beat the peanut butter, honey, cream cheese, condensed milk, sour cream and vanilla until smooth; stir into the pudding mixture. Set aside. In a large bowl, beat whipping cream until it begins to thicken. Add sugar and beat until stiff peaks form. Fold half into pudding mixture. Pour into crust.

For the Garnish: Pipe remaining whipped cream over top. If desired, garnish with sweetened whipped cream, chocolate curls, chopped honey roasted peanuts, chopped Butterfinger, and mini Nutter Butter cookies. Refrigerate until completely chilled.

Honey Roasted Peanut Butter Pie

PEANUT BUTTER AND CRACKER PIE

Andrea Spring, Bradenton, FL
2013 American Pie Council Crisco National Pie Championships
Professional Division Best of Show and 1ˢᵗ Place Peanut Butter

CRUST
3 egg whites
1 cup sugar
1 teaspoons vanilla
1 teaspoons baking powder
1 cup honey roasted peanuts, ground fine
1 cup Ritz crackers
½ cup semisweet mini chocolate chips

FILLING
4 ounces cream cheese
¼ cup granulated sugar
1 cup creamy peanut butter
8 ounces whipped topping

TOPPING
¼ cup Reese's peanut butter chips
¼ cup white chocolate chips
¼ cup heavy cream
¼ cup semisweet mini chocolate chips
¼ cup heavy cream

GARNISH
1 cup whipped sweetened heavy cream
Extra peanut and cracker crumbs

For the Crust: Preheat oven to 350°F. Whip egg whites until foamy, add sugar, and whip until glossy. Add vanilla, baking powder, peanuts, crackers, and chips. Pour into greased 10-inch pie pan. Bake for 45 minutes. Chill crust.

For the Filling: Beat cream cheese and sugar, add peanut butter and beat well. Add whipped topping and pile in cooled crust. Chill well.

For the Topping: Place peanut butter chips and white chips in two different cups. Divide heavy cream between the two cups and microwave until melted. Swirl the two over the chilled pie. Melt the cream with the mini semisweet chocolate chips and swirl it over the top of pie.

Garnish with whipped cream rosettes and crumbs. Chill well.

Cracker and Peanut Butter Pie

AN AFFAIR TO REMEMBER

Janet Ropp, Edgewater, FL
2013 American Pie Council Crisco National Pie Championships
Amateur Division 1st Place Peanut Butter

CRUST
1 (16.8-ounce) box brownie mix
1 cup chopped honey roasted
  peanuts
24 saltine crackers, crushed
2 tablespoons powdered peanut
  butter (PB2)
6 tablespoons butter, melted

FILLING ONE
4 (3-ounce) packages cream cheese
2 tablespoons unsalted butter,
  softened
2 cups plus 3 tablespoons
  confectioners' sugar, divided
Pinch salt
1 cup smooth peanut butter

5 tablespoons powdered peanut
  butter, divided
1 cup whipping cream

FILLING TWO
1¾ cup reserved peanut butter filling
2 cups chopped brownies
3 teaspoons Three Chilies Chocolate
  Sauce
1 teaspoon chocolate extract

TOPPING
3 cups whipping cream
9 tablespoons confectioners' sugar
9 tablespoons powdered peanut
  butter

For the Crust: Preheat oven to 350°F. Bake brownies according to package directions. Cool completely. Lightly grease 9½-inch glass pie plate. In bowl, combine 2 cups of crumbled brownies (reserving the rest for the filling), peanuts, saltines, and powdered peanut butter and toss to mix well. Add melted butter and mix completely. Press into pie plate and blind bake for 12 minutes. Cool on wire rack.

For Filling One: In a bowl, beat whipping cream until soft peaks start to form. Add 3 tablespoons confectioners' sugar and 1 tablespoon powdered peanut butter and beat until firm. Set aside. In large mixing bowl, beat together cream cheese and butter until

smooth. Add remaining confectioners' sugar, salt, and 4 tablespoons powdered peanut butter and mix well. Add peanut butter and mix until well blended. Stir in whipped cream mixture. Spoon out 1¾ cup mixture and set aside. Pour remaining mixture into prepared crust. Chill while preparing filling two.

For Filling Two: Mix together all the chocolate filling ingredients and blend well. Spread over filling one. Chill while preparing topping.

For the Topping: Beat cream until soft peaks form. Add confectioners' sugar and powdered peanut butter and beat until set. Spread on top of pie. Refrigerate. Serve cold.

An Affair to Remember Peanut Butter Pie

AMAZING PEANUT BUTTER EXPERIENCE

Valarie Enters, Sanford, FL
2013 American Pie Council Crisco National Pie Championships
Professional Division Honorable Mention Peanut Butter

CRUST
24 Nutter Butter cookies, finely chopped
5 tablespoons butter
¼ cup roasted peanuts
3 tablespoons sugar

FILLING
1 (8-ounce) package cream cheese
1 cup marshmallow cream
½ cup peanut butter
1 teaspoon vanilla
2 cups heavy whipping cream
1 teaspoon gelatin, softened (soften in water)

GANACHE
6. 5 ounces chocolate chips
6. 5 ounces heavy whipping cream

2 teaspoons corn syrup
1 tablespoon unsalted butter

TRUFFLES
1 (8-ounce) package cream cheese
¼ cup peanut butter
24 nutter butters, pulverized
3 tablespoons powdered sugar
12 ounces peanut butter chips
1 tablespoon oil
Mini nutter butters
¼ cup roasted peanuts

For the Crust: Preheat oven to 350°F. Pulsate crust ingredients in a food processor until a nice dough is formed. Press into a crust and bake for 10 minutes till set.

For the Filling: Beat cream cheese, marshmallow cream, peanut butter, and vanilla. In a separate bowl, whip cream and add softened gelatin. Fold into filling and pour into cooled pie crust.

For the Ganache Topping: Heat the cream in a microwave till hot. Add chocolate chips and let sit for a minute so it melts the chocolate. Add butter and corn syrup. Stir until melted and silky. Sieve to remove any lumps and pour over cooled pie.

For the Truffles: Mix together cream cheese, peanut butter, nutter butters, and powdered sugar and form into small balls. Set aside. Melt together peanut butter chips and oil. Dip truffles in peanut butter chip mixture. Garnish with the truffles and a mini nutter butter and top with roasted peanuts.

Amazing Peanut Butter Experience

FUDGY BOTTOM PEANUT BUTTER CRUNCH PIE

Alberta F. Dunbar, San Diego, CA
2013 American Pie Council Crisco National Pie Championships
Amateur Division 2nd Place Peanut Butter

CRUST
1½ cup all-purpose flour
½ teaspoon salt
½ cup Crisco shortening
3 to 4 tablespoons ice water

FILLING ONE
¾ cup semisweet chocolate chips melted and cooled
½ cup chocolate peanut butter
¾ cup heavy cream whipped

FILLING TWO
8 ounces cream cheese softened,
1 cup milk
4-ounce serving Hershey's white chocolate instant pudding mix

1 cup peanut butter
10 ounces peanut butter chips, melted and cooled
1 cup heavy cream whipped
¾ cup unsalted dry roasted peanuts, ground
½ cup toffee baking bits

TOPPING
2½ cups heavy cream
¼ cup sifted powdered sugar
¾ teaspoon vanilla extract

GARNISH
½ cup chocolate curls or flakes
Whole unsalted dry roasted peanuts

For the Crust: Preheat oven to 450°F. Mix flour and salt together, cut in shortening using a pastry blender or 2 knives until flour is blended and forms pea-size chunks. Sprinkle with 1 tablespoon of water at a time. Toss lightly with a fork until dough forms a ball. Roll on a lightly floured surface until pastry is large enough to fit a 9-inch deep dish pie pan, with ½" overlap. Transfer pastry to pie pan and fold edges under and flute using fingers. Prick bottom with fork and bake for 10 to 12 minutes or until golden brown. Cool completely before adding filling.

For Filling One: In a small bowl combine melted chocolate and chocolate peanut butter; beat well. Fold in whipped cream and pour into a cooled crust. Smooth top and chill.

For Filling Two: In a large bowl beat cream cheese until smooth. Slowly beat in milk until well combined and smooth. Slowly add pudding mix; beat well for 1 minute. Add melted peanut butter chips and fold in whipped cream. Blend well. Gently fold in ground peanuts and toffee bits. Carefully and evenly spread over first layer. Smooth top and chill until set.

For the Topping: Combine heavy cream, powdered sugar, and vanilla extract in a medium bowl. Beat until stiff. Reserve one third of mixture for rosettes. Frost top of pie, smooth. Pipe rosette border around edge and top each rosette with a whole peanut. Sprinkle center with chocolate flakes or curls.

Fudgy Bottom Peanut Butter Crunch Pie

PUMPKIN

BROWN SUGAR PUMPKIN PIE

Sarah Spaugh, Winston Salem, NC
2004 American Pie Council Crisco National Pie Championships
Amateur Division 1st Place Pumpkin

CRUST
3 cups flour
1½ teaspoon salt
1 cup butter-flavored Crisco
9 tablespoons cold milk
1 egg white, slightly beaten

FILLING
4 cups cooked mashed pumpkin
½ cup apple butter
2½ cups brown sugar, loosely
   packed

¼ cup maple syrup
¼ cup orange juice
¾ teaspoon salt
2 tablespoons cinnamon
4 eggs, beaten well
1½ cups undiluted evaporated milk

GARNISH
1 cup whipping cream
¼ cup confectioners' sugar
¼ teaspoon vanilla

For the Crust: Sift together flour and salt. Cut in shortening until particles are about the size of peas. Add cold milk, a little at a time, to make a dough that will barely stick together. Refrigerate 20 minutes. Divide dough into 2 equal parts. Roll each out on a floured surface and fit into 9-inch pie pans. Brush bottom crusts with beaten egg white. Crimp edges.

For the Filling: Preheat oven to 425°F. Beat eggs well in a large bowl. Add brown sugar, maple syrup, pumpkin, apple butter, orange juice, salt, and cinnamon. Mix well. Add evaporated milk and mix well. Pour into prepared pie crusts. Bake 10 minutes at 425°F. Turn oven down to 350°F and continue cooking for 30 to 40 minutes until filling in middle does not stick to tester.

Garnish after pie is cooled. Whip 1 cup whipping cream with ¼ cup confectioners' sugar and ¼ teaspoon vanilla. Sprinkle with toffee bits or chopped pecans.

Brown Sugar Pumpkin

CARAMELIZED PUMPKIN PIE

Sarah Spaugh, Winston-Salem, NC
2002 American Pie Council Crisco National Pie Championships
Amateur Division 1st Place Pumpkin

CRUST
1½ cups unsifted all-purpose flour
2 tablespoons confectioners' sugar, sifted
½ teaspoon salt
½ cup unsalted butter, chilled
4 tablespoons vegetable shortening, chilled
½ cup chopped pecans
3 to 4 tablespoons ice water

FILLING
3 large eggs
2 cups fresh pumpkin, mashed, or 15-ounce can solid pack pumpkin
½ cup granulated sugar
¼ cup firmly packed dark brown sugar

¼ cup 100 percent amber maple syrup
½ teaspoon salt
¼ cup apple butter
1 teaspoon allspice
½ teaspoon cinnamon
¼ teaspoon freshly grated nutmeg
⅛ teaspoon ground cloves
¾ cup milk
¼ cup cream

GARNISH
1 cup heavy cream
3 tablespoons pulverized sugar
¼ cup caramel toffee bits for topping on cream

For the Crust: Whisk together the first three ingredients in a large bowl. Cut or work the fats into the dry ingredients until the mixture resembles coarse meal. Add the pecans and toss with a fork to incorporate. Add the ice water, 1 tablespoon at a time, drizzling it around the edge of the bowl. Stir with the fork until moist clumps form. With lightly floured hands, shape the dough into a 5-inch flat disk. Score the pastry with the side of your hand to relax the gluten, cover the dough with plastic wrap, and refrigerate for 30 minutes. Roll dough to fit a 9-inch pie pan.

For the Filling: Preheat the oven to 350°F. Beat the eggs lightly with a whisk in a large bowl. Stir in pumpkin and apple butter. Combine the sugars, salt, and spices. Stir in maple syrup. Slowly stir in the milk and cream, mixing just until smooth. Do not over-mix. Pour into pie shell. Cover the edges to prevent burning. Bake for about 50 minutes or until the center is set. Remove the cover from the edges. Bake for an additional 5 to 10 minutes if edges need browning. Cool. Whip cream with sugar for topping, and garnish as desired. Sprinkle on toffee-bits.

PUMPKIN PECAN SURPRISE PIE

Alberta Dunbar, San Diego, CA
2011 American Pie Council Crisco National Pie Championships
Amateur Division 1st Place Pumpkin

CRUST

1⅓ cups all-purpose flour

½ teaspoon salt

½ stick Crisco all-vegetable shortening

3 to 6 tablespoons ice water

FILLING FIRST LAYER

12 ounces cream cheese, softened

2 tablespoons heavy cream

¼ cup sugar

1 large egg, slightly beaten

¾ cup finely chopped candied pecans

¾ teaspoon vanilla extract

FILLING SECOND LAYER

15-ounce can pumpkin

½ cup granulated sugar

¼ cup packed brown sugar

2 teaspoons pumpkin pie spice

¼ teaspoon salt

2 large eggs, slightly beaten

12-ounce can evaporated milk

TOPPING AND GARNISH

2 cups heavy cream

¼ cup powdered sugar, sifted

1 teaspoon vanilla extract

1 cup candied pecans, ground

For the Crust: Preheat oven to 400°F. Spoon flour into measuring cup and level. Mix flour and salt in a medium bowl. Cut in shortening using pastry blender or 2 knives until flour is blended and forms pea-size chunks. Sprinkle with 1 tablespoon of water at a time. Toss lightly with a fork until dough forms a ball. Roll on lightly floured board to fit a 9-inch pie plate with ½ inch overlap. Turn into pie plate and flute edges and prick bottom with fork. Bake for 10 minutes or until golden brown. Cool on rack completely before filling.

For Filling Layer One: Combine cream cheese, heavy cream, and sugar in a medium bowl; beat well on high. Add egg and beat to combine. With spoon, stir in nuts and extract. Spread evenly in shell. Smooth top of pie and set aside.

For Filling Layer Two: Preheat oven to 425°F. Combine pumpkin, granulated and brown sugars, pumpkin pie spice, and salt in a large bowl. Beat to mix well. Beat in egg. Gradually stir in milk with a spoon, mix well. Slowly pour over first layer. To prevent over browning, cover outer edges of pie with foil or pie ring. Bake for 15 minutes. Reduce heat to 350°F and bake 40 to 50 minutes or until knife inserted in center comes out clean. Cool on rack and chill until set for about an hour.

For the Topping and Garnish: Combine all ingredients in a medium bowl. Beat on high until stiff. Fit pastry bag with large rosette tip. Pipe large rosettes. Sprinkle nuts around pie. Pipe smaller rosettes and then sprinkle nuts in a row of small rosettes ending with nuts in center.

Pumpkin Pecan Surprise Pie

GINGERBREAD PUMPKIN PIE WITH DOUBLE STREUSEL

Karen Hall, Elm Creek, NE
2006 American Pie Council Crisco National Pie Championships
Amateur Division 2nd Place Pumpkin

CRUST
3 cups unbleached flour
1 tablespoon buttermilk powder
½ teaspoon baking powder
1 teaspoon salt
1 teaspoon sugar
½ cup plus 1 tablespoon butter-flavored Crisco, cut into ¼ inch pats
½ cup unsalted butter, cut into ¼ inch pats
1 egg
⅓ cup plus 3 tablespoons cold water
1 tablespoon vinegar

STREUSEL BOTTOM
3 tablespoons butter, melted
¼ cup chopped pecans
¼ cup light brown sugar, packed
1 tablespoon crushed gingerbread cookie crumbs or ginger snaps
½ cup raisins

FILLING
2 eggs
15-ounce can pumpkin
14-ounce can sweetened condensed milk
2 tablespoons maple syrup
1 teaspoon cinnamon
⅛ teaspoon nutmeg
⅛ teaspoon cloves
⅛ teaspoon ginger

TOPPING
2 tablespoons butter, melted
⅓ cup light brown sugar, packed
¼ cup crushed gingerbread or gingersnap crumbs
⅓ cup pecans, chopped

GARNISH (OPTIONAL)
Pecan halves
Pastry cut outs or miniature gingerbread men
8-ounce container whipped topping

For the Crust: In a large mixing bowl, combine flour, buttermilk powder, baking powder, salt, and sugar. With pastry blender, cut in Crisco and butter until mixture resembles coarse crumbs. In a small bowl, beat egg, water, and vinegar. With a pastry fork, add egg mixture slowly to flour mixture while tossing with fork until mixture is moistened. Do not over mix. Divide dough and shape into 3 balls. Flatten each to form a disk. Wrap each disk with plastic wrap and refrigerate at least 30 minutes before using. Use only one disk for this recipe for one 9-inch pie shell. After at least 30 minutes, roll out pastry and place in a 9-inch pie dish. Flute edge.

For Streusel Bottom: In a small bowl, stir together melted butter, pecans, brown sugar, crushed gingerbread crumbs, and raisins. Spread mixture over bottom of unbaked pie shell.

For the Filling: Preheat oven to 425°F. In a large mixing bowl, beat eggs until light in color.

Add pumpkin, milk, maple syrup, cinnamon, nutmeg, cloves, and ginger; mix until well combined. Carefully pour filling over streusel in bottom of pie shell. Protect edge of pie with foil to prevent over browning. Bake at 425°F for 15 minutes. Reduce oven temperature to 350°F; bake an additional 25 to 30 minutes or until center is set.

For Streusel Topping: In a small bowl, combine melted butter, brown sugar, crushed cookie crumbs, and pecans. Sprinkle over top of pie and bake an additional 5 to 8 minutes. Cool pie on rack.

Dollop or pipe whipped topping on top of pie as desired. Garnish as desired.

PRETTY AS A PICTURE PUMPKIN PIE

Beth Campbell, Belleville, WI
2008 American Pie Council Crisco National Pie Championships
Amateur Division 3rd Place Pumpkin

CRUST
1 cup flour
½ cup shortening
¼ cup cold water
Pinch of salt

PRALINE LAYER:
3 tablespoons butter
⅓ cup brown sugar
⅓ cup chopped pecans

FILLING
1 cup evaporated milk and ½ cup
    water, scalded
3 eggs

1½ cups pumpkin
½ cup sugar
½ cup brown sugar
1¼ teaspoons cinnamon
½ teaspoon ginger
½ teaspoon nutmeg (freshly ground
    recommended)
½ teaspoon ground cloves
½ teaspoon salt

GARNISH
Whipped Cream
Caramel Sauce
Toasted Pecan Halves

For the Crust: Cut the shortening into the flour and salt until the particles are the size of small peas. Sprinkle in the water until the flour mixture is moistened. Gather the pastry into a ball and refrigerate overnight. Roll pastry out on floured board. Fold the pastry into quarters, unfold and ease into the pie pan.

For the Praline Layer: Preheat oven to 450°F. Mix the butter and brown sugar. Add the pecans and spread on unbaked pie shell. Bake 10 minutes.

For the Filling: Preheat oven to 350°F. Beat the eggs; add pumpkin, sugars, and spices. Mix well. Beat in slightly cooled milk/water mixture. Pour on top of praline layer. Bake for 50 minutes or until the custard is set.

Garnish with whipped cream, hot caramel sauce, and pecan halves (toasted) as desired.

PUMPKIN PECAN CRUMBLE PIE

Marles Riessland, Riverdale, NE
2003 American Pie Council Crisco National Pie Championships
Amateur Division 1st Place Pumpkin

CRUST
3 cups all-purpose flour
1 teaspoon salt
1 teaspoon sugar
1 cup plus 1 tablespoon butter-
  flavored shortening, chilled
1/3 cup ice water
1 tablespoon vinegar
1 egg, beaten

FILLING
2 eggs, beaten
16-ounce can pumpkin

3/4 cup sugar
1/2 teaspoon salt
1 teaspoon cinnamon
1/4 teaspoon ginger
1/4 teaspoon cloves
2 tablespoons pure maple syrup
12-ounce can evaporated milk

TOPPING
1/2 cup flour
1/2 cup chopped pecans
1/4 cup packed brown sugar
3 tablespoons butter, softened

For the Crust: Chill all ingredients, including the flour and vinegar. Combine the flour, salt, and sugar. Cut in shortening with a pastry blender until the mixture resembles cornmeal. In another bowl, mix water and vinegar with the beaten egg. Add the liquid mixture, one tablespoon at a time, to the flour mixture, tossing with a fork to form a soft dough. Shape into three disks. Wrap in plastic wrap and chill in refrigerator at least three hours (overnight works best), before attempting to roll out. Hold no more than three days in refrigerator. For longer storage, place in a freezer bag and freeze. Use one disk for a single crust pie. Use two disks for a double crust pie.

To roll out for pies, work quickly on a floured pastry cloth (store pastry cloth in freezer). Flip the dough at least once, adding a little more flour to the pastry cloth. Roll out to fit pie pan.

For the Filling: Preheat oven to 375°F. Beat eggs until frothy. Add all remaining ingredients in order given, beating only until well blended. Pour filling into crust. Bake for 25 minutes.

For the Topping: Combine ingredients. Remove pie from oven and sprinkle topping over filling. Return pie to oven and bake 25 minutes more or until center is set.

PUMPKIN PIE WITH A KICK

Phyllis Bartholomew, Columbus, NE
2004 American Pie Council Crisco National Pie Championships
Amateur Division 3rd Place Pumpkin

CRUST
2 cups flour
1 cup cake flour
2 tablespoons Super Rich butter
  powder
1 cup Crisco shortening
1 whole egg
1 tablespoon cider vinegar
½ teaspoon salt
⅓ cup ice water

FILLING
¾ cup pureed pumpkin
½ cup sugar

⅛ teaspoon ground ginger
2 eggs
2 tablespoons blackstrap molasses
¼ teaspoon cinnamon
Dash of nutmeg
¾ cup half-and-half
¼ teaspoon salt

TOPPING
¾ cup sour cream
1½ tablespoons lemon juice
3 tablespoons brown sugar
Chopped pecans or pecan halves
  for garnish

For the Crust: Mix the flours and butter powder together. Cut in the shortening until it resembles coarse crumbs. Beat together the other ingredients and stir into the flour. Mix just until incorporated. Form dough into a disk and wrap in plastic wrap. Refrigerate to chill. Roll out about a third of the dough between 2 sheets of plastic wrap. Place crust in a 9-inch pie dish.

For the Filling: Preheat oven to 450°F. Blend all of the ingredients together and pour into a pastry-lined dish. Bake at 450°F for 10 minutes on bottom shelf. Then lower the temperature to 325°F and move the pie to the middle rack. Bake for an additional 40 to 45 minutes. Remove from oven (leave oven on) and add topping (recipe below).

For the Topping: Blend together sour cream, lemon juice, and brown sugar and pour on top of hot pie. Bake an additional 10 minutes. Garnish with a ring of chopped pecans or pecan halves. Let cool.

Pumpkin Pie with a Kick

PUMPKIN PIE WITH WALNUT GINGERSNAP TOPPING

Beth Campbell, Belleville, WI
2004 American Pie Council Crisco National Pie Championships
Amateur Division 2nd Place Pumpkin

CRUST
1 cup flour
½ cup Crisco shortening
Pinch of salt
¼ cup water

FILLING
1½ cups or small can of solid pack
   pumpkin
¾ teaspoon salt
¼ teaspoon mace
¾ teaspoon cinnamon
1 tablespoon flour
1 cup sugar

2 eggs, beaten
¾ cup scalded milk (don't boil; stop
   when you get a thin skin on the
   milk)
¾ cup scalded half-and-half (don't
   boil; stop when you get a thin skin
   on the cream)

TOPPING
1 cup chopped walnuts
¾ cups packed brown sugar
½ cup crushed gingersnaps
4 tablespoons butter, melted
½ teaspoon cinnamon

For the Crust: Cut shortening into flour and salt until pea-sized pieces form. Mix in cold water. Refrigerate until chilled. Roll out crust on floured board. Place into pie pan and prick the crust with a fork so it doesn't bubble.

For the Filling: Preheat oven to 350°F. Combine salt, mace, cinnamon, flour, and sugar. Add pumpkin. Add beaten eggs. Put milk and half-and-half in a pan and scald at the same time. Gradually pour milk mixture into the pumpkin mixture, stirring. Mix until well combined. Pour into the pie shells. Bake for 1 hour and 20 minutes or until knife in center comes out clean.

For the Topping: Prepare the walnut topping by mixing all of the ingredients together. Spoon the topping evenly over the prepared pie. About 5 to 7 inches away from the source of heat, broil the pie for 3 minutes or until the topping is golden brown. Watch carefully to avoid burning. Cool the pie on a wire rack.

Can be garnished with sweetened whipping cream that has a touch of cinnamon in it, if desired.

PUMPKIN PIE SURPRISE WITH CRYSTALLIZED GINGER SOUR CREAM TOPPING

Alberta Dunbar, San Diego, CA
2009 American Pie Council Crisco National Pie Championships
Amateur Division 2nd Place Pumpkin

CRUST
1½ cups flour
½ teaspoon salt
½ cup Crisco vegetable oil
¼ cup whole milk

FILLING LAYER ONE
¾ cup sugar
16 ounces can pumpkin
½ teaspoon salt
2½ teaspoons pumpkin pie spice
2 large eggs, slightly beaten
12 ounces can evaporated milk

FILLING LAYER TWO
16-ounce can pumpkin
14-ounce can condensed milk
3.4-ounce package French vanilla instant pudding

2½ teaspoons pumpkin pie spice
1 cup heavy whipping cream

GINGER CREAM TOPPING
1 cup heavy whipping cream
8-ounce carton sour cream
2 tablespoons sugar
1 teaspoon rum extract
½ teaspoon pure vanilla extract
⅓ cup crystallized ginger, minced

GARNISH
1 cup heavy whipping cream
¼ cup sifted powdered sugar
1 teaspoon rum extract
2 teaspoons crystallized ginger, minced

For the Crust: Preheat oven to 425°F. Combine all ingredients in a medium bowl. Mix well with a fork to form a ball. Flatten and place between two sheets of waxed paper. Roll out to fit a 10-inch pie dish. Place in dish and crimp edges. Bake 10 to 15 minutes and cool.

For Filling Layer One: Place sugar, pumpkin, salt, and pumpkin pie spice in a large bowl. Mix well with a wooden spoon. Stir in eggs and mix well. Stir in milk until smooth. Pour into prepared shell. Bake for 15 minutes at 425°F. Reduce heat to 350°F and bake from 40 to 50 minutes or until knife inserted comes out clean. Cool on rack or place in freezer to speed cool.

For Filling Layer Two: Place pumpkin, condensed milk, instant pudding, and pie spice in a medium bowl, beat well with an electric mixer on high for 2 minutes. Whip cream until stiff peaks form. With wooden spoon, carefully fold into pumpkin mixture. Carefully spread over cooled first layer. Refrigerate until set (2 to 3 hours) or place in freezer (30 minutes) until set.

For the Topping: Combine cream, sour cream, and sugar in a small bowl. Beat on high for 2 minutes. Fold in extracts and ginger with a wooden spoon. Carefully spread over pie and chill 30 minutes or until set.

For the Garnish: Place all ingredients except ginger in small bowl and beat on high until stiff. Place in a pastry bag fitted with a large rosette tip. Pipe large rosettes around outer edge of pie. Sprinkle with the crystallized ginger in center of pie. Chill until ready to serve.

PUMPKIN PIE WITH PECAN TOPPING

Phyllis Bartholomew, Columbus, NE
2006 American Pie Council Crisco National Pie Championships
Amateur Division 1st Place Pumpkin

CRUST
2 cups flour
1 cup cake flour
1 cup Crisco shortening
1 whole egg
1 tablespoon apple cider vinegar
½ teaspoon salt
⅓ cup ice water

FILLING
¾ cup brown sugar
½ teaspoon salt

2 teaspoons pumpkin pie spice
2 eggs
2 cups pumpkin pulp or canned pumpkin
1½ cups heavy cream

TOPPING
⅔ cup brown sugar
3 tablespoons milk
2 tablespoons syrup
⅓ cup chopped pecans

For the Crust: Cut the shortening into the flours. Beat together the rest of the ingredients and add to the flour mixture. Mix just until incorporated. Form into a disk and wrap in plastic and chill. Roll out and line pie dish.

For the Filling: Preheat oven to 400°F. Blend all ingredients together and pour into 9-inch pastry lined pie dish. Bake for about an hour. Cool and then add the pecan topping.

For the Topping: In a small saucepan, heat the sugar, milk, and syrup just until sugar is melted. Add the pecans and cool. Pour on top of the cooled pie. Serve with whipped topping or ice cream.

AMAZING PUMPKIN PIE

Jennifer Morris, Debary, FL
2013 American Pie Council Crisco National Pie Championships
Amateur Division 1st Place Pumpkin

CRUST
2 cups finely crushed ginger snaps
⅓ cup butter

GANACHE
80 pumpkin spice Hershey kisses
¼ cup heavy whipping cream
1 tablespoons butter
1 tablespoons Karo Syrup

FILLING ONE
1¼ cup Ready-To-Eat Cheesecake
   Filling

FILLING TWO
⅛ teaspoon nutmeg
¾ cup milk

1 cup heavy whipping cream
1 box Jell-O pumpkin spice instant
   pudding
1 teaspoon pumpkin pie spice

TOPPING
Whipping cream
2 tablespoons confectioners' sugar
½ teaspoon vanilla extract
Piping gel (to stabilize whipped
   cream)
Remaining ganache

For the Crust: Preheat oven to 325°F. Melt butter. Process gingersnaps in a food processor until fine crumbs form. Mix gingersnap crumbs and butter together, pack firmly in pie pan. Cook for 8 to 10 minutes.

For the Ganache: Melt Hershey Kisses, butter and heavy cream in microwave for about 45 seconds, then mix. Then add Karo syrup. Push mixture through strainer. Take ¾ of mixture and put on bottom of cooled pie crust. Put in refrigerator.

For Filling One: Take cheesecake filling and spread evenly over ganache.

For Filling Two: Mix together nutmeg, milk, heavy cream, pumpkin pudding, and pumpkin pie spice. Mix till thick and creamy. Spoon over cheesecake layer evenly.

For the Topping: Mix together whipping cream and confectioners' sugar about 10 minutes until soft peaks form. Continue mixing and add piping gel and vanilla extract. Keep mixing until stiff peaks form. Pour leftover ganache from center spreading out over top of pie. Pipe with whipped cream.

Amazing Pumpkin Pie

HOLIDAY PUMPKIN SURPRISE

David Harper, Richland Center, WI
2013 American Pie Council Crisco National Pie Championships
Amateur Division 3rd Place Pumpkin

CRUST
½ cup butter-flavored Crisco
1 cup flour
1 teaspoon salt
5 tablespoons ice-cold water

FILLING ONE
1 cup dark corn syrup
1 cup white sugar
4 eggs
2 teaspoons vanilla
6 tablespoons melted butter
2 cups chopped pecans

FILLING TWO
½ cup sugar
1 teaspoon salt
1 (15-ounce) can pumpkin

8 ounces cream cheese, softened to
    room temperature
1 can sweet condensed milk
⅓ cup instant vanilla pudding
1¼ teaspoon unflavored gelatin
2 tablespoons water
1 teaspoon cinnamon
¼ teaspoon nutmeg

WHIPPED CREAM TOPPING
1½ cups heavy whipping cream
¼ cup powdered sugar
¼ teaspoon nutmeg
1 teaspoon vanilla

GARNISH
½ cup pecans, chopped
Sprinkling of nutmeg

For the Crust: Preheat oven to 350°F. Whisk the flour and the salt together in a large bowl. Add the Crisco and mix with your fingers until combined. Add the ice water and use a fork to combine. Turn pie dough out onto a floured surface and gather into a circular disk. Roll out the dough big enough to fit into a pie plate. Flute edges for decoration. Place into the refrigerator until ready to use.

For Filling One: Combine first five ingredients in a large bowl and whisk until smooth. Remove crust from refrigerator and place 2 cups of chopped pecans on the bottom of shell. Pour the filling over the pecans. Place in oven and bake for 50 to 60 minutes or until filling is just set when jiggled. Remove from oven and cool on wire rack until room temperature. Chill in the refrigerator for at least 6 hours. Wait to make the pumpkin filling until pecan pie is sufficiently chilled.

For Filling Two: Place sugar and cream cheese in mixer bowl and mix until smooth. Add the can of sweetened condensed milk, pudding mix, salt, and pumpkin and mix until smooth. Place the water in a small bowl and sprinkle the gelatin over the water. Microwave for 15 seconds. With mixer running, add the gelatin mixture to the pumpkin mixture. Mix in cinnamon and nutmeg. Pour pumpkin mixture on top of the chilled pecan pie. You may have more filling than will fit on the pie. Just slowly add the filling and mound the top as much as you can. Chill the pie until set, about 3 hours.

For the Whipped Cream Topping: Combine all ingredients and whip until stiff peaks form. Top chilled pie with whipped cream and sprinkle with chopped pecans and nutmeg.

Holiday Pumpkin Surprise

PUMPKIN CHOCOLATE SURPRISE PIE

Alberta Dunbar, San Diego, CA
2012 American Pie Council Crisco National Pie Championships
Amateur Division 1st Place Pumpkin

CRUST
1⅓ cups all-purpose flour
½ teaspoon salt
½ stick Crisco all vegetable
   shortening
3 to 6 tablespoons ice water

FILLING
12 ounces cream cheese, softened
¼ cup granulated sugar
1 egg, lightly beaten
6 ounces semisweet chocolate,
   chopped

15-ounce can pumpkin
⅔ cup brown sugar, packed
2 teaspoons pumpkin pie spice
4 eggs, lightly beaten
¾ cup light cream

GARNISH
2½ cups heavy cream
¼ cup powdered sugar, sifted
1 teaspoon vanilla extract
Chocolate curls

For the Crust: Preheat oven to 400°F. Spoon the flour into measuring cup and level. Mix flour and salt in a medium bowl. Cut in shortening using pastry blender or two knives until flour is blended and forms pea-size chunks. Sprinkle with 1 tablespoon of water at a time. Toss lightly with a fork until dough forms a ball. Roll out on lightly floured board to fit a 9-inch deep dish pie plate with ½-inch overlap. Fold under and flute edges. Prick bottom and sides with a fork. Line pastry with a double layer of foil. Bake 8 minutes. Remove foil; bake 5 to 6 minutes more or until golden brown. Cool on rack completely before filling. Lower oven temperature to 375°F.

For the Filling: In a medium mixing bowl, beat cream cheese, sugar, and egg on low speed until smooth. Spread cream cheese mixture on bottom of cooled pastry shell. Sprinkle with chopped chocolate. In a bowl, combine pumpkin, brown sugar, and spice. Stir in 4 eggs. Gradually stir in light cream. Slowly pour pumpkin mixture on chocolate layer. To prevent overbrowning, cover pie edge with foil. Bake 60 to 65 minutes or until knife inserted near center comes out clean. Remove foil. Cool on wire rack. Cover and refrigerate within 2 hours.

For the Garnish: In a medium bowl, combine cream, sugar, and extract; with an electric beater, beat on high speed until stiff. Fill a pastry bag with small tip and decorate top of pie as desired. Add chocolate curls to top of pie.

Pumpkin Chocolate Surprise Pie

MAPLE CRUNCH PUMPKIN PIE

Jill Jones, Palm Bay, FL
2012 American Pie Council Crisco National Pie Championships
Amateur Division 2nd Place Pumpkin

CRUST
1 cup flour
½ teaspoon salt
½ cup shortening
¼ tablespoon sugar
¼ tablespoon vinegar
1 egg
1½ tablespoons ice cold water

FILLING
6- or 7-inch cooking pumpkin
    (to make 2 cups pumpkin)
¾ cup sugar
½ teaspoon salt
1 teaspoon cinnamon
1½ teaspoons pumpkin pie spice
Smidgen nutmeg
¼ teaspoon vanilla

2 tablespoons maple syrup
2 eggs
14-ounce can sweetened condensed
    milk

TOPPING
½ cup walnuts, chopped fine
2 tablespoons brown sugar
½ teaspoon cinnamon
1 teaspoon pumpkin pie spice
¼ cup oatmeal
2 tablespoon maple syrup

GARNISH
1 cup heavy whipping cream
2 tablespoons sugar

For the Crust: Mix flour, salt, and sugar together. Cut in shortening with a fork or pastry cutter until mixture is crumbly. Add egg, vinegar, and water to mixture until it comes together and is a little sticky. Scrape out bowl onto a floured surface. Roll into a ball. Wrap in plastic wrap and refrigerate for 1 hour. Roll out on a floured surface and place in a pie dish.

For the Filling: Cut the pumpkin in half, scrape out seeds, string membranes, and the stem and cut into quarters. Steam pumpkin pieces in a double boiler until pumpkin is soft and skin peels off, about 45 to 60 minutes. Peel and mash pumpkin with a potato masher.

Squeeze water out by using a cheese cloth. Mix pumpkin with salt, sugar, cinnamon, pumpkin pie spice, nutmeg, vanilla, and syrup. Mix well, and then add eggs and milk. Mix until blended. Pour into an unbaked pie shell.

For the Topping: Mix ingredients together and sprinkle over pie. Bake pie at 425°F for 15 minutes. Then reduce temperature to 350°F. Place pie guard on pie and bake for 40 to 50 minutes. Let cool.

For the Garnish: Mix ingredients until stiff peaks form. Top pie to your liking before serving.

Maple Crunch Pumpkin Pie

PUMPKIN CHEESECAKE PIE

Bev Johnson, MN
2012 Amateur American Pie Council Crisco National Pie Championships
Amateur Division 3rd Place Pumpkin

CRUST
1½ cups flour
1 tablespoon sugar
½ teaspoon salt
½ cup cold shortening, cut into
  pieces
¼ cup cold water

CHEESE LAYER
4 ounces white chocolate
4 ounces cream cheese, softened
1 tablespoon honey
1 egg, room temperature
½ cup heavy cream

PUMPKIN LAYER
1 envelope unflavored gelatin
¼ cup cold water

1½ cups pumpkin
1 cup light brown sugar
3 eggs, separated
½ teaspoon salt
½ teaspoon ginger
½ teaspoon plus ¼ teaspoon
  cinnamon
2 tablespoons sugar
½ cup heavy whipping cream

TOPPING
2 cups heavy whipping cream
½ cup Coffee-mate Italian Sweet
  Crème
2 tablespoons powdered sugar
6 teaspoons piping gel

For the Crust: Combine flour, sugar, and salt; mix well. Cut shortening into dry ingredients. Mix in cold water. Flatten the dough into a disk about ¾ inch thick. Wrap in plastic and refrigerate for at least an hour or overnight. Roll out and place pastry in a 9-inch deep dish pie plate; flute edges. Place it in the freezer for 15 minutes. Line un-pricked shell with double thickness of aluminum foil. Preheat oven to 450°F and bake pie crust for 8 minutes. Remove foil; bake for 5 minutes. Cool.

For the Cheese Layer: Melt white chocolate in double boiler over simmering water. Beat cream cheese and honey until fluffy. Beat in white chocolate. Add egg, beat well. Beat in cream and continue beating until smooth. Pour into crust, cover edges with foil. Bake at 325°F for 30 minutes until set. Cool for one hour; cover with plastic wrap, and refrigerate overnight.

For the Pumpkin Layer: Soften gelatin in cold water. Combine pumpkin, brown sugar, egg yolks, spices, and salt in the top of a double boiler; cook over hot (not boiling) water until thickened, stirring constantly. Add softened gelatin to hot pumpkin mixture and stir until dissolved. Remove from hot water, chill until mixture begins to thicken. Beat egg whites until stiff; beat in granulated sugar. Fold into cooled pumpkin mixture. Whip cream and fold into pumpkin mixture, Pour onto cheese layer; chill.

For the Topping: Whip cream, then add Coffee-mate and powdered sugar; mix in piping gel. Spread topping on top of pie and pipe around the edge.

Pumpkin Cheesecake Pie

RAISIN

21ST NIGHT OF SEPTEMBER

John Sunvold, Orlando, FL
2010 American Pie Council Crisco National Pie Championships
Amateur Division 3rd Place California Raisin

CRUST
1½ cups graham cracker crumbs
¼ cup sugar
6 tablespoons butter, melted
Pinch of cinnamon (optional)

FILLING
1 cup California raisins
15-ounce can of pumpkin
1 cup chunky applesauce
   (sweetened)
3 eggs, beaten
½ cup dark brown sugar
½ teaspoon salt

¼ cup cream or half-and-half
1½ tablespoons all-purpose flour
1 teaspoon vanilla extract
2½ teaspoons pumpkin pie spice

TOPPING
8 ounces cream cheese
½ cup butter, softened
2 cups powdered sugar
1 teaspoon vanilla extract

GARNISH
Chopped nuts or other nut topping
   (optional)

For the Crust: Preheat oven to 350°F. Mix all ingredients together and press mixture into a 9-inch deep dish pie plate. Bake for 10 minutes, or until brown. Allow to cool down to room temperature.

For the Filling: Mix pumpkin, eggs, brown sugar, salt, cream, flour, vanilla, and spice together until blended. Gently mix in the chunky applesauce, being careful not to break up the chunks of apple. Pour a third of this mixture into the piecrust and then sprinkle half of the raisins over the entire pie. Pour another third gently over the raisins, and cover with the rest of the raisins. Finally, top off pie with the rest of the pumpkin filling. Bake at 350°F for 45 to 55 minutes. Pie is done when it is set in the center. Remove from heat and cool on a cooling rack. Chill pie for least four hours.

For the Topping: Cream butter, cream cheese, and vanilla together, then add powdered sugar until blended. Spread over pie. Top with chopped walnuts or favorite nut topping, if desired.

APPLE RAISIN STRUDEL PIE

Christine Montalvo, Windsor Heights, IA
2008 American Pie Council Crisco National Pie Championships
Amateur Division 3rd Place California Raisin

CRUST
2 cups all-purpose flour
1 cup cake flour
½ teaspoon salt
1 cup butter-flavored Crisco shortening, frozen and cut into small pieces
1 large egg
1 tablespoon apple cider vinegar
⅓ cup cold water

FILLING
5 cups of thinly sliced Granny Smith, Golden Delicious, and Red Delicious apples (about 2 each)
1 cup brown sugar
¼ cup water
1 tablespoon lemon juice
1½ cups California raisins
¼ cup flour
2 tablespoons sugar
¾ teaspoon salt
1 teaspoon cinnamon
¼ teaspoon nutmeg
⅛ teaspoon ground cloves
1 teaspoon vanilla
3 tablespoons butter

STRUDEL TOPPING
⅛ cup butter
¼ cup sugar
¾ teaspoon vanilla
½ cup cake flour

For the Crust: Preheat oven to 425°F. In food processor, combine the flours and salt. Add the shortening pieces and pulse until dough resembles coarse crumbs. Set aside. In a small bowl, beat together the egg, vinegar, and water. Add egg mixture to the flour mixture and combine with a fork, just until the dough comes together. Do not over mix. Form dough into 2 disks, wrap in plastic, and chill for a least one hour or overnight. Roll out one piece of crust into a 12-inch circle. Fit into a 9-inch deep dish pie plate. Flute edges.

For the Filling: Combine apples, brown sugar, water, lemon juice, and raisins in a large pot.

Cover and cook over medium heat about five minutes or until the apples are just tender. In a small bowl, mix flour, sugar, salt, cinnamon, nutmeg, and ground cloves until combined. Stir into apple mixture. Cook, stirring constantly until the syrup thickens, about 2 minutes. Remove from heat and stir in vanilla and butter. Pour into crust.

For the Strudel Topping: Knead butter and sugar by hand; add vanilla. Add cake flour a little at a time and mix by hand until crumbs are formed. Do not over mix. Sprinkle evenly over pie. Bake 40 to 45 minutes or until the crust is golden brown. Remove from oven and cool.

Apple Raisin Strudel Pie

CALIFORNIA DREAM RAISIN AND SOUR CREAM PIE WITH SURPRISE MAPLE RAISIN STUFFED CRUST

Karen Hall, Elm Creek, NE
2008 American Pie Council Crisco National Pie Championships
Amateur Division 1st Place California Raisin

CRUST
3 cups unbleached flour
1 cup plus 1 tablespoon butter-
    flavored Crisco, cold
½ teaspoon baking powder
1 egg
1 teaspoon sea salt
¼ cup plus 1 tablespoon ice-cold
    water
1 tablespoon sugar
1 tablespoon rice vinegar

STUFFING FOR STUFFED CRUST
1 cup California raisins
½ cup hot water
2 tablespoons water
2 teaspoons cornstarch
2 tablespoons butter
½ cup pure maple syrup
½ teaspoon cinnamon
¼ cup chopped walnuts

FILLING
1 cup California raisins
½ cup hot water
⅔ cup sugar
1 teaspoon cinnamon
2 tablespoons cornstarch
½ cup half-and-half
1 cup sour cream
3 egg yolks, beaten
1 teaspoon vanilla
2 tablespoons butter

MERINGUE
4 egg whites
3 tablespoons sugar
¼ teaspoon cream of tartar
½ teaspoon vanilla

For the crust: In a large bowl, combine flour, baking powder, salt, and sugar. With a pastry blender, cut in Crisco until mixture resembles coarse crumbs. In a small bowl, beat egg, water, and vinegar together. Add egg mixture slowly to flour mixture, tossing with a fork until mixture is moistened. Do not over mix. Divide dough and shape into 3 balls; flatten each to form a disk. Wrap each disk with plastic wrap and refrigerate for at least 30 minutes before using. Makes 3 single crusts. Use two disks for this recipe.

For the Stuffed Crust: Preheat oven to 425°F. To plump raisins, place raisins and ½ cup hot water in a small bowl and set aside. Combine 2 tablespoons water and the cornstarch in a small bowl. In a small saucepan, melt butter; add maple syrup, cinnamon, and cornstarch mixture. Cook over medium heat 3 to 4 minutes or until thickened. Drain raisins; stir raisins and walnuts into mixture. Cook 1 to 2 minutes longer. Set aside.

Roll out a single crust and place in a 9-inch pie dish. Trim and flute edge. Roll out second crust; cut out one 8-inch circle from pastry. Spread raisin maple filling into bottom of pie pastry. Place 8-inch pastry on top of maple raisin filling; pat together gently. Protect edge with foil. Bake for 12 to 15 minutes, or until golden.

For the Filling: To plump raisins, place raisins and hot water into a small bowl; set aside. In a medium saucepan, combine sugar, cinnamon, and cornstarch. Stir in half-and-half and sour cream; cook over medium heat 8 to 10 minutes or until mixture begins to thicken; whisk in egg yolks. Drain raisins and stir into pudding; cook until thickened. Stir in vanilla and butter. Spoon pudding into pie shell, then prepare meringue.

For the Meringue: Preheat oven to 375°F. In a large mixing bowl, beat egg whites until frothy; continue beating, adding sugar one tablespoon at a time. Add cream of tartar and vanilla, beating until stiff peaks form. Dollop meringue onto pie. Bake for 8 to 10 minutes or until golden. Keep pie refrigerated.

FALL'S IN THE AIR RAISIN PIE

Barbara Polk, Albuquerque, NM
2011 American Pie Council Crisco National Pie Championships
Amateur Division 3rd Place California Raisin

CRUST
1½ cups all-purpose flour plus 2 tablespoons for roll out
½ teaspoon salt
⅝ cup butter-flavored Crisco
1 small egg, beaten
½ tablespoon white distilled vinegar
2 to 3 tablespoons cold water

FILLING
1 cup dark California raisins
1¾ cups Granny Smith apples, peeled and chopped
½ cup canned jellied cranberry sauce, chopped
1 cup chopped walnuts
¾ teaspoon lemon zest
¼ cup lemon juice
1 cup granulated sugar
⅛ teaspoon salt
¼ teaspoon ginger
¼ teaspoon cloves
¾ teaspoon cinnamon

GINGERSNAP STREUSEL
½ cup gingersnap cookies, finely ground
½ cup brown sugar
¼ cup butter, cold

For the Crust: Preheat oven to 400°F. Cut in Crisco, flour, and salt. In a cup mix egg, vinegar, and 2 tablespoons cold water. Sprinkle on flour and fluff in. Add more water if too dry. Form dough into a ball. Flour wide wax paper and place dough in center. Top with another piece of wax paper and roll out 3 inches larger than pie plate. Remove top wax paper and invert dough into 9-inch pie plate. Trim to ½ inch larger than pie plate, fold under and flute edges. Roll out dough trimmings and cut into fall leaves for decorations. Bake in a tin for 10 minutes. Put fall leaves on crumb top when pie is done.

For the Filling: Combine raisins, apples, cranberry sauce, walnuts, lemon zest, and lemon juice in a large bowl. In a smaller bowl mix sugar and spices together, then stir into apple mixture. Pour into crust.

For the Gingersnap Streusel: Cut butter into cookie crumbs and brown sugar. Sprinkle on filling. Bake at 400°F for 45 minutes.

Falls in the Air Raisin Pie

ORANGE-RAISIN-CARROT PIE

Naylett LaRochelle, Miami, FL
2008 American Pie Council Crisco National Pie Championships
Amateur Division 2nd Place California Raisin

CRUST
2½ cups flour
1 tablespoon sugar
1 teaspoon salt
½ cup solid Crisco butter-flavored
    shortening
1 stick unsalted butter, cold
5 to 6 tablespoons ice water mixed
    with 1 teaspoon red wine vinegar
Egg wash

FILLING
3 large eggs
¾ cup brown sugar corn syrup or
    light corn syrup
¼ cup brown sugar
½ cup granulated sugar

¼ cup butter or margarine, melted
1 teaspoon ground cinnamon
½ teaspoon ground ginger
¼ teaspoon ground nutmeg
¼ teaspoon salt
1 cup California dark raisins
1 teaspoon orange extract
1 tablespoon orange peel, grated
1 cup finely shredded carrots
¾ cup chopped walnuts

TOPPING
1 cup powdered sugar
8 ounces cream cheese, softened
1½ tablespoons fresh orange juice
1 tablespoon orange peel, grated

For the Crust: Combine dry ingredients in a large bowl. Add Crisco with a pastry blender, then add water 1 tablespoon at a time until coarse and pea-like. Refrigerate for ½ hour. Roll out crust and place in pie plate. Brush a thin layer of egg wash onto the bottom and sides of the dough.

For the Filling: Preheat oven to 375°F. In a large bowl, whisk eggs. Add the remaining ingredients and stir. Pour the carrot-raisin mixture into pie crust and bake until the center of the filling is set but quivery, about 45 to 50 minutes.

Let cool completely on a rack, about 2 to 3 hours.

For the Topping: In a medium bowl, beat powdered sugar and cream cheese until smooth and creamy; add orange juice and orange peel. Pour topping into medium-sized Ziploc bag, snip a small piece off one corner. Pipe rosettes on pie. Garnish with more orange zest/peel, if desired.

Orange-Raisin-Carrot Pie

SUNSHINE RAISIN PIE

Janet Ropp, Edgewater, FL
2009 American Pie Council Crisco National Pie Championships
Amateur Division 3rd Place California Raisin

CRUST
30 saltine crackers
2 cups pecans, toasted
1 teaspoon sugar
Pinch of salt
1 tablespoon orange zest
1½ teaspoon cinnamon
5 tablespoons butter, melted

FILLING ONE
2 cups orange juice
1 cup jumbo red raisins
½ cup golden raisins
2 tablespoons maple syrup
1 teaspoon cinnamon extract
1 teaspoon butter extract

FILLING TWO
⅔ cup flour
¾ cup sugar
4 eggs, beaten
¼ cup light brown sugar
4 tablespoons butter, melted
1 cup white corn syrup
¼ cup maple syrup
3 teaspoons vanilla extract
2 tablespoons orange zest
½ cup dates
½ cup pecans

For the Crust: Grind crackers and pecans in food processor until finely ground. Add sugar, salt, orange zest, and cinnamon, then blend well. With food processor running, add melted butter and mix well. Lightly grease 9-inch glass pie pan. Press mixture into pan.

For Filling One: In medium saucepan, combine orange juice, raisins, maple syrup, cinnamon extract, and butter extract. Cook over low heat until raisins are plump, about 30 minutes. With slotted spoon, spoon raisins into pie crust.

For Filling Two: Preheat oven to 350°F. Combine flour and sugars. Add eggs, syrups, vanilla extract, orange zest, and melted butter, mixing well. Stir in dates. Spoon mixture over raisins in pie crust. Sprinkle on the pecans. Bake on cookie sheet for 25 minutes with edge of crust shielded. Remove shield and bake for another 20 minutes or until filling is set. Remove from oven and cool on wire rack. Garnish with candied orange peel, if desired.

DUAL RAISINS AND OTHER GOODIES PIE

Alberta F. Dunbar, San Diego, CA
2013 American Pie Council Crisco National Pie Championships
Amateur Division 1st Place California Raisin

CRUST
1½ cups all-purpose flour
½ teaspoon salt
½ cup Crisco shortening
3 to 4 tablespoons ice water

FILLING
1½ cups golden raisins
1½ cups raisins
1 cup maple syrup
½ cup packed brown sugar
½ cup sugar
1 tablespoon molasses
2 tablespoons cornstarch or pie enhancer
¼ cup butter
½ teaspoon salt
6 extra-large egg yolks, slightly beaten

2 tablespoons fresh lemon juice
½ cup heavy cream
½ cup orange marmalade
¾ cup chopped toasted walnuts

TOPPING
1½ cups sour cream
½ cup sugar
½ teaspoon orange extract
1½ teaspoons finely grated orange peel

GARNISH
1½ cups heavy cream
2 tablespoons sifted powdered sugar
½ teaspoon vanilla extract
2 teaspoons finely grated orange peel
Thin slice of a fresh orange, twisted

For the Crust: Preheat oven to 450 °F. Mix flour and salt together, cut in shortening using pastry blender or 2 knives until flour is blended and forms pea-size chunks. Sprinkle with 1 tablespoon of water at a time. Toss lightly with a fork until dough forms a ball. Roll on a lightly floured surface until pastry is large enough to fit a 9-inch deep dish pie pan, with ½-inch overlap. Transfer pastry to pie pan and fold edges under and flute using fingers. Prick bottom with fork and bake for 10 to 12 minutes or until golden brown. Cool completely before adding filling.

For the Filling: Place raisins in microwave safe bowl, cover with water. Microwave 2½ minutes on high setting. Set aside. Combine maple syrup, brown sugar, sugar, salt, molasses, and butter in a medium sauce pan. Stir lemon juice into cornstarch to dissolve, mix well with first mixture. Stir in cream and marmalade and mix well. Bring to a boil over medium heat, stirring constantly, and cook 3 minutes. Add one cup to eggs, mix well, and return to pan stirring constantly cook 2 minutes. Drain raisins well and pat dry add to pan with the nuts mix well. Cool 5 minutes. Pour into pie shell. Chill 10 minutes.

For the Topping: In a small bowl, combine topping ingredients. Pour over pie evenly. Place in a 350°F oven for 5 minutes. Chill until set about 1 hour.

For the Garnish: Combine cream, powdered sugar, and vanilla extract in a small bowl. Beat on high until stiff. Pipe a border around pie of large rosettes. Top each with the grated orange peel. Place the twisted orange slice in center of pie.

Duel Raisin and Other Goodies Pie

CALIFORNIA GOLDEN RAISIN BUTTERSCOTCH PIE

Carol Socier, Bay City, MI

CRUST
1 cup all-purpose flour
½ cup cake flour
½ teaspoon salt
½ teaspoon sugar
¼ teaspoon baking powder
½ cup butter-flavored Crisco
¼ cup cold water
2 teaspoons rice vinegar
1 small egg, beaten

FILLING
1½ cups California golden raisins
½ cup 7UP
1½ cups packed brown sugar

¼ cup all-purpose flour
⅛ teaspoon salt
3 egg yolks, beaten
1½ cups whole milk
2 tablespoons margarine or butter
1 teaspoon vanilla
½ cup finely chopped walnuts
1 cup miniature marshmallows

TOPPING
1 cup powdered sugar
8 ounces cream cheese, softened
1 teaspoon vanilla paste

For the Crust: Preheat oven to 425°F. In medium size bowl, combine flours, salt, sugar, and baking powder. Add shortening, cutting with a fork until coarse pieces form. In shaker, mix water, vinegar, and egg. Shake well. Add to flour mixture small amounts at a time, tossing with a fork until dough ball forms. Shape into a disk. Roll to fit a 9-inch deep dish pie pan. Flute edges, trimming excess dough. Chill for 30 minutes. Prick all over with a fork. Bake for about 12 to 14 minutes or until golden brown.

For the Filling: In small saucepan bring raisins and 7 UP to a boil. Cover and let set overnight or at least 1 hour. In non-stick saucepan, stir together the brown sugar, flour, and salt. Add egg yolks and milk. Cook while stirring until thick and bubbly. Cook and stir 2 minutes more. Remove from heat. Stir in margarine or butter and vanilla. Fold in raisin mixture, nuts, and marshmallows. Pour into prepared crust.

For the Topping: Beat powdered sugar, cream cheese, and vanilla paste together until smooth. Place in decorating gun and using rosette tip, pipe rosettes on top of pie.

California Golden Raisin Butterscotch Pie

SOUR CREAM RAISIN CRUNCH

Nikki Penley, Tipton, IN
2013 American Pie Council Crisco National Pie Championships
Amateur Division 3rd Place California Raisin

CRUST
¾ cup butter-flavored Crisco
2 cups all-purpose flour
2 teaspoons sugar
5 tablespoons cold water

FILLING
1½ cups white raisins
1½ cups dark raisins
1½ cups sour cream

3 egg whites
1 teaspoon cinnamon
1 tablespoon lemon juice
2 tablespoons flour

TOPPING
1 cup flour
1 cup sugar
1 stick softened butter

For the Crust: Preheat oven to 350°F. Combine flour and sugar. Cut in Crisco until crumbly. Add water one tablespoon at a time until dough starts to come together. Ball and flatten to a disk. Refrigerate ½ hour. Roll out and place in pie dish. Blind bake for 12 to 15 minutes or until golden brown.

For the Filling: Boil raisins until plump, drain, let cool. Add remaining ingredients, mix, and pour into baked pie shell.

For the Topping: Combine ingredients and spread evenly over raisin mixture. Bake for 40 minutes.

Sour Cream Raisin Crunch

SPECIAL CATEGORIES

Each year at the American Pie Council Crisco National Pie Championships we have a new category that we add in. Sometimes they are holiday oriented, date oriented, or just plain fun. The recipes in this chapter are from those categories.

BLUEBERRY POMEGRANATE CHEESE PIE

Evette Rahman, Orlando, FL
2011 American Pie Council Crisco National Pie Championships
Amateur Division 3rd Place Crisco Innovation

CRUST
2 cups shortbread cookie crumbs
½ cup flaked coconut
¼ cup finely chopped almonds
3 tablespoons sugar
½ cup Crisco shortening, melted

FILLING
8 ounces cream cheese, softened
½ cup powdered sugar
8 ounces extra creamy whipped topping

TOPPING
1 cup pure pomegranate juice
1 teaspoon fresh lemon juice
¼ cup sugar
1 tablespoon cornstarch
1 cup fresh blueberries
Sweetened whipped cream

For the Crust: Preheat oven to 350°F. Mix together crumbs, coconut, almonds, and sugar. Add in shortening and combine well. Press in bottom and up sides of a 9-inch pie plate. Bake for 10 minutes. Cool completely.

For the Filling: In large mixing bowl, beat together cream cheese and sugar. Fold in whipped topping and spread in prepared pie shell. Chill for 1 hour.

For the Topping: In saucepan over medium heat, whisk together juices, sugar, and cornstarch. Cook until thickened and starch taste is gone. Cool until slightly warm. Stir in blueberries. Chill in refrigerator. Spread over pie. Pipe on sweetened whipped cream.

Garnish if desired with any of the following: shaved white chocolate, fresh berries, toasted sliced almonds, and mint leaves.

Blueberry Pomegranate Cheese Pie

BOSTON CREAM PIE???

Kathryn Hanson, Orlando, FL
2011 American Pie Council Crisco National Pie Championships
Professional Division 3rd Honorable Mention Crisco Innovation

CRUST
1 cup pastry flour (sifted)
½ cup all-purpose flour (sifted)
½ teaspoon salt
4 teaspoons cocoa powder
4 teaspoons granulated sugar
½ cup Crisco shortening (cold)
3 to 4 tablespoons water (ice cold)

BAVARIAN CREAM
1 cup heavy cream
1 cup whole milk
1 vanilla bean pod, scraped,
¼ teaspoon salt
1 teaspoon powdered gelatin,
    dissolved in ¼ cup water
6 eggs yolks
⅔ cup granulated sugar

¼ cup cornstarch
1 tablespoon unsalted butter

CAKE LAYER
1 cup cake flour, sifted
⅔ cup sugar
1½ teaspoons baking powder
¼ teaspoon salt
½ cup milk
¼ cup Crisco cooking oil
2 eggs, separated
1 teaspoon vanilla extract
¼ teaspoon cream of tartar

CHOCOLATE GANACHE
½ cup heavy cream
½ cup 45 percent chocolate

For the Crust: Combine the flours, salt, cocoa powder, and sugar in a mixing bowl. Cut the cold shortening into the flour mixture. The mixture should have the appearance of tiny, irregular flakes and bits. Sprinkle the cold water over the mixture a tablespoon at a time, using just enough to form the dough into a ball. Pat the dough into small disks, wrap in plastic wrap, and chill.

On floured, dusted surface, roll the dough until it is about ⅛-inch thick and about 12 inches in diameter.

For the Filling: Slit vanilla bean pod and scrape out the insides; discard seeds. In small saucepan, combine heavy cream, milk, vanilla bean pod, salt, and granulated sugar. Stir until sugar is dissolved. Remove the vanilla bean pod. Soften the gelatin in ice-cold water and add to the cream mixture. Whisk the egg yolks and cornstarch together in separate bowl. Temper the egg yolks and cornstarch with the cream mixture. Return to heat and cook until thickened. Remove from heat; add the unsalted butter, mixing well. Strain the cream mixture through a china cap strainer, removing any possible lumps. Set aside to cool. Pour 1½ cups of the filling into the crust. Reserve the rest of filling.

For the Cake Layer: Preheat oven to 350°F. In a medium mixing bowl, combine flour, sugar, baking powder, and salt. Add milk, oil, egg yolks, and vanilla. Beat on medium low speed until combined, then on high for 3 minutes.

Boston Cream Pie???

In separate mixing bowl, whip the egg whites and cream of tartar until soft peaks form. Gently fold the egg yolk mixture into the egg whites. Pour batter into an 8-inch prepared cake pan. Bake for 25 to 30 minutes or until the top springs back when lightly touched. Invert onto a wire rack. Cool completely. Slice into 2 layers. Only half of the cake will be used in the pie. Place 1 layer on top of the Bavarian cream filling. Pour the rest of the Bavarian cream filling (approximately 1½ cups) on top of cake layer.

For the Chocolate Ganache: Chop the chocolate into small pieces and place in small bowl. Warm the heavy cream, making sure not to scald it. Pour the heavy cream over the chocolate and whisk quickly. Pour the ganache over the top of the pie.

Chill until ready to serve.

PILGRIM APPLE MINCEMEAT PIE

Marles Riessland, Riverdale, NE
2006 American Pie Council Crisco National Pie Championships
Amateur Division 1st Place Favorite Thanksgiving Pie

CRUST
1 cup pastry flour
2 cups all-purpose flour
1 teaspoon salt
1 teaspoon sugar
½ teaspoon baking powder
1 cup plus 1 tablespoon Crisco butter
   flavored shortening, chilled
⅓ cup water (ice cold)
1 tablespoon vinegar
1 egg, beaten
1 egg white, slightly beaten
1 tablespoon sugar

APPLE LAYER
4 cups apples (Rome or Jonathan)
2 teaspoons lemon juice

2 tablespoons butter
½ cup sugar
1 tablespoon tapioca
½ teaspoon cinnamon
⅛ teaspoon nutmeg
⅛ teaspoon salt
¼ teaspoon vanilla
1 tablespoon heavy cream

MINCEMEAT LAYER
27-ounce jar mincemeat
   (None Such brand Classic Original)

GARNISH (OPTIONAL)
Pastry cut-outs or dollops of
   whipped topping

For the Crust: Preheat oven to 450°F. In large bowl, combine the flour, salt, sugar, and baking powder. Cut in shortening with a pastry blender until the mixture resembles cornmeal. In small bowl, mix water and vinegar with the beaten egg. Add the liquid mixture, one tablespoon at a time, to the flour mixture, tossing with a fork to form a soft dough. Shape into three disks. Wrap in plastic wrap and chill in refrigerator. Use two disks when making this pie. Freeze remaining dough for later use. Roll out one pastry and place into a 9-inch pie dish for bottom crust. Mix egg white and sugar and use as an egg wash for top crust.

For the Apple Layer: Preheat oven to 450°F. Peel and slice apples. Sprinkle with lemon juice.

In heavy skillet, sauté apples and butter together over medium heat for about 8 minutes. Cool slightly. In medium bowl, combine sugar, tapioca, cinnamon, nutmeg, and salt. Add slightly cooled apples and mix well. Stir in vanilla and cream. Place apple mixture into bottom of pie crust, spreading evenly.

For the Mincemeat Layer: Spread the mincemeat on top of apple filling. Adjust top crust, seal, flute edge and vent top. Bake 15 minutes at 450°F. Reduce oven temperature to 350°F and bake 30 to 35 minutes longer or until golden.

Garnish is optional. Top pie with baked pastry cut outs or whipped topping, if desired.

RED VELVET CREAM PIE

Patricia Lapiezo, La Mesa, CA
2011 American Pie Council Crisco National Pie Championships
Amateur Division 2nd Place Crisco Innovation

CRUST
1½ cups all-purpose flour
⅓ cup powdered sugar
¼ cup plus 2 tablespoons finely
  chopped pecans
¼ teaspoon salt
½ cup butter-flavored Crisco
  shortening
3 to 4 tablespoons ice water
Melted white chocolate

FILLING
9-inch layer of a red velvet cake
  (either a mix or homemade)
12 ounces cream cheese, softened

½ cup powdered sugar
6 ounces white chocolate
¼ cup heavy cream
2 tablespoons white chocolate coffee
  syrup
¼ teaspoon cream cheese flavoring
  or vanilla extract
1½ cups heavy whipping cream,
  stiffly beaten

GARNISH
Sweetened whipped cream
Red velvet cake crumbs

For the Crust: Preheat oven to 400°F. Combine flour, powdered sugar, finely chopped pecans, and salt; cut in shortening until flour is blended to form pea-size chunks. Sprinkle mixture with water, 1 tablespoon at a time. Toss lightly with fork until dough forms a ball. Form a disk. Roll and press crust into a 9-inch pie plate. Flute edges. Prick bottom and sides with a fork and bake blind for 15 minutes. Remove pie weights and bake an additional 10 minutes or until golden brown. Lightly brush bottom and sides of crust with melted white chocolate. Cool while preparing filling.

For the Filling: Divide the cake layer into 2 layers. Trim one layer to fit into the bottom of the pie crust. Measure the top of the pie dish and trim the remaining layer to fit the top of the pie dish (reserve crumbs). Set aside the top piece. Place the smaller cake on the bottom of pie crust.

Heat ¼ cup heavy cream and the white chocolate until just melted. In a large mixing bowl, beat the cream cheese and powdered sugar until creamy and well blended. Blend in melted chocolate mixture. Blend in coffee syrup and flavoring. Fold in whipped cream. Spread over cake. Top with second cake layer.

Top pie with sweetened whipped cream and sprinkle center of pie with reserved cake crumbs. Garnish edge of pie with chopped pecans. Chill 2 hours to set.

Red Velvet Cream Pie

STRAWBERRY NAPOLEON

Michele Stuart, Norwalk, CT
2011 American Pie Council Crisco National Pie Championships
Professional Division 2nd Runner Up Crisco Innovation

CRUST
4 cups flour
2 teaspoons salt
½ cup Crisco
10 tablespoons ice water

CREAM FILLING
3 egg yolks, beaten
½ cup sugar
¼ teaspoon salt
⅓ cup flour

1⅓ cups whole milk
¾ cup water
1 vanilla bean
15 medium strawberries, thinly sliced

STRAWBERRY GLACÉ
1 cup fresh strawberries, mashed
1 cup sugar
3 tablespoons cornstarch
½ cup water

For the Crust: Preheat oven to 375°F. Combine ingredients until dough begins to form. Use about enough dough to prepare a single crust in a 9-inch ceramic deep dish. Brush edge of crust with cream. Bake the crust for about 20 minutes or until golden brown. Set aside and cool completely. With the remaining dough, on a floured surface, thinly roll out pie dough to a thickness of about ⅛ inch. With a sharp knife, using the bottom of a 9-inch pie pan, trace the circle so you have a circular disk. Repeat two more times so you have 3 circular disks. Place on a baking sheet. Brush with heavy cream and bake for 10 minutes at 375°F or until golden brown. Set aside and allow to cool completely.

For the Cream Filling: Combine the sugar, salt, and flour in a medium-sized saucepan and whisk them together. Add the milk and water to the whisked dry ingredients and heat the saucepan over medium heat, constantly whisking and scraping the sides of the pan. Monitor the mixture carefully; when it begins to simmer and becomes thick and bubbly after approximately 4 minutes, let it cook for 1 more minute. Mix 2 tablespoons of the heated mixture into the egg yolks (this will temper the egg yolks and prepare them so they cook properly in the cream). Pour the egg yolks into the cream in the saucepan and let the cream simmer for 2 minutes, stirring and scraping the sides constantly to prevent burning. Scrape vanilla bean and mix into saucepan. Pour ¾ cup cream mixture on the bottom of

Strawberry Napoleon Pie

the pie shell. Place a layer of the thinly sliced strawberries on top of the cream.

For the Glacé: Combine the mashed strawberries, sugar, cornstarch, and water in a medium-sized saucepan over high heat. Stir while the ingredients heat, for about 10 minutes or until the mixture attains a thick consistency. Let the glacé cool to room temperature and then place in the refrigerator prior to use. Spread a layer of strawberry glacé on the bottom of one of the pie dough disks. Place the dough disks with the glacé facing down on top of the strawberries. Repeat this layering three times until you have a disk on top. Refrigerate the pie overnight.

Spread a layer of whipped cream over the top disk. Garnish with the chocolate napoleon lines and strawberries.

LIZZY'S LEMON PIE

Johnna Poulson, Celebration, FL
2003 American Pie Council Crisco National Pie Championships
Amateur Division 2nd Place Celebration

CRUST
1⅓ cup all-purpose flour
½ teaspoon salt
½ cup shortening
3 to 4 tablespoons cold water

FILLING
1 cup sugar
2 tablespoons cornstarch
2 tablespoons flour
1 cup water
2 egg yolks, beaten

1 tablespoon butter
½ teaspoon fresh grated lemon peel
¼ cup fresh lemon juice
6 ounces chopped white chocolate
    baking bar
8 ounces cream cheese, softened

ALMOND TOPPING
1 cup whipping cream
1 tablespoon powdered sugar
1 teaspoon almond extract
1 tablespoon toasted sliced almonds

For the Crust: Preheat oven to 475°F. Combine flour and salt. Cut in shortening with pastry blender until mixture resembles coarse meal. Sprinkle in cold water one tablespoon at a time. Stir with a fork until dry ingredients are moistened. Shape into a ball and chill. Roll dough to 1/8-inch thickness on a lightly floured surface. Place in pie plate, trim off excess pastry along edges. Bake for 9 to 10 minutes until golden brown. Cool.

For the Filling: In a saucepan, combine sugar, cornstarch, and flour. Gradually add water until mixture is smooth. Cook over medium heat until mixture boils, stirring constantly. Lower heat and cook an additional 2 minutes. Remove from heat. Stir 1/4 cup of hot mixture into egg yolks. Add egg yolk mixture to the other mixture in the saucepan. Cook over low heat until the mixture boils. Cook 2 minutes, stirring constantly. Remove from heat. Stir in butter, lemon peel and lemon juice. Transfer third of the hot lemon filling to a smaller saucepan. Add chopped white chocolate baking bar. Stir over low heat until chocolate is melted. Cool remaining lemon mixture 15 minutes. Beat cream cheese until fluffy. Add melted white chocolate mixture. Beat until well blended. Spread over bottom of cooled baked pie shell. Spoon lemon mixture over cream cheese layer. Refrigerate 2 hours until set or overnight.

For the Almond Topping: In a small bowl, beat whipping cream. Add sugar and extract. Beat until cream forms soft peaks. Pipe over pie and garnish with toasted almonds.

CRANBERRY-RIBBON APPLE PIE

Christine Montalvo, Windsor Heights, IA
2007 American Pie Council Crisco National Pie Championships
Amateur Division 1st Place Holiday Pie

CRUST
2½ cups all-purpose flour
½ tablespoon sugar
¼ teaspoon salt
1½ cups chilled butter, cut into pieces
¼ cup chilled butter-flavored Crisco, cut into pieces
3 to 6 tablespoons (or more) iced water

FILLING
1½ cups plus 1 tablespoon sugar, divided
1 cup frozen 100 percent cranberry juice, thawed

2 (8-ounce) packages frozen cranberries
2 pounds Granny Smith apples, peeled, cored, and thinly sliced
1¾ pounds Golden Delicious apples, peeled, cored, thinly sliced
2 tablespoons flour
1 teaspoon lemon juice
½ teaspoon ground cinnamon

EGG WASH
1 egg white
1 tablespoon water

For the Crust: In food processor, combine flour, sugar, and salt. Pulse to blend. Add butter and Crisco pieces. Pulse until the flour mixture looks like coarse meal. Add about 3 tablespoons of the ice water and blend just until moist clumps form. Add additional water if needed. Do not over work. Remove dough and divide into 2 equal balls. Flatten each ball into a disk and wrap in plastic wrap. Chill in refrigerator for at least one hour before using. Roll out one dough disk on a floured surface into a 12-inch round. Transfer the dough to a 9-inch deep dish glass pie dish. Trim edges to 1 inch evenly around edge of pie plate.

For the Filling: Preheat oven to 400°F. In a medium saucepan, stir in ¾ cup of sugar and cranberry juice and cook over medium high-heat. Add frozen cranberries and bring to a simmer. Reduce heat and simmer until almost all the liquid is absorbed, stirring often, about 25 minutes. Remove from heat and cool completely. In a small bowl, blend cinnamon, flour, and remaining ¾ cup sugar together. Place sliced apples into a large mixing bowl and toss with lemon juice. Toss with cinnamon-sugar mixture so apples are evenly covered. Spread half of the cranberry mixture evenly on pie crust. Spread half of the apples over the cranberry filling; spread remaining cranberry mixture over apple layer. Finally, spread remaining apples over the cranberry layer.

Roll out remaining disk of dough on a floured surface into a 12-inch round. Carefully place

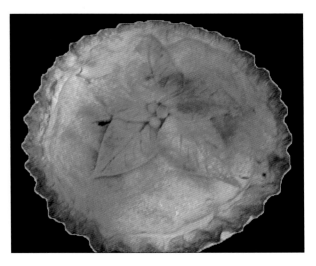

Cranberry-Ribbon Apple Pie

it over the filled pie dish. Trim edges and press crust edges and decoratively crimp the edges. Vent top with a sharp knife. Roll out remaining dough scraps and cut 5 large poinsettia petal shapes. Mix egg white and water together in small bowl. With a pastry brush, gently brush the back of each petal with the egg wash and arrange on top and center of the pie so that it looks like a poinsettia flower. Brush rest of top crust with egg white and sprinkle with remaining sugar and cinnamon that have been mix together.

Bake pie 15 minutes at 400°F. Reduce temperature to 375°F and bake until golden brown, about 50 minutes. Remove from oven and cool completely before serving.

RASPBERRY JALAPEÑO CREAM CHEESE PIE

Tammi Carlock, Chickamauga, GA
2013 American Pie Council Crisco National Pie Championships
Amateur Division 1st Place Crisco Innovation

CRUST
2 cups flour
1 teaspoon salt
⅔ cup Crisco
4 to 6 tablespoons ice water

FILLING
4 (8-ounce) packages cream cheese, softened
1⅔ cups sugar
2 eggs
¼ cup cornstarch
3 teaspoons vanilla
¾ cup heavy cream

TOPPING
1 cup raspberries
1 cup sugar
¼ cup cornstarch
2 teaspoons finely chopped jalapeños (without seeds)
½ cup water

GARNISH
1 cup heavy cream
2 tablespoons sugar
1 teaspoon vanilla
Fresh raspberries

For the Crust: Preheat oven to 425°F. Mix together flour and salt. Cut in shortening until you have pea-sized crumbs. Slowly add water, fluffing with a fork until dough holds together. Form ball and flatten to a disk. Roll out onto floured surface and fit into a 9-inch pie pan. Crimp edges. Line shell with foil and fill with pie weights. Bake for 15 minutes. Remove foil and weights and continue baking an additional 10 minutes or until golden brown. Set aside to cool on wire rack.

For the Filling: In the large bowl of an electric mixer, beat the cream cheese until very creamy. Add in the sugar and cornstarch gradually while beating at medium speed. Add eggs one at a time until completely mixed in. Add the vanilla and heavy cream and blend together. Pour into pie shell and bake at 350°F for 35 to 40 minutes or until pie is set (may still jiggle slightly in the middle). Let cool on wire rack.

For the Topping: Crush the raspberries in a small saucepan. Stir together the sugar and cornstarch and add to the raspberries; blend well. Stir in the water and jalapeños. Cook over medium heat until mixture has thickened. Boil and stir for 1 minute. Set aside to cool to room temperature.

For the Garnish: Spread top of pie with raspberry mixture. Beat heavy cream, sugar, and vanilla together until stiff peaks form. Pipe whipped cream onto edges of pie and top with raspberries.

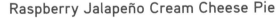

Raspberry Jalapeño Cream Cheese Pie

STRAWBERRY KIWI GREEN TEA PIE

Evette Rahman, Orlando, FL
2012 National Pie Championships
Amateur Division 1st Place Crisco Innovation

CRUST
2 cups fine vanilla wafer cookie crumbs
2 tablespoons sugar
½ cup butter-flavored Crisco shortening, melted
¼ teaspoon lemon extract

STRAWBERRY KIWI FILLING
2½ cups sliced strawberries, divided
1½ cups diced kiwi
½ cup sugar
½ tablespoon lemon juice
2 tablespoons cornstarch
2 tablespoons water
2 tablespoons strawberry flavored gelatin powder

3 tablespoons strawberry jam, melted
3 tablespoons apricot jam, melted

GREEN TEA FILLING
4 ounces cream cheese, softened
⅓ cup sweetened condensed milk
1 tablespoon green tea powder (Matcha)
1 tablespoon lemon juice
½ cup powdered sugar
8-ounce container of extra creamy frozen whipped topping, thawed

TOPPING
Sweetened whipped cream
Mint sprig for optional garnish

For the Crust: Preheat oven to 350°F. Mix together cookie crumbs and sugar. Stir in melted Crisco shortening and lemon extract. Press in bottom and up sides of a deep dish pie plate. Bake for 8 minutes. Cool completely.

For the Strawberry Kiwi Filling: In small blender, puree 1 cup of strawberries with 2 tablespoons of water. In small saucepan over medium heat, place pureed strawberries, sugar, lemon juice, and cornstarch. Cook, stirring frequently, until mixture is very thick. Remove from heat and stir in gelatin powder. Scrape into a medium size bowl. Cool 10 minutes. Stir in 1 cup of sliced strawberries and 1 cup of diced kiwi. Refrigerate. Mix remaining ½ cup of strawberries with melted strawberry jam. Mix remaining ½ cup of kiwi with melted apricot jam. Save for garnish.

For the Green Tea Filling: In large bowl, beat cream cheese until fluffy. Add in condensed milk, lemon juice, green tea powder (Matcha), lemon juice, and powdered sugar. Beat until well combined. Fold in whipped topping. Spread green tea filling in prepared pie crust. Top with strawberry kiwi filling.

For the Topping: Garnish pie with remaining strawberry and kiwi mixtures as desired. Top with dolloped or piped sweetened whipped cream. Garnish with mint sprig.

Strawberry Kiwi Green Tea Pie

BIRTHDAY CAKE SURPRISE

Michele Stuart, Norwalk, CT
2012 American Pie Council Crisco National Pie Championships
Professional Division Honorable Mention Crisco Innovation

CRUST
2 cups flour
1 teaspoon salt
¾ cup Crisco
5 tablespoons very cold water
Heavy cream to brush on crust

WHITE CAKE LAYER
2½ cups cake flour
1⅔ cups sugar
1 tablespoon baking powder
¾ teaspoon salt
¾ cup unsalted butter, softened
4 egg whites
1 egg
1 cup milk
3 teaspoons vanilla

VANILLA CREAM LAYER
3 egg yolks, beaten
½ cup sugar
¼ teaspoon salt
⅓ cup flour
1⅓ cups whole milk
¾ cup water
1 vanilla bean

BUTTERCREAM TOPPING
6 tablespoon butter, room
   temperature
2½ cups confectioners' sugar
3 tablespoon milk
¾ teaspoon vanilla
Sprinkles to decorate

For the Crust: Combine flour and salt. Cut Crisco into flour until the consistency resembles coarse meal. Sprinkle water over flour mixture one tablespoon at a time until dough forms a ball. Form dough into two disks. Wrap in plastic and chill in refrigerator for at least 1 hour. Roll out 1 disk and place in a 9-inch pan. Brush edge of crust with cream. Blind bake the pie shell at 425°F for 15 to 20 minutes or until golden brown. Let crust cool.

For the White Cake Layer: Mix all dry ingredients. Add the soft butter and mix. Add the egg whites and then the whole egg, one egg at a time. Slowly add the milk and vanilla. Beat for 1 minute. Pour the cake batter into a greased and floured 9-inch pan. Bake at 350°F for 20 to 25 minutes. Remove from the oven and cool. Once cooled, cut the cake into two equal layers.

For the Vanilla Cream Layer: Place the egg yolks in a mixing bowl and set them aside. Combine the sugar, salt, and flour in a medium-sized saucepan and whisk them together. Add the milk and water to the whisked dry ingredients and heat the saucepan over medium heat, constantly whisking and scraping the sides of the pan. Monitor the mixture carefully; when it begins to simmer and becomes thick and bubbly, after approximately four minutes, let it cook for one more minute. Add 2 tablespoons of the heated mixture to the egg yolks and mix them together

Birthday Cake Surprise Pie

well. Pour the egg yolks into the cream in the saucepan and let the cream simmer for 2 minutes, stirring and scraping the sides constantly to prevent burning. Add the vanilla bean and stir. Let stand to cool. Remove the bean before filling pie. Pour ½ of the vanilla cream into the bottom of the pie shell. Lay one layer of the cake on top of the cream. Then add the remaining cream on top of the cake. Add the second cake layer. Refrigerate the pie for at least 2 hours to set.

For the Buttercream Topping: In a mixing bowl, blend the butter until fluffy. Add the confectioners' sugar, the milk, and the vanilla. Beat at least 2 minutes or until light and fluffy. Decorate as you like with buttercream and sprinkles.

GOING BANANAS PIE

Susan Boyle, Debary, FL
2012 American Pie Council Crisco National Pie Championships
Professional Division 1st Place Crisco Innovation

CRUST
3 cups flour
1 egg
1 tablespoon white vinegar
1/8 teaspoon salt
1 cup Crisco (original or
  butter-flavored)
7 to 9 tablespoons cold water

GANACHE
2 cups chocolate chips
1/2 tablespoon white corn syrup
2 teaspoons butter, unsalted
1 pint regular whipping cream

WHIPPED TOPPING
2 cups heavy whipping cream
1/3 cup sugar

FILLING
1 bar white Lindt chocolate, melted
1/2 cup ganache (recipe above)
1 large box banana cream
  pudding mix
3 cups heavy whipping cream
1/4 cup sugar
1/2 cup pineapple juice
4 large semi-green bananas,
  sliced thin

GARNISH
8 or 9 vanilla wafers

For the Crust: Preheat oven to 400°F. In a large cold bowl, add flour and salt and mix well. Blend in Crisco until it resembles cornmeal. In a separate bowl, whip egg, vinegar, and water. Pour over flour mixture, stirring it with a fork until it forms a ball. Separate dough into two equal halves. Refrigerate one half of dough to use later for another pie. On a floured board, roll out dough 2 inches larger than your pie pan. Place in pie pan and flute the edges. Refrigerate while making the filling. Bake prepared crust at 400°F for 12 to 18 minutes or until golden brown. Place a guard over the edges of the pie to prevent burning. Cool before filling.

For the Ganache: Combine all ingredients except for corn syrup in a saucepan. Cook on medium heat. When mixture reaches 90°F, remove from heat. Strain to remove any large particles from chocolate chips. Add corn syrup and stir slowly trying not to add air bubbles. Refrigerate until firm. Spread ½ cup ganache on bottom of prebaked, cooled crust

For the Filling: Dip sliced bananas in pineapple juice to prevent browning. See aside. Whip 3 cups of heavy whipping cream, melted chocolate, sugar, and pudding mix. Whip until creamy but not stiff. Reserve ½ cup for garnish before adding bananas. Fold in the sliced bananas. Spoon filling onto the ganache. Whip cream and sugar together until firm but creamy. Cover very quickly with whipped topping to seal the banana filling.

Swirl the banana cream around edge of pie and decorate with a vanilla wafer.

Going Bananas Pie

AVOCADO DREAM PIE

Lois Spruytte, Richland, MI
2013 American Pie Council Crisco National Pie Championships
Amateur Division 3rd Place Crisco Innovation

CRUST
⅓ cup crushed almonds
1¼ cup flour
⅓ cup sugar
¼ teaspoon salt
½ cup butter-flavored Crisco
2 egg yolks, beaten and divided.

FILLING
2 mashed and pureed avocados
12 ounces softened cream cheese
1 cup sugar
¼ cup flour
½ teaspoon salt

2 eggs
4 ounces crème fraîche

TOPPING
1 small jar of Smucker's Strawberry
   jam
2 tablespoons water
3 tablespoons cornstarch

GARNISH
1 star fruit, cut
2 kiwis, cut
Mandarin oranges

For the Crust: Preheat oven to 400°F. Mix all but the Crisco in a medium bowl. Cut the Crisco in with a pastry blender or 2 butter knives. Add more than half of the egg yolks and toss with a fork. Pat down in an Emile Henry pie dish. Dock the crust, then bake it for 18 to 22 minutes. Add about 1 tablespoon of water to the remaining egg yolk. When the crust is done brush the egg yolk mixture all over. Reduce oven to 325°F and bake for 2 minutes longer.

For the Filling: In a mixer, beat cream cheese and sugar until nice and fluffy. Add flour and salt. Mix well, scraping the bowl. Add eggs, one at a time. Mix well. Add the crème fraîche and mix very well. Lastly, add the pureed avocado and bring mixer to a higher speed. Place in crust and bake in the 325°F oven for 45 to 55 minutes.

For the Topping: Add ingredients to a small pot and reduce over medium heat until smooth and thick. Once pie is out of the oven let it cool for about 10 to 20 minutes. Then spread the strawberry jam mixture over the top.

Garnish with cut up fruit. Let cool completely and place in fridge for a few hours before serving.

SPECIAL DIETARY

We have added some special categories that might help with some dietary restrictions such as gluten free or no sugar added. This chapter includes some of those recipes.

CREAMY PINEAPPLE PISTACHIO PIE

Carol Socier, Bay City, MI
2011 American Pie Council Crisco National Pie Championships
Amateur Division 3rd Place No Sugar Added

CRUST
1½ cups all-purpose flour
1 cup butter, softened
1 cup finely chopped pistachios

FILLING ONE
8 ounces cream cheese, softened
1 teaspoon pineapple extract
1½ cups Cool Whip Free whipped
    topping
1 cup pineapple tidbits, well drained
2 cups miniature marshmallows

FILLING TWO
1 box Jell-O Sugar Free instant
    pistachio pudding mix
8-ounce can no-sugar-added
    crushed pineapple
1 cup vanilla low-fat yogurt
1 cup Cool Whip Free whipped
    topping

GARNISH
Cool Whip Free, sugar free chocolate
    syrup, and chopped pistachios

For the Crust: Preheat oven to 400°F. In large bowl, beat flour and butter with electric mixer on low speed for 1 minute. Continue beating on high speed until creamy. Stir in chopped pistachios. Press mixture evenly onto bottom and sides of 9-inch pie dish. Bake 12 to 15 minutes or until edges are golden brown. Cool completely before filling.

For Filling One: With beater, whisk cream cheese and extract until smooth. Fold in Cool Whip, blending well. Add pineapple tidbits and marshmallows. Spoon into cooled pie shell. Cool in refrigerator until set.

For Filling Two: Stir together pudding mix, pineapple, and yogurt in large bowl until well blended. Gently fold in whipped topping. Spoon over first layer.

Garnish with more whipped topping. Drizzle with chocolate syrup and sprinkle with chopped pistachios. Refrigerate for at least 1 hour before cutting.

Creamy Pineapple Pistachio Pie

CITRUS SUMMER BREEZE

Liza Ludwig, Curlew, IA
2010 American Pie Council Crisco National Pie Championships
Amateur Division 3rd Place Splenda

CRUST
1 cup flour
½ cup sugar free lemon cookie
  crumbs
1 tablespoon Splenda
½ teaspoon salt
2 tablespoons milk
½ cup lard

FILLING
¼ cup lemon juice
¼ cup lime juice
¼ cup grapefruit juice

1½ cups water
3 pinches of salt (one for each of the
  citrus layers)
12 ounces cream cheese, room
  temperature
6 tablespoons Splenda
9 tablespoons cornstarch

TOPPING
1½ cups whipping cream
1 tablespoon Splenda
1 teaspoon lemon zest
1 teaspoon lime zest

For the Crust: Preheat oven to 375°F. Combine all ingredients with pastry cutter. Roll out and place in 9-inch pie dish. Chill until needed. Bake for 10 to 15 minutes until done. Set aside to cool.

For the Filling: Combine the salt, ½ cup water, lemon juice, 2 tablespoons Splenda, and 3 tablespoons cornstarch in a medium saucepan. Bring to a low boil, allowing mixture to thicken. Let cool. Repeat Step 1 for the lime juice and grapefruit juice layers.

Whip cream cheese and divide into thirds. Gently fold into each citrus filling. Pipe into the pie shell one layer at a time. Refrigerate for 2 hours minimum.

For the Topping: Combine Splenda with the whipped cream. Whip until stiff peaks form. Gently dollop the whipped cream on top of your pie just before serving. Garnish with the lemon and lime zest.

BODACIOUS SWEETIE PIE WITH STRAWBERRIES AND BANANAS

Karen Hall, Elm Creek, NE
2008 American Pie Council Crisco National Pie Championships
Amateur Division 3rd Place Splenda

CRUST
2 cups crushed sugar free chocolate
   filled cookie crumbs
1/3 cup butter, melted

BOTTOM STRAWBERRY LAYER
8-ounce package Philadelphia cream
   cheese, softened
2 packets Splenda flavors for coffee,
   French vanilla flavor
1/3 cup Splenda granular
2 tablespoons Smucker's strawberry
   sugar free preserves
4 ounces sugar free Cool Whip
3 tablespoons chopped nut topping

STRAWBERRY BANANA LAYER
2 bananas, thinly sliced
1½ cups fresh strawberries, cut into
   ¼ to ½ inch pieces

½ cup Smucker's sugar free
   strawberry preserves

TOP CREAM CHEESE LAYER
8-ounce package Philadelphia cream
   cheese, softened
2 packets Splenda flavors for coffee,
   French vanilla flavor
1/3 cup Splenda granular
4 ounces sugar free Cool Whip

TOPPING AND GARNISH
8-ounce container sugar free
   Cool Whip
2 tablespoons sugar free Smucker's
   chocolate fudge topping
2 tablespoons nut topping
Fresh strawberries or sugar free
   chocolate covered strawberries

For the Crust: Toss together crumbs and butter in medium bowl until well blended. Press into bottom and up sides of 10-inch deep dish pie pan. Chill.

For the Bottom Strawberry Layer: In a large mixing bowl, beat Philadelphia cream cheese, Splenda coffee flavor, Splenda granular, and Smucker's preserves until smooth. Fold in Cool Whip; beat until smooth. Spoon mixture into bottom of chocolate crust; smooth. Sprinkle nut topping over layer.

For the Strawberry Banana Layer: Layer bananas over nut topping. In a medium bowl, combine strawberries and Smucker's preserves. Spoon over bananas and smooth this layer.

For the Top Cream Cheese Layer: In a large mixing bowl, beat Philadelphia cream cheese, Splenda coffee flavor, and Splenda granular until smooth. Fold in Cool Whip; beat until smooth. Spoon mixture over strawberry layer; smooth top.

For Topping and Garnish: Pipe Cool Whip on top of pie as desired. Drizzle pie top with Smucker's sugar free fudge topping and sprinkle with nuts. Garnish with strawberries. Chill pie.

Bodacious Sweetie Pie with Strawberries and Banana

JAMMIN' BANANA CREAM PIE

Phyllis Szymanek, Toledo, OH
2007 American Pie Council Crisco National Pie Championships
Amateur Division 1ˢᵗ Place Splenda

CRUST
1⅓ cups flour
½ teaspoon salt
½ cup Crisco
3 tablespoons cold water

FILLING
¾ cup Smucker's sugar free blackberry Jam
3 bananas
3 tablespoons cornstarch

½ teaspoon salt
3 egg yolks, lightly beaten
1½ teaspoons vanilla
⅔ cup Splenda
1 tablespoon flour
3 cups 2 percent milk
1 tablespoon butter

GARNISH
Cool Whip
Blackberries, optional

For the Crust: Preheat oven to 425°F. Mix flour and salt in mixing bowl. Add Crisco. With pastry cutter, cut into pea-size pieces. Add water, one tablespoon at a time, until dough forms into a ball. Roll out on floured surface one inch larger than 9-inch pie pan. Place into pie plate and flute edges. Prick bottom and sides of pie crust. Bake for 12 to 15 minutes. Remove from oven and cool on wire rack.

For the Filling: In a saucepan, combine Splenda, cornstarch, flour, and salt. Gradually stir in milk until smooth. Bring to a boil. Cook and stir for 2 minutes or until thickened. Remove from heat. Gradually stir one cup of hot filling into egg yolks; return all to pan, stirring constantly. Bring to a gentle boil. Cook and stir for 2 minutes. Remove from heat; stir in butter and vanilla. Set aside to cool, stirring often. When cooled, spoon jam into prepared pie crust. Slice bananas and layer over jam. Add cooled filling. Chill for at least 3 hours.

Garnish with Cool Whip and blackberries.

JUST SPLENDA'D RASPBERRY RIPPLE PIE

Marles Riessland, Riverdale, NE
2006 American Pie Council Crisco National Pie Championships
Amateur Division 1st Place Splenda

CRUST
1 cup pastry flour
2 cups all-purpose flour
1 teaspoon salt
½ teaspoon baking powder
1 cup plus 1 tablespoon butter-flavored
    Crisco shortening, chilled
⅓ cup water (ice cold)
1 tablespoon vinegar
1 egg, beaten

CREAM CHEESE FILLING
8-ounce package cream cheese
½ cup Splenda No Calorie, granular
½ teaspoon vanilla
⅓ cup reserved pineapple juice from
    pineapple layer

RASPBERRY FILLING
⅓ cup Splenda No Calorie, granular
1 tablespoon cornstarch
1 cup frozen raspberries, thawed
2 tablespoons raspberry juice
¼ teaspoon almond extract
¼ teaspoon red food coloring

PINEAPPLE FILLING
20-ounce can crushed pineapple
    (juice packed), divided, reserve
    ⅓ cup juice
4 egg yolks, slightly beaten
1 tablespoon water
⅓ cup cornstarch, firmly packed
1⅓ cups white chocolate chips
¼ teaspoon salt
2 cups milk
2 tablespoons butter
1 teaspoon vanilla

CRÈME FRAÎCHE TOPPING
1 cup cold whipping cream
2 tablespoons Splenda No Calorie,
    granular
⅓ cup sour cream

GARNISH (OPTIONAL)
Fresh raspberries and/or mint leaves

For the Crust: Preheat oven to 425°F. In large bowl, combine the flours, salt, and baking powder. Cut in shortening with a pastry blender until the mixture resembles cornmeal. In small bowl, mix water and vinegar with the beaten egg. Add the liquid mixture, one tablespoon at a time, to the flour mixture, tossing with a fork to form a soft dough. Shape into three disks. Wrap in plastic wrap and chill in refrigerator. Use one disk for this recipe. Roll out one disk of pie dough to fit a 9-inch pie pan. Adjust crust into pan, flute edge and prick bottom. Bake 15 to 20 minutes or until golden brown. Cool completely before filling.

For the Cream Cheese Filling: Beat together cream cheese and Splenda until smooth.

Add vanilla and the 1/3 cup of pineapple juice. Mix well. Spread filling over bottom of cool baked pie shell.

For the Raspberry Filling: In small bowl, combine the Splenda and cornstarch. In small saucepan, mix together the raspberries and juice. Stir in the Splenda-cornstarch mixture. Cook over medium heat 3 to 4 minutes or until thickened. Remove from heat and stir in the almond extract and red food coloring. Cool. When mixture has cooled, spread over cream cheese layer.

For the Pineapple Filling: Drain pineapple (reserve 1/3 cup for cream cheese filling). Combine the egg yolks and water in small bowl; stir in cornstarch. Set aside. Combine white chocolate, salt, milk, and pineapple in saucepan. Cook and stir on medium heat until mixture almost boils. Reduce heat to low. Slowly stir in egg yolk mixture; cook, and stir until thickened. Add butter and vanilla. Remove from heat; cover surface with plastic wrap. Refrigerate 30 minutes or longer, stirring once or twice. When mixture has cooled, spread over raspberry mixture.

For the Topping: In a medium-size mixing bowl, beat the cream on high speed until frothy. Add the Splenda and beat until thickened. Fold in sour cream. Cover and refrigerate. Spoon topping onto pie before serving.

Garnish as desired with fresh raspberries and/or mint leaves. Refrigerate.

NESSY'S NESSELRODE PIE

John Michael Lerma, St. Paul, MN
2006 American Pie Council Crisco National Pie Championships
Amateur Division 3rd Place Splenda

CRUST
1¼ cups chocolate wafer or cookie crumbs
1 tablespoon Splenda No Calorie, granular
5 tablespoons unsalted butter, melted

FILLING
1 tablespoon good quality rum extract
¼ cup candied fruit, chopped
2 teaspoons unflavored gelatin

2 cups milk, divided
½ cup Splenda No Calorie, granular, divided
½ teaspoon salt
3 eggs, separated
1 cup heavy whipping cream

GARNISH
Chocolate curls or shavings for decorating

For the Crust: Preheat oven to 350°F. Spray 9-inch pie plate with cooking spray and set aside. Add chocolate wafers or cookies to food processor or crush with mortar and pestle. Pulse until wafers or cookies are broken down. Add Splenda. Mix well. Pour butter over crumb mixture and process until mixture begins to hold together. Spread crumb mixture in pie plate and press into bottom and up the sides. Bake for 10 to 12 minutes. Cool and place in refrigerator for 10 minutes before filling.

For the Filling: In a small bowl, combine the rum extract and candied fruit. Set aside. Sprinkle gelatin in a small bowl and pour ½ cup of the milk over it. Let stand 5 minutes to soften. In a heavy bottom saucepan over low heat, combine ¼ cup of the Splenda, the remaining milk, and salt. Stir in the gelatin mixture. Cook, stirring constantly, until the gelatin dissolves. Whisk in the egg yolks and cook, stirring, until thick enough to coat the spoon. Do not boil. Pour the mixture over the candied fruit and rum extract. Set in a bowl of ice water to cool.

Whisk or beat the cream until soft peaks form. Set aside. With an electric mixer, beat the egg whites until they hold soft peaks. Add the remaining Splenda and beat just enough to blend. Fold in a large dollop of the egg whites into the cooled gelatin mixture. Pour gelatin mixture into the remaining egg whites and carefully fold together. Fold in the whipped cream. Pour filling into the chilled pie shell and chill for at least 2 hours or until firm.

Garnish with chocolate curls or shavings.

PINA COLADA SPLENDA CREAM PIE

Carol Socier, Bay City, MI
2008 American Pie Council Crisco National Pie Championships
Amateur Division 2nd Place Splenda

CRUST
1½ cups all-purpose flour
¼ cup crushed vanilla wafers
1 teaspoon Splenda sweetener
⅔ cup Crisco shortening
5 to 6 tablespoons ice water

FILLING
20-ounce can pineapple tidbits,
  well drained
4 tablespoons flour, divided
4 tablespoons butter, softened

1 cup Splenda
¼ teaspoon salt
3 large eggs
¾ cup cream of coconut
2 teaspoons rum flavoring
1 cup whipping cream, whipped
2 tablespoons Splenda

GARNISH
Pineapple chunks
Maraschino cherries

For the Crust: In a mixing bowl, combine flour, crushed wafers, and Splenda. Cut in shortening until pea-size pieces form. Sprinkle one tablespoon ice water at a time over mixture. Gently toss with fork until all is moistened. Form dough into ball. On lightly floured surface, flatten dough with hands. Roll into a 12-inch circle. Transfer into pie plate. Trim and flute edges. Set aside while preparing filling.

For the Filling: Preheat oven to 325°F. Toss drained pineapple in 2 tablespoons flour.

Set aside. In a large bowl, beat butter, Splenda, and salt until light and fluffy. Add eggs, one at a time, beating well after each addition. Beat in cream of coconut and rum flavoring. Stir in remaining 2 tablespoons flour, just until blended. Fold in flour-coated pineapple. Put filling into crust. Bake 50 to 55 minutes. Cool completely. Whip cream, add Splenda. Top pie with whipped cream and garnish with chunks of pineapple and maraschino cherries. Keep refrigerated.

Pina Colada Splenda Cream Pie

SPLENDA CARAMEL APPLE PIE

Patti Sharrard, Ruby, MI
2009 American Pie Council Crisco National Pie Championships
Amateur Division 1ˢᵗ Place Splenda

CRUST
1¼ cups all-purpose flour
4 to 5 tablespoons ice cold water
⅓ cup Crisco shortening
Pinch of salt and Splenda

FILLING
7 to 8 Michigan Ida Red apples, sliced
1 cup Splenda
2 teaspoons cinnamon
½ cup flour

TOPPING
1 cup Splenda brown sugar
½ cup flour
½ cup oatmeal
1 stick butter, softened

GARNISH
½ cup Marzetti's caramel sauce
½ cup chopped pecans

For the Crust: Stir together flour and shortening. Add pinch of salt and Splenda. Work until crumbly. Add water and work together with pastry blender until dough forms. Roll out dough and place in 9-inch pie pan.

For the Filling: Mix all ingredients together and put in pie shell.

For the Topping: Preheat oven to 350°F. Mix all ingredients together until crumbly. Cover apples with topping, sealing to edge of crust. Bake for one hour and 15 minutes.

For the Garnish: Remove pie from oven and drizzle caramel over top of pie. Sprinkle chopped pecans over top of pie.

GLUTEN FREE THREE CHEESE PUMPKIN PIE

Cordella LaRoe, Orlando, FL
2012 American Pie Council Crisco National Pie Championships
Amateur Division 1st Place Gluten Free

CRUST
1½ cups gluten free gingersnaps
  (about 26), finely ground
4 tablespoons butter, melted
2 tablespoons sugar

FILLING
8-ounce package cream cheese
8-ounce package Nuefchâtel cheese

1 cup cottage cheese, blended until
  smooth
15-ounce can pumpkin
1 cup sugar
1½ teaspoons pumpkin pie spice
1 teaspoon vanilla
4 eggs

For the Crust: Preheat oven to 350°F. Mix together gingersnap crumbs, sugar, and melted butter. Press into bottom and sides of pie pan. Chill until ready to use.

For the Filling: Beat cheeses together until smooth. Add pumpkin, sugar, spice, and vanilla. Mix well. Add eggs and mix until blended. Pour into prepared pie crust. Bake for 1 hour to 1 hour and 20 minutes until center is almost set. Refrigerate 4 hours or overnight. Serve with whipped cream. Sprinkle with a dusting of pumpkin pie spice for garnish.

Gluten Free 3 Cheese Pumpkin Pie

SPLENDA PEANUT BUTTER CARAMEL PIE

Laura Francese, Gerry, NY
2010 American Pie Council Crisco National Pie Championships
Amateur Division 1st Place Splenda

CRUST
15 reduced fat Nutter butter cookies, crushed
3 tablespoons sugar free caramel syrup, melted
1½ cups quick oats
2 tablespoons flour
1 stick light butter, melted
Pinch of salt
2 tablespoons roasted unsalted peanuts, crushed

CARAMEL FILLING LAYER
⅓ cup sugar free caramel syrup
4 ounces low-fat cream cheese
8 ounces fat-free whip topping
¼ cup Splenda

CENTER LAYER AND TOPPING
¼ cup light cream
1 cup semisweet chocolate chips

½ cup chopped roasted unsalted peanuts
1 cup crust crumbles (from 1 cup crust baked on cookie sheet)

PEANUT BUTTER FILLING
1 cup reduced fat creamy peanut butter
8 ounces package low fat cream cheese
½ cup Splenda
½ cup reduced sugar vanilla frosting
1 teaspoon vanilla
12 ounces fat free whipped topping

GARNISH
Caramel topping
Chocolate shavings

For the Crust: Preheat oven to 350°F. Combine all crust ingredients. Press into a large stone pie plate, reserving 1 cup of crust mixture to bake separately on a cookie sheet. Bake both stone pie plate and cookie sheet mixture 8 to 10 minutes, watching closely not to over bake. Crust should be slightly golden brown. Remove and cool completely.

For the Caramel Filling Layer: Cream together syrup and cream cheese until smooth. Add Splenda until completely combined. Fold in whipped topping. Refrigerate for at least 20 minutes. Pour into cooled crust.

For Center Layer and Topping: Heat cream slowly over double boiler and add chocolate until smooth. Add chopped peanuts. Drizzle half of this mixture over the caramel layer. Sprinkle ½ cup of crust crumbles over chocolate drizzle.

For the Peanut Butter Filling: Mix cream cheese and peanut butter until smooth. Add Splenda, vanilla frosting, and vanilla. Fold in whipped topping and refrigerate for at least 20 minutes. Spoon on top of the center layer and crumbles. Top with remaining half of center layer mixture and remaining crumbles. Refrigerate.

For the Garnish: Top with chocolate shavings and caramel topping. Refrigerate for at least 30 minutes before serving.

SPLENDALIOUS FRENCH VANILLA RASPBERRY PIE

Alberta Dunbar, San Diego, CA
2010 American Pie Council Crisco National Pie Championships
Amateur Division 2nd Place Splenda

CRUST
2 cups sugar free shortbread cookie crumbs
6 tablespoons butter, melted

LAYER ONE
16 ounces cream cheese, divided and softened to room temperature
¾ cup milk
½ cup heavy whipping cream
3.4-ounce package sugar free vanilla instant pudding mix
½ cup Splenda
½ teaspoon vanilla extract
1½ cups heavy whipping cream, whipped and divided

LAYER TWO
⅓ cup raspberry jam
3 tablespoons raspberry dry dip mix

0.35-ounce package Whip It
½ teaspoon raspberry extract
2 to 3 drops red food coloring

TOPPING
2 cups heavy whipping cream
1 teaspoon Splenda
¾ teaspoon vanilla extract
Large rosette tip
Pastry bag

GARNISH (OPTIONAL)
Fresh raspberries
Sprig of fresh mint

For the Crust: Mix all ingredients in a medium bowl with a fork until well combined. Press on bottom and sides of a 9-inch deep pie plate. Place in freezer.

For Layer One: In a large mixing bowl, beat cream cheese, milk, and ½ cup heavy whipping cream on high with an electric mixer. Add pudding mix and Splenda, mix well. Divide cream cheese mixture into two medium bowls. Set one bowl aside for use in second layer. In one of the bowls, add vanilla and ¾ cup of the whipped cream. Carefully spread in prepared pie crust. Place pie in freezer while preparing next layer.

For Layer Two: In the remaining cream cheese mixture, blend with a wooden spoon all the ingredients for the second layer. Carefully fold in remaining whipped cream. Remove pie from freezer and gently spoon mixture over first layer. Smooth top of pie and chill until set, about 45 minutes to an hour.

For Topping: Place all ingredients in a mixing bowl and beat with an electric mixer until stiff. Reserve ⅓ of topping for piping around edge. Spread remaining topping over pie and smooth top. Pipe a border around the outer edge of the pie. Place fresh raspberries, if available, in center of pie and place a sprig of fresh mint in the center to garnish.

STRAWBERRIES AND CHAMPAGNE

John Sunvold, Winter Park, FL
2012 American Pie Council Crisco National Pie Championships
Amateur 3rd Place Gluten Free

CRUST
16 Mi-Del Royal Vanilla Gluten Free
  Cookies
3 tablespoons butter

CHOCOLATE LAYER
2 tablespoons butter
2 tablespoons corn syrup
2 tablespoons milk
$\frac{1}{3}$ cup gluten free chocolate chips
  (semisweet)
1 cup gluten free powdered sugar
1 to 2 ounces strawberry Pop Rocks

FILLING
4 ounces cream cheese
$\frac{1}{3}$ cup gluten free powdered sugar
4 ounces gluten free whipped
  topping

STRAWBERRY TOPPING
Fresh strawberries, enough
  to cover pie
16-ounce package frozen strawberries
  in syrup, reserving 1 cup juice
1 to 2 tablespoons cornstarch

GARNISH
Chopped nuts (pecans, walnuts,
  almonds, or nut toppings)
Favorite gluten free whipped topping
Chocolate covered strawberries

For the Crust: Preheat oven to 375°F. Place whole cookies in food processor and pulse until cookies resemble wet sand. Melt butter and pour over cookie crumbs and mix until butter is evenly distributed. Press crumbs evenly into pie pan. Bake crust for 10 minutes. Let cool.

For the Chocolate Layer: Mix butter, corn syrup, and milk in a saucepan. Heat over medium heat until boiling. Stir constantly. Add chocolate chips and stir until melted. Once fully combined, slowly add powdered sugar. Mix completely, then set aside to cool. Place in an air tight container and place in the refrigerator. Once chilled, place on wax paper and roll it out into a 1/3-inch layer. Quickly place pop rocks on this fudge mixture and gently press them into the fudge. Fold up the fudge and gently squeeze the fudge back into an airtight bag. Spread into chilled pie crust and cover quickly with cream cheese filling.

For the Filling: Beat cream cheese and powdered sugar until smooth. Fold in the Cool Whip. Spread onto cooled chocolate layer and chill in refrigerator.

For the Topping: Strawberries may be sliced, whole, or a combination of both. A pie with sliced

Strawberry and Champagne Pie

strawberries should be served immediately. Once cut, pat strawberries dry and allow to air dry. Drain the syrup from a 16-ounce frozen strawberries (in syrup) package. Let drain until you have 1 cup of syrup. Mix 1 to 2 tablespoons of cornstarch into syrup and bring to a boil. Heat until thick. Let cool and chill. After pie crust has chilled, dip strawberries into glaze and place on pie until the top is filled with strawberries. Use glaze to fill in spaces between strawberries.

Garnish pie as desired.

BERRY KEY LIME PIE

Jeanne Ely, Mulberry, FL
2012 American Pie Council Crisco National Pie Championships
Amateur Division 2nd Place Gluten Free Category

CRUST
4 egg whites
½ teaspoons cream of tartar
¼ teaspoon salt
1 teaspoon vanilla bean paste
1 cup white sugar

FILLING
16-ounce package cream cheese, softened
1 can sweetened condensed milk
⅔ cup key lime juice

TOPPING
1 cup sugar
2 tablespoons cornstarch
8-ounce can 7UP
1 teaspoon lemon juice
3-ounce box strawberry Jell-O
1 pint strawberries

GARNISH
¾ cup heavy whipping cream
¼ cup confectioners' sugar
¼ teaspoon vanilla bean paste

For the Crust: Preheat oven to 300°F. In a large bowl, beat egg whites, cream of tartar, and salt until soft peaks form. Add vanilla and slowly beat in sugar until very stiff and glossy. Spread the mixture into a 9-inch pie plate to form a shell. Bake for 50 minutes. Turn off the oven and leave the meringue in the oven for 1 more hour. Cool.

For the Lime Filling: Whip the cream cheese until light and fluffy, whip in the sweetened condensed milk, whip in the key lime juice, and whip some more. Hint: the more you whip this, the better it is. Spoon into cooled pie shell. Cool in refrigerator until set.

For the Topping: Combine sugar, cornstarch, and 7UP in a small sauce pan. Heat, stirring constantly, until mixture becomes clear and thickens. Stir in strawberry Jell-O and lemon juice. Cool. Clean strawberries and slice in half. Dip in the strawberry Jell-O mixture and place on top of the set chocolate filling until the filling is covered. Cool.

For the Garnish: Whip all ingredients together until stiff. Spoon into star tipped pastry bag. Swirl into rosettes around just inside the crust. Keep cold in the refrigerator until ready to serve.

Berry Key Lime Pie

SWEET POTATO

BROWN ANGEL SWEET POTATO PIE HEAVEN

Saposta Foster, Atlanta, GA
2004 American Pie Council Crisco National Pie Championships
Amateur Division 3rd Place Sweet Potato

CRUST
1¾ cups graham cracker crumbs
⅓ cup margarine or butter, melted
¼ cup sugar

FILLING
4 to 5 large sweet potatoes
1 cup Crisco all-vegetable shortening
1½ cups sugar
¾ cup brown sugar

2 large eggs
2 teaspoons vanilla
1 tablespoon cinnamon
1 teaspoon nutmeg
¼ cup lemon juice
1½ teaspoons lemon zest

GARNISH
Whipped cream and/or
Caramel

For the Crust: Preheat oven to 375°F. Mix crumbs, margarine or butter, and sugar in a bowl. Press mixture onto bottom and up sides of 8- or 9-inch spring form pie pan. Form a layer about 2½ inches on the sides. Set aside.

For the Filling: Boil potatoes until tender. Let cool and then peel. Put the potatoes in a large mixing bowl and mash thoroughly with a potato masher. Add shortening to potatoes and begin mixing well at a low speed using an electric mixer. Add sugars and eggs, one at a time, and continue mixing at a medium speed. Blend in vanilla, cinnamon, nutmeg, lemon juice, and lemon zest. Pour into prepared crust. Bake at 375°F for 45 minutes or until toothpick inserted in the center comes out clean. Cool pie on a cooling rack for an hour. Serve with whipped cream and or caramel for garnish if desired.

MAPLE PECAN SWEET POTATO PIE

Jennifer Nystrom, Morrow, OH
2012 American Pie Council Crisco National Pie Championships
Amateur Division 1st Place Sweet Potato

CRUST
3 cups all-purpose flour
1 teaspoon table salt
¾ cup vegetable shortening
½ cup butter (not margarine)
1 egg, slightly beaten
⅓ cup cold water
1 tablespoon cider vinegar

FILLING
40-ounce can sweet potatoes,
   drained
14-ounce can sweetened
   condensed milk
½ cup pure maple syrup
½ cup cream

1 tablespoon pumpkin pie spice
1 teaspoon cinnamon
2 large eggs

TOPPING
¼ cup packed brown sugar
¼ cup quick oats
¼ cup all-purpose flour
½ cup chopped pecans
¼ cup butter, melted

MAPLE DRIZZLE
3 tablespoons heavy cream
Scant ½ teaspoon maple extract
1 cup powdered sugar

For the Crust: Preheat oven to 425°F. In a large bowl, mix together the flour and the salt. With a pastry blender, cut in shortening until flour resembles cornmeal. Cut in butter until it resembles small peas. In a small bowl, beat egg with a fork. Beat in water and vinegar. Quickly mix egg mixture in with the flour until flour just begins to hold together. Separate dough into halves and form each half into a disk. Wrap each disk tightly with plastic wrap and let rest in refrigerator for at least an hour and up to two days. Take one disk of prepared and refrigerated dough and roll it out and place in a 9-inch deep dish pie plate that has been sprayed with cooking spray.

For the Filling: In a food processor, place drained sweet potatoes and process until smooth, about 20 seconds. Add maple syrup, sweetened condensed milk, cream, pumpkin pie spice, cinnamon, and eggs. Process until well incorporated and smooth, about 10 more seconds. Pour mixture into prepared pie pan. Cover edge with foil or pie shield. Bake at 425°F for 15 minutes. While pie is baking, prepare topping.

For the Topping: In a medium-sized bowl, mix the brown sugar, oats, flour, and pecans until combined. Stir in melted butter until very well incorporated. Set aside until ready to use.

When pie has baked for 15 minutes, take out of the oven and remove pie shield. Turn the oven down to 375°F. Sprinkle topping over the top of

Maple Pecan Sweet Potato Pie

the pie, spreading evenly. Replace pie shield and cover top very loosely with a piece of foil so topping does not burn. Put the pie back in the oven and bake an additional 45 to 60 minutes at 375°F. Check pie after 45 minutes. If a knife inserted in the center comes out clean (or almost clean), the pie is done. If not, return to the oven for another 10 to 15 minutes and check again.

For the Drizzle: While pie is baking, make the drizzle by mixing the maple extract with the cream then adding to the powdered sugar. With a fork, mix thoroughly until drizzle is smooth. Set aside.

When pie is done, remove to a wire rack and let cool completely. After pie is completely cooled, put the drizzle in a small zip top plastic bag. Snip off a very small corner of the bag. Squeeze drizzle over the pie. Refrigerate for at least one hour before serving.

GINGERBREAD SWEET POTATO PIE WITH RAISIN MAPLE GLAZE

Karen Hall, Elm Creek, NE
2008 American Pie Council Crisco National Pie Championships
Amateur Division 2nd Place Sweet Potato

CRUST
3 cups unbleached flour
1 cup plus 1 tablespoon
    butter-flavored Crisco, cold
½ teaspoon baking powder
1 egg
1 teaspoon sea salt
¼ cup plus 1 tablespoon ice cold
    water
1 tablespoon sugar
1 tablespoon rice vinegar

CREAM CHEESE LAYER
4 ounces cream cheese, softened
3 tablespoons sugar
1 egg white
¼ teaspoon vanilla

FILLING
2 cups cooked mashed sweet
    potatoes
3 eggs, slightly beaten
¾ cup light brown sugar, packed

¼ cup pure maple syrup
½ cup evaporated milk
½ teaspoon cinnamon
⅛ teaspoon cloves
⅛ teaspoon ginger
½ teaspoon vanilla
1 tablespoon gingerbread or
    gingersnap cookie crumbs,
    finely crushed

GINGERBREAD RAISIN GLAZE
2 tablespoons water
2 teaspoons cornstarch
2 tablespoons butter
½ cup pure maple syrup
½ cup raisins
¼ cup chopped pecans

GARNISH
8 ounces frozen whipped topping,
    thawed
Pastry cutouts, as desired
    (gingerbread men recommended)

For the Crust: In a large bowl, combine flour, baking powder, salt, and sugar. With a pastry blender, cut in Crisco until mixture resembles coarse crumbs. In a small bowl, beat egg, water, and vinegar together. Add egg mixture slowly to flour mixture, tossing with a fork until mixture is moistened. Do not over mix. Divide dough and shape into three balls, flatten each to form a disk. Wrap each disk with plastic wrap and refrigerate for at least 30 minutes before using. Makes three single crusts. Use only one disk for this recipe. When ready, roll out a single crust and place in a 9-inch pie dish. You can freeze remaining disks for another use.

For the Cream Cheese Layer: In a small mixing bowl, blend together cream cheese, sugar, egg white, and vanilla until smooth. Spread cream cheese mixture on bottom of pie shell.

For the Filling: Preheat oven to 425°F. In a large mixing bowl, stir together sweet potatoes, eggs, brown sugar, maple syrup, milk, cinnamon, cloves, ginger, and vanilla until well blended. Pour mixture over cream cheese layer. Protect edge of pie with foil to prevent over browning. Bake at 425°F for 10 minutes. Reduce oven temperature to 375°F and bake 30 to 35 minutes or until center is set. Sprinkle gingerbread cookie crumbs over hot pie top. Cool pie on rack.

For the Glaze: While pie cools, prepare glaze. Stir together water and cornstarch. In a small saucepan over medium heat, melt butter; add maple syrup, and cornstarch mixture. Cook and stir until thickened. Stir in raisins and pecans. Cool slightly; spoon onto cooled pie.

Before serving, pipe or dollop whipped topping on top of pie and garnish with pastry cutouts as desired.

Gingerbread Sweet Potato Pie

GEORGIA LOWCOUNTRY SWEET POTATO PIE

John Sunvold, Orlando, FL
2012 American Pie Council Crisco National Pie Championships
Amateur Division 2nd Place Sweet Potato

CRUST
1½ cups gingersnap crumbs
3 to 4 tablespoons butter, melted

FILLING
8 ounces cream cheese
2 cups sweet potato puree
3 eggs
1½ teaspoons vanilla
1 stick melted butter
3 cups powdered sugar
1 teaspoon cinnamon

½ teaspoon mace
½ teaspoon nutmeg

CREAM TOPPING
2½ cups heavy cream
6 ounces white chocolate (broken
   into small pieces)

GARNISH
Praline pecans
Caramel sauce

For the Crust: Mix all ingredients together and press mixture into a 9-inch pie plate. Bake in a 375°F oven for 8 to 10 minutes, or until brown. Allow to cool down to room temperature before filling.

For the Filling: Mix sweet potato, cream cheese, eggs, butter, and vanilla until smooth. Add sugar and spices and blend with mixer. Pour in pie crust.

Bake in a 350°F oven for about 45 minutes. Begin checking after 40 minutes. Pie is done when it is set in the center. Remove from heat and cool on a cooling rack. Chill pie for least four hours.

For the Topping: Bring one cup of cream to a boil over medium heat. Add white chocolate and stir constantly until the chocolate is melted and mixture is combined. Remove from heat and let cool to room temperature. Refrigerate for at least four hours. In a large bowl, beat the rest of the cream with an electric mixer set on high speed. Beat until soft peaks form. Slowly add the white chocolate mixture and continue to beat until stiff. Cover and refrigerate for 2 hours.

For the Garnish: Top pie with praline pecans. Drizzle with caramel sauce, if desired. Decorate pie as desired.

Georgia Low Country Sweet Potato Pie

SOUTHERN SWEET POTATO PIE

Sarah Spaugh, Winston-Salem, NC
2007 American Pie Council Crisco National Pie Championships
Amateur Division 2nd Place Sweet Potato

CRUST
2 cups flour
¾ cup chilled Crisco
¾ teaspoon salt
¼ teaspoon baking powder
1 egg yolk, beaten and added to
    ¼ cup ice water
1 teaspoon vinegar

NUT LAYER
²/₃ cup finely chopped pecans
²/₃ cup firmly packed brown sugar
3 tablespoons butter, softened

FILLING
3 cups mashed sweet potatoes
14-ounce can sweetened
    condensed milk

2 eggs, beaten
1 teaspoon cinnamon
½ teaspoon salt
½ teaspoon vanilla
⅛ teaspoon mace
½ teaspoon nutmeg

TOPPING
1 cup whipping cream
½ cup sugar
¼ teaspoon vanilla

OPTIONAL GARNISH
Chopped nuts
Nutmeg

For the Crust: Combine the flour, salt, and baking powder. Mix the vinegar into the egg and water. Cut the Crisco into the flour mixture until it resembles coarse meal. Gradually add the liquid mixture until a ball can form. Chill dough. Roll out in a 12-inch circle and place in pie pan. Trim and crimp edges.

For the Nut Layer: Combine pecans and brown sugar. Then stir in softened butter. Place this in the bottom of the crust, pressing down evenly.

For the Filling: Preheat oven to 400°F. Combine all of the ingredients. Mix well and gently pour on top of the nut layer in pie shell. Bake for 10 minutes, then reduce temperature to 350°F and bake for an additional 35 to 40 minutes or until a knife inserted near the center comes out clean. Cool.

For the Topping: Whip ingredients together until stiff peaks form. Place on top of pie and garnish with a few chopped nuts if desired. May also sprinkle very lightly with nutmeg.

SPICY SWEET POTATO PIE

Carolyn Blakemore, Fairmont, WV
2006 American Pie Council Crisco National Pie Championships
Amateur Division 1st Place Sweet Potato

CRUST
1½ cups flour, sifted
½ teaspoon salt
½ cup Crisco buttered-flavored
  shortening
3 tablespoons cold water

BOTTOM OF PIE AND TOPPING
¼ cup brown sugar
1 tablespoon butter
¼ cup chopped pecans

FILLING
2½ cups cooked mashed sweet
  potatoes

¾ cup sugar
¼ teaspoon salt
½ teaspoon cinnamon
⅛ teaspoon cloves
¼ teaspoon nutmeg
½ teaspoon ginger
1 teaspoon pumpkin spice
½ teaspoon vanilla
2 eggs, beaten
⅔ cup Carnation evaporated milk

For the Crust: Combine flour and salt in a bowl. Cut in shortening with a pastry blender until crumbly. Sprinkle on water, stirring with a fork to form a ball. Wrap in wax paper. Chill. Roll out on wax paper. Place in pie plate.

For the Bottom of Pie Crust and Topping: In a small dish, combine brown sugar and butter until crumbly. Sprinkle half of pecans on crust bottom in pie plate. Reserve 2 tablespoons of topping, sprinkle remainder over pecans.

For the Filling: Preheat oven to 425°F. Place cooked mashed sweet potatoes in a bowl; add sugar, spices and vanilla. Mix well. Add eggs and milk. Mix all together. Pour in crust.

For the Topping: Sprinkle remaining topping and pecans over filling. Cover fluted crust rim with foil strips. Bake in 425°F oven 10 minutes; reduce heat to 350°F and bake for 20 minutes. Cool completely.

MAPLE PECAN CRUNCH SWEET POTATO PIE

Jill Jones, Palm Bay, FL
2012 American Pie Council Crisco National Pie Championships
Amateur Division 3rd Place Sweet Potato

CRUST
1 cup flour
½ teaspoon salt
½ cup shortening
¼ tablespoon sugar
¼ tablespoon vinegar
1 egg
1½ tablespoon ice cold water

FILLING
1 cup brown sugar
1 teaspoon cinnamon
2 tablespoons flour
2 eggs, slightly beaten
¼ teaspoon salt
1 teaspoon nutmeg

1 teaspoon vanilla
2 tablespoons maple syrup
2½ cups mashed sweet potatoes
15-ounce can evaporated milk
½ teaspoon pumpkin pie spice

TOPPING ONE
1 cup pecans, chopped fine
2 tablespoons maple syrup
¼ cup oatmeal
2 tablespoons brown sugar
1 teaspoon cinnamon

TOPPING TWO
1 cup heavy whipping cream
2 tablespoons sugar

For the Crust: Mix flour, salt, and sugar together. Cut in shortening with a fork or pastry cutter until mixture is crumbly. Add egg, vinegar, and water to mixture until it comes together and is a little sticky. Scrape out bowl onto a floured surface. Roll into a ball. Wrap in plastic wrap and refrigerate for 1 hour. Roll out on a floured surface and place in a pie dish.

For the Filling: Mix sugar, cinnamon, flour, salt, nutmeg, pumpkin pie spice, and maple syrup with mashed sweet potatoes. Mix well. Add eggs, milk, and vanilla. Pour into an unbaked pie shell.

For Topping One: Mix pecans, oatmeal, cinnamon, maple syrup, and brown sugar until well combined. Sprinkle over top of pie. Bake pie at 450°F for 15 minutes. Reduce heat to 325°F. Place pie guard on crust and bake for 30 to 45 minutes more or until filling appears done. Cool 4 hours before cutting.

For Topping Two: Combine heavy cream and sugar. Mix until stiff peaks form. Top pie to your liking before serving.

Maple Pecan Crunch Sweet Potato Pie

STREUSEL TOPPED SWEET POTATO DESSERT PIE

Carol Socier, Bay City, MI
2010 American Pie Council Crisco National Pie Championships
Amateur Division 3rd Place Sweet Potato

CRUST
1½ cups all-purpose flour
¼ cup sugar
¼ cup powdered sugar
½ cup cold butter

FILLING
2½ cups cooked, mashed sweet
   potatoes
½ cup sugar
¼ cup brown sugar
½ teaspoon salt
1½ teaspoons cinnamon
1 teaspoon allspice
1 teaspoon vanilla

2 eggs, beaten
1 cup evaporated milk

TOPPING
¼ cup packed brown sugar
2 tablespoons all-purpose flour
½ teaspoon cinnamon
2 tablespoons cold butter
½ cup chopped pecans
½ cup mini vanilla chips

GARNISH (OPTIONAL)
Whipped cream
Cinnamon sticks

For the Crust: Preheat oven to 350°F. Combine flour and sugars; cut in butter until crumbly. Press into ungreased 9.5-inch deep dish pie plate. Bake for about 15 minutes or until edges begin to brown. Set aside while preparing filling and topping.

For the Filling: In large bowl, combine sweet potatoes, sugars, salt, and spices. Mix well. Gradually add beaten eggs, vanilla, and milk, mixing until smooth. Set aside while preparing topping.

For the Topping: Preheat oven to 350°F. Combine brown sugar, flour, and cinnamon. Cut in butter until crumbly. Add chopped pecans and vanilla chips. Pour sweet potato mixture into prepared crust. Sprinkle with topping. Bake for 55 to 60 minutes or until a knife inserted near center comes out clean. Cool on wire rack. Garnish with whipped cream and cinnamon sticks when served.

SWEET POTATO PIE CROWNED WITH STREUSEL

Phyllis Bartholomew, Columbus, NE
2004 American Pie Council Crisco National Pie Championships
Amateur Division 2nd Place Sweet Potato

CRUST
2 cups flour
1 cup cake flour
2 tablespoons Super Rich butter powder
1 cup Crisco shortening
1 whole egg
1 tablespoon cider vinegar
½ teaspoon salt
⅓ cup ice water

STREUSEL TOPPING
2 tablespoons brown sugar
½ cup chopped pecans
½ teaspoon cinnamon
1 tablespoon butter, melted

FILLING
1 cup cooked sweet potato
¾ cup brown sugar
½ teaspoon salt
2 large eggs
1 teaspoon cinnamon
1 teaspoon ground ginger
¼ teaspoon ground allspice
1¼ cups heavy cream

GARNISH
Sweetened whipped cream

For the Crust: Mix the flours and butter powder together. Cut in the shortening until it resembles coarse crumbs. Beat together the other ingredients and stir into the flour. Mix just until incorporated. Form dough into a disk and wrap in plastic wrap. Refrigerate to chill. Roll out about ⅓ of the dough between 2 sheets of plastic wrap. Place crust in a 9-inch pie dish.

For the Topping: Combine ingredients in mixing bowl. Set aside until ready to sprinkle on top of pie filling while baking.

For the Filling: Preheat oven to 400°F. Cook potato in microwave until done. Scoop out the inside to measure 1 cup. Place sweet potato and the rest of filling ingredients in a food processor and blend until smooth. Pour into pastry-lined pie dish. Bake on the bottom shelf of the oven for 15 minutes. Then move the pie to the middle of the oven and reduce heat to 350°F. Continue to bake for about 10 minutes more and remove pie from oven. Quickly sprinkle on the streusel topping and return pie to oven. Bake an additional 15 to 20 minutes or until center is firm. Serve with sweetened whipped cream.

SWEET POTATO PRALINE PIE

Christine Montalvo, Windsor Heights, IA
2009 American Pie Council Crisco National Pie Championships
Amateur Division 2nd Place Sweet Potato

CRUST
2 cups all-purpose flour
1 cup cake flour
½ teaspoon salt
1 cup butter-flavored Crisco, frozen
   and cut into small pieces
1 large egg
⅓ cup ice cold water
1 tablespoon apple cider vinegar

FILLING
1 cup baked sweet potato (peeled),
   packed
3 eggs, slightly beaten
2 (3-ounce) packages cream cheese,
   softened

½ cup brown sugar
½ cup sugar
1 teaspoon vanilla
¼ cup butter, melted and cooled

PRALINE TOPPING
3 tablespoons butter
½ cup packed brown sugar
2 tablespoons half-and-half
½ cup chopped pecans

GARNISH
Whipped Cream

For the Crust: In a food processor, combine the flours and salt. Add the shortening pieces and pulse until dough resembles coarse crumbs. Set aside. In a small bowl, beat together the egg, vinegar and water. Add egg mixture to the flour mixture and combine with a fork, just until the dough comes together. Do not over mix. Form dough into two disks, wrap in plastic, and chill for a least one hour or overnight. Roll out one piece of pie crust into a 12-inch circle. Fit into a 9-inch deep dish pie pan and flute edges. Set aside.

For the Filling: Preheat oven to 350°F. Mash sweet potatoes. Add all the other ingredients to sweet potatoes and mix with mixer and beat until smooth. Pour into pie shell. Bake for 20 to 30 minutes or until set. While pie is baking, prepare praline topping.

For the Topping: In a small saucepan, stir together butter, brown sugar, and half-and-half. Bring to boiling; remove from heat. Stir in pecans. Remove pie from oven and place on a cookie sheet. Pour praline mixture evenly over hot pie. Bake 5 minutes more. Remove from oven and cool completely. Garnish with whipped cream.

SWEET POTATO PIE WITH EGGNOG

Sarah Spaugh, Winston-Salem, NC
2003 American Pie Council Crisco National Pie Championships
Amateur Division 2nd Place Sweet Potato

CRUST
1½ cups all-purpose flour
½ teaspoon salt
½ cup plus 1 tablespoon Crisco
  shortening
3 to 4 tablespoons cold water

FILLING
1 tablespoon granulated sugar
¾ teaspoon ground cinnamon
2 tablespoons butter, melted

¾ cup eggnog
1 egg
½ cup granulated sugar
½ cup packed brown sugar
½ teaspoon vanilla
2 cups cooked, mashed sweet
  potatoes

GARNISH
Whipped Cream
Nutmeg

For the Crust: Spoon flour into measuring cup and level. Combine flour and salt in medium bowl. Cut in Crisco until all flour is blended to form pea-size chunks. Sprinkle with water, 1 tablespoon at a time. Toss lightly with fork until dough will form a ball. Press dough between hands to form a 5- to 6-inch pancake. Flour rolling surface and rolling pin lightly. Roll dough into circle. Trim 1 inch larger than upside down pie plate. Loosen dough carefully. Fold dough into quarter. Unfold and press into pie plate. Fold edge under. Flute

For the Filling: Preheat oven to 400°F. Combine 1 tablespoon granulated sugar and ¼ teaspoon of cinnamon; sprinkle in pastry shell. Bake for 5 minutes. Remove to wire rack. Reduce oven temperature to 350°F. With electric mixer, beat butter, eggnog, egg, remaining cinnamon, sugars and vanilla into potatoes. Pour into pastry. Bake for 50 minutes or until a knife inserted off-center comes out clean. Cool. Cover and chill to store.

For the Garnish: If desired, top with whipped cream and sprinkle with nutmeg.

CREDITS

American Pie Council
Board of Directors

Rick Barton, D&W Fine Pack

Joseph DiPaolo, Pinnacle Foods LLC

Dennis Dipo, Cyrus O'Leary's Pies

Barbara Dolbee, Bonert's Slice of Pie

Richard Hoskins, Colborne Foodbotics

Chris Kelley, Publix Super Markets

Mary Pint, Legendary Baking

Christine Valley, Jessie Lord Bakery

Marsha Wickersham, Wick's Pies

Susan Mahoney, Associate Board Member

Photography Courtesy of…

Sue Ade, Food Columnist, Morris Publishing Group

Brion Price Photography

California Raisin Marketing Board

Catherine Colombo

Christie's Photography

Linda Hundt

Tye Ridolfi

Gunnar Soderlind Photography

Sarah Spruytte

SPECIAL THANKS

Compiling all of the recipes for this cookbook was a big undertaking and I couldn't have done it without the help of my family and friends for being great editors, taste testers, and supporters. And, of course, my pie family, without whom, none of this would be possible.

My Family – Rich, Lysa, Joe, Rick, Niki, Richie, Riley, Braden

My Proofreading Friends – Laurie, Julia, Marianne, Marsha

My Pie Family – You know who you are! Keep on Baking!

INDEX

Maple Pecan Crunch Sweet Potato Pie, 430–431, *431*
Maple Pecan Sweet Potato Pie, 420–421, *421*
maple syrup
    Cashew Coconut Pie, Date Night, 238–239
    Lattice-Topped Apple Pie, 34–35
    Pecan Chess Pie, Caramelized, 236–237
    Pecan Pie, Vermont Maple, 230–231
    Pumpkin Gingerbread Pie with Double Streusel, 318–319
    Pumpkin Pecan Crumble Pie, 322–323
    Pumpkin Pie, Brown Sugar, 312–313
    Pumpkin Pie, Caramelized, 314–315
    Pumpkin Pie, Maple Crunch, 338–339
    Raisin Pie, California Dream Raisin Pie, 348–349
    Raisin Pie, Dual, 356–357
    Raisin Pie, Sunshine, 354–355
    Sweet Potato Pie, Gingerbread, 422–423
    Sweet Potato Pie, Maple Pecan, 420–421
    Sweet Potato Pie, Maple Pecan Crunch, 430–431
maraschino cherries. *see* cherries, maraschino
marmalade, orange, 356–357
marshmallow cream
    Chocolate Pie, Happy Pigs, 82–83
    Malted Milk-Marshmallow Pie, *275*
    Peanut Butter Experience, 306–307
    Pineapple Pistachio Pie (No Sugar Added), 390–391
    Strawberry Twist Pie, 272–273
marshmallow fluff, 286–287
marshmallows
    Candy Cane Express, 268–269
    Clem 'N Mellow Pie, 124–125
    Raisin Butterscotch Pie, 358–359
mascarpone, 88–89
meringue mix, 290–291
meringues
    Chocolate Cream Pie, 72–73
    Orange Meringue, 112–113
    Peanut Butter Pie, 298–299
    Raisin Pie, California Dream Raisin Pie, 348–349
Meyer Lemon Cheese Pie, 132–133
Michigan apples. *see* apples, Michigan
Mile High Key Lime Pie, 120–121, *121*
milk chocolate. *see* chocolate, milk
mincemeat, 368–369
mint, 78–79
Mint Chocolate Chip Cream Pie, 78–79
mint cookies

Chocolate Mint Parfait Pie, 250–251
    Strawberry Twist Pie, 272–273
mint extract, 80–81
mints, chocolate, 250–251
molasses
    Pecan Pie, Sweet Southern, 240–241
    Pumpkin Pie with a Kick, 324–325
    Raisin Pie, Dual, 356–357
Morello cherries. *see* cherries, Morello
mousse pies
    Blueberry Mousse Pie, 156–157, *157*
    Caramel Nut Pie, Salted, 242–243, *243*
    Chocolate Mousse Mint Pie, 80–81, *81*
    Key Lime Mousse Dream Pie, 100–101
Mrs. Kelly's Date Pie, 266–267

N

Nana's Crumb Dutch Apple Pie, 10–11, *11*
nesselrode pie, 400–401
Nessy's Nesselrode Pie (No Sugar Added), 400–401
Nilla Wafers. *see* vanilla wafers
no bake pies, 282–283
no sugar added pies
    Banana Cream Pie, Jammin' (No Sugar Added), 396–397
    Caramel Apple Pie, 404–405
    Citrus Summer Breeze, 392–393
    French Vanilla Raspberry Pie (No Sugar Added), 410–411
    Nesselrode Pie, 400–401
    Peanut Butter Caramel Pie, 408–409
    Pina Colada Splenda Cream Pie, 402–403, *403*
    Pineapple Pistachio Pie, 390–391, *391*
    Raspberry Ripple Pie, 398–399
    Strawberry and Banana Pie (No Sugar Added), 394–395, *395*
Nuefchâtel cheese, 406–407
nut pies
    Apple Pecan Pie, Mama Flipped It, 18–19, *19*
    Apple Pecan Pie, Terrific Topsy-Turvy, 12–13, *13*
    Caramel Nut Pie, 218–219
    Cashew Coconut Pie, Date Night, 238–239, *239*
    Fruits of the Forest Pie, 232–233
    Green Tea Pie, 258–259, *259*
    Macadamia Cappuccino Crunch Pie, 214–215
    Macadamia Madness Pie, 224–225, *225*
    Pecan Chess Pie, Caramelized, 236–237
    Pecan Pie, 220–221

Pecan Pie, Award Winner's Chocolate, 234–235
    Pecan Pie, Caramel Chocolate, 212–213, *213*
    Pecan Pie, Chocolate Chip, 216–217, *217*
    Pecan Pie, Extreme, 222–223, *223*
    Pecan Pie, Heath Toffee, 244–245, *245*
    Pecan Pie, Perfect, 228–229, *229*
    Pecan Pie, Sweet Southern, 240–241, *241*
    Pecan Pie, Vermont Maple, 230–231, *231*
    Pecan Toffee Supreme, 226–227
    Pumpkin Pecan Crumble Pie, 322–323
    Pumpkin Pecan Surprise Pie, 316–317
    Salted Caramel Nut Pie, 242–243
nut topping
    Peanut Butter Fluff Pie, 286–287
    Raisin Pie, 21st Night of September, 344–345
    Strawberry and Banana Pie (No Sugar Added), 394–395
    Strawberry Banana Nut Goodie Pie, 264–265
Nutella, 88–89
Nutter Butter cookies
    Peanut Butter Caramel Pie (No Sugar Added), 408–409
    Peanut Butter Experience, 306–307
    Peanut Butter Explosion, 294–295
    Peanut Butter Pie, Honey Roasted, 300–301

O

oatmeal
    Caramel Apple Pie (No Sugar Added), 404–405
    Pumpkin Pie, Maple Crunch, 338–339
    Sweet Potato Pie, Maple Pecan Crunch, 430–431
oatmeal cookies, 162–163
oats, quick
    Lip Smackin' No Bakem' Peanut Butter Pie, 282–283
    Peanut Butter Caramel Pie (No Sugar Added), 408–409
    Sweet Potato Pie, Maple Pecan, 420–421
oats, rolled, 20–21
    apple pie topping, 28–29
Old Time Butterscotch Cream Pie, 168–169, *169*
Old-Time Blackberry Pie, 188–189, *189*
open pies
    Black Forest Cream Pie, 248–249
    Candy Cane Express, 268–269, *269*
    Chocolate Decadence Pie, 252–253